iPhone®
Fully Loaded

THIRD EDITION

iPhone®
Fully Loaded

THIRD EDITION

Andy Ihnatko

Wiley Publishing, Inc.

iPhone® Fully Loaded, Third Edition

Published by
Wiley Publishing, Inc.
111 River Street
Hoboken, N.J. 07030
www.wiley.com

Copyright © 2010 by Wiley Publishing, Inc.

Published by Wiley Publishing, Inc., Indianapolis, Indiana
Published simultaneously in Canada

ISBN: 978-0-470-54213-2

Manufactured in the United States of America

10 9 8 7 6 5 4 3 2 1

For general information on our other products and services or to obtain technical support, please contact our Customer Care Department within the U.S. at (800) 762-2974, outside the U.S. at (317) 572-3993 or fax (317) 572-4002.

Wiley also publishes its books in a variety of electronic formats. Some content that appears in print may not be available in electronic books.

Library of Congress Control Number: 2009933757

Trademarks: Wiley, the Wiley logo, and related trade dress are trademarks or registered trademarks of John Wiley & Sons, Inc. and/or its affiliates in the United States and other countries, and may not be used without written permission. All trademarks are the property of their respective owners. Wiley Publishing, Inc. is not associated with any product or vendor mentioned in this book.

Colophon: This book was produced using the Adobe Warnock Pro typeface for the body copy, Helvetica Neue for the headline, caption, and sidebar text, and Lucida Grande for section titles.

Acknowledgments

First, last, and always, I dedicate this book to my Dad and my sadly sainted Mom. But how can I properly thank the usual team that works with and behind me on the *Fully Loaded* books? Shout-outs go to the many folks who helped me finish this book as I steadily contemplated and re-contemplated how the App Store had changed the landscape: Courtney Allen at Wiley, Carol Person and the book's designer, Galen Gruman. Props as usual go to my agent, Carole McClendon, for once again doing that which agents do best … allow the writer to get on with the writing.

But last as first, and for always, my true thanks go to Mom and Dad. To my eye, these books are a thick stew of victories and defeats, joys and sorrows, bits that surpassed my highest and hardest expectations and (infrequently, thank Thor) bits that are marked for Serious Reconsideration when the next edition comes around.

For Mom and Dad, a new book was cause for pleasure and pride and joy. Which is another reason for me to thank the aforementioned group of folks who have helped me get four editions of this book out the door.

Credits

Acquisitions Editor
Courtney Allen

Editorial Director
Robyn B. Siesky

**Vice President &
Executive Group Publisher**
Richard Swadley

**Vice President &
Executive Publisher**
Barry Pruett

Business Manager
Amy Knies

Marketing Manager
Sandy Smith

Editor
Carol Person, The Zango Group

Layout and Production Editor
Galen Gruman, The Zango Group

Book Designer
Galen Gruman, The Zango Group

Cover Image
Michael E. Trent

**Copy Editing, Proofreading,
and Indexing**
The Zango Group

About the Author

The Wikipedia entry for Andy Ihnatko categorizes him as "Living Person — American Journalist." That's just about right.

He's been writing regular columns about technology since 1989, contributing to mainstream publications as well as every magazine that ever carried the prefix "Mac-." He's currently a regular columnist for *Macworld* and a co-host of the popular *MacBreakWeekly* podcast. When he can afford to get his good jacket out of the cleaners, he makes appearances on the *CBS Early Show*, too.

His weekly tech column in *The Chicago Sun-Times* might very well be worthy of a Pulitzer. But just try convincing the Pulitzer committee. Seriously. Andy's tried and failed. And he wants that Pulitzer *so damned badly*.

If you wear that Pulitzer medallion around your neck, you can park wherever the hell you want. If you're ever in Chicago and you see a Mercedes parked across two handicapped spaces and part of the sidewalk, you know Roger Ebert must be nearby.

Andy is kind to animals, donates blood regularly, and returns his library books on time. He lives in Boston with his two goldfish, Click and Drag.

You can visit Andy on the Web at Andy Ihnatko's Celestial Waste of Bandwidth: `http://ihnatko.com`.

Contents

PART III: THE DEATH OF PRINT   75

Chapter 9: Books and Huge-ish Documents   77

Chapter 10: Comic Books   91

Chapter 11: Comic Strips   99

Chapter 12: Crosswords   107

PART IV: THE INTERNET   113

Chapter 13: News, Blogs, and Bookmarks   115

Introduction

Welcome again, fellow sensation-seekers, to yet another book introduction. If you've read my previous books, you know how I feel about these things. This is the point in the book where I stand like Mr. Roarke at the start of every episode of *Fantasy Island*, raise my margarita glass in a welcoming toast, and hope like hell that you're not looking around at the caliber of your fellow guests (typically: Anson Williams and Barbi Benton) and feeling like you've just been profoundly ripped off.

Yes, it's where I Explain Myself. There's a good chance that you're leafing through this book at a major retailer, or at a friend's house. The book pulses with a certain resonance of destiny, and it's available at attractive prices, but should you follow your heart?

Well, it depends on what your heart is telling you. If your heart is telling you, "I should just stroll off with it," then I urge you to bring a couple of other organs in on the conference call.

Your wrists, for instance, will have much to say. It remembers the time your older brother snapped those novelty handcuffs on them and then "forgot" where he left the key. Your feet report that they will do their best to propel you out of the store or your friend's house well ahead of any pursuers, but nonetheless they don't feel as though they should speak for the knees, which would need to be ready for a great deal of praying and begging, should worse come to worst.

But why am I talking nonsense? Your moral compass is so powerful that it can be used for street navigation. You understand how important it is that I buy a plasma TV that's so large I could serve dinner for six on it. And not for my own distraction, you understand. My dear mother doesn't like to pry but she *does* appreciate these little tangible reminders that my writing career is going well.

Besides, why steal, when this bookstore has so many plush, comfy chairs, and a full coffee bar? And if you ask to *borrow* this book from your friend instead of swiping it, well, that's a built-in excuse to get together again, isn't it? Perhaps you could buy this friend a dinner, in gratitude? It's these small touches that reinforce the gossamer threads that keep Our Grand Society together.

Also, if you happen to dribble salsa all over it, you'll have to do the right thing and replace it. So that's the copy you bought for yourself *plus* the replacement copy *plus* the friend's original copy. This will put me well on my way towards sliding a Blu-ray player underneath the TV. With a full high-def setup in my living room, maybe Mom won't be shy about setting me up with her friend's daughter, the periodontist. She's damned cute and my gums would no longer lack for caring attention.

And yes, I mean it *that* way, as well.

The Point of All This

But an Introduction isn't merely here to help hook me up with a dental professional. It's also here to tell you a bit about the book in general.

A good pal recently gave me a 1910 book on housekeeping and its introduction truly is a world-beater. With just a couple of easy search-and-replaces it'll work perfectly for *iPhone Fully Loaded:*

"This book is designed to help the intelligent (iPhone or iPod Touch user) of limited means who looks upon the (usage of said device) as one worthy of her best efforts, and who fully realizes that the business of (having a kick-ass phone) is the most important as well as the most complicated business in the world. Between the covers of this book she will find an extensive and eminently practical fund of (iPhone and iPod Touch) information upon which she can draw, almost without limit, to meet the various (iPhone and iPod Touch) problems that inevitably present themselves from year to year. The table of contents is a convincing argument as to the value of this work. The compiler has taken much pleasure in preparing it, and bespeaks for it a kindly welcome and hearty appreciation in thousands and thousands of (worldwide) homes."

There you go. Sets the stage nicely. Also: It's in the public domain.

Like the other books in my *Fully Loaded* series, the purpose of this book is *not* to give you a ground-up explanation of how the iPhone works. The philosophy of this series has always been that there are already *plenty* of books out there that teach you the usual stuff. This book won't teach you how to configure your iPhone for push e-mail. Nor will it show you how to purchase music from the iTunes Store. I refuse to explain that if you hold your finger on the virtual keyboard's Symbols key and *drag* it across instead of tapping, the QWERTY keyboard will automatically return after you lift your finger above the symbol you wanted to enter, thus saving you a couple of taps.

Oh. I just did. Well, that's a freebie.

No, the goal of *Fully Loaded* has always been to look upon a device like the iPhone as an empty vessel that you can fill to the brim with every type of material you need or want in your personal or professional life. The iPhone is a pretty damned scary-crazy-nice bit of tech, but just because the manual says nothing about syncing YouTube videos on it, or storing Microsoft Office documents, or converting your e-mails into podcasts that you can listen to during your morning commute doesn't mean that you can't *do* any of those things with it.

And it *also* doesn't mean that the standard methods in the standard books necessarily represent the best way to do things.

So what does it mean? Well, it means that there's a certain knack to getting the full potential out of your iPhone. And my honorable and trusty friend — if you did in fact steal this book despite my call to your higher nature, obviously I'm not talking to you, here — you can call me Doug Fieger.

Doug Fieger. You know? Founder and lead singer for The Knack? "My Sharona" — that was probably their biggest hit.

Okay, that's not really important. The point is that if you're looking for the basic stuff that you can either get from any other book or from just fooling around with your iPhone for a week, this isn't the book for you.

This book is for people who want someone to ask them, "Wait ... how did you get *Raiders of the Lost Ark* on your iPhone? That movie isn't in the iTunes store!" with incredulous eyes and trembling hands that daren't touch the hem of your robe for fear of being reduced to ash by the awesome power bottled within your corporeal form.

Oh, and if you own an iPod Touch instead of an iPhone ... jump right in, the water's just fine. Not *everything* in this book will apply to you but you'll find that any technique or trick that relies on the Music, Video, or Photo viewers on your iPod, or on the Safari browser, or on third-party apps, will work just fine. That's a pretty big chunk of the book.

I think I've said everything I wanted to say here. Let's get started. Final words:

If you're reading this in a bookstore,

I think you'll wind up buying the book if you read Chapter 4, "Ripping DVDs" and Chapter 20, "Putting Terabytes Worth of Files on Your iPhone." All this stuff is good, but those two will quickly convince you that your money's well spent.

If you're reading this because you spotted it on a friend's bookshelf, you should compliment this friend on his or her fine taste. If it's a dating situation, that'll put you in good. If it's a friendship situation, it might lay the groundwork for getting this person to lend you something way more valuable. In the meantime, tear out the aforementioned two chapters when the friend is distracted. They're some of the most useful bits of the book, so the person is bound to buy a new copy. Plus you'll read them at home and buy a copy of your own. Two more royalties for Andy. Awesome: I'm on my way to a Wii console as well.

If you're reading this because you're robbing some dude's house: Police response time is typically about two and a half minutes. So take the book and *go*, already. I've just Googled for information on alarm codes and it seems that the default disarm password for the two most popular home security systems are 2287 and 1111.

Just remember who your friends are. Maybe you could tear out those chapters and leave the book and the chapters in the next two houses you rob? Again, I'm convinced that your next victims will be so taken by the incomplete book that they'll both buy fresh copies.

Which will work out well for you, too, because remember, my house will soon contain a 72-inch plasma HDTV, a Blu-ray player, and a Wii ... which means that I'll finally have stuff worth stealing.

Mouse, Touchpad, and Other Conventions

Okay. I did say this book is not your regular how-to for using the iPhone. And I meant it. But every once in a while I need to give you instructions in the computerese that the iPhone, Mac OS, and Windows use.

On those very rare occasions, here's what I mean when I talk about using the mouse or the touchpad on the iPhone or iPod Touch:

- Click: Most Mac mice have only one button, but some have two or more; all PC mice have at least two buttons. If you have a multibutton mouse, quickly press and release the leftmost mouse button once when I say to click the mouse. (If your mouse has only one button — you guessed it — just press and release the button you have.)
- Double-click: When I say to double-click, quickly press and release the leftmost mouse button twice (if your mouse has only one button, just press and release twice the button you have). On some multibutton mice, one of the buttons can function as a double-click (you click it once, the mouse clicks twice); if your mouse has this feature, use it — it saves strain on your hand.
- Right-click: a Windows feature since Windows 95, right-clicking means clicking the right-hand mouse button. On a Mac's one-button mouse, hold the Control key when clicking the mouse button to achieve the right-click effect. On multibutton Mac mice, Mac OS X automatically assigns the righthand button to Control+click.
- Tap: This is the equivalent of clicking on a touchscreen, using your finger

rather than a mouse.

- Drag: Dragging is used for moving and sizing items in a document. To drag an item on a computer, position the mouse pointer on it. Press and hold down the mouse button, and then slide the mouse across a flat surface to drag the item. Release the mouse button to drop the dragged item in its new location. On a touchpad, just touch and hold on the item to be dragged, and then drag your finger until the item is in its new position; then let go.
- Swipe: On a touchpad, move your finger in a sideways motion.

The commands that you select with the mouse (or touch) by using the program menus appear in this book in normal typeface. When you choose some menu commands, a related pull-down menu or a pop-up menu appears. If I describe a situation in which you need to select one menu and then choose a command from a secondary menu or list box, I use an arrow symbol. For example, "Choose Edit ▶ Paste" means that you should choose the Paste command from the Edit menu.

Okay, that's everybody. Yoiks and away.

PART I

The Basics of Content

Remedial iTunes

The Skim

Good heavens! I spent all that time in the introduction explaining that this book certainly isn't meant to be a ... *For Dummies*–style guide to the fundamentals of using the iPhone and iPod Touch. And now here I am, using the first chapter of the book to explain some of the fundamentals of using the iPhone and iPod Touch.

Blame my friend Roy. He broke my car.

Or at least, he *let* me break my car. Yes, the thing was 10 years old. Yes, it was pushing 100,000 miles. But I was looking after it very carefully and I'd expected to get another couple of years out of it. Just to be sure, I had my friend Roy teach me about basic maintenance. Roy was definitely the man to ask. He knows so much about cars that I imagine he has a second, ancillary brain down near his butt solely to store information about the correct tire pressure for hundreds of late-model sedans and SUVs.

He told me about the importance of checking the oil. "It's going to be leaking somewhere," he said, after walking me through the procedure. "If you don't know you're low on oil, you'll blow the engine and that's a career-ending injury even on a *new* car."

I followed his advice religiously. About two months later, I blew the engine.

It seems that when he told be about checking the oil, he neglected to point out the importance of being parked on a level surface. My house is on a big hill and apparently the dipstick was only reaching the deep end of the pool.

I am convinced that I am not an idiot. When I explain this to Roy, he usually asks for 10 minutes of airtime for partisan rebuttal.

The way I see it, this chapter is a win-win. The remainder of this book is peppered with phrases like "…and then add the file to your iTunes library" and "…just create a new, special playlist for this new content." If you don't already know all about iTunes, this chapter will save you a world of frustration. It'll also save me hours and hours

of obsequious begging for you to please change the horrifically negative review you posted on Amazon.com after dead-ending somewhere around Chapter 2.

And if you already know iTunes inside and out … well, I myself occasionally enjoy a good sneer as I skip over something I already understand well.

It's just never anything to do with cars, that's all. Not any *more*.

THE VERY VERY (VERY) BASICS

The one slight bummer about iPhones and iPods is that you, the humble hard-working user, are never allowed to access the device directly. Media phones and players made by other companies may be slightly tawdry, but they're like little hard drives. If you don't want to use a slick piece of software to manage the device's contents, you can just drag music and videos and other files into the thing manually. Even the stunningly shameless iPhone knockoff I bought in China for $70 allows you to add content to the device this easily.

For a million reasons — some in your best interest, some not — Apple doesn't extend you that same courtesy. The iTunes app always, always, *always* acts as the gatekeeper. The iTunes app acts as a central library and file manager for all your media (see Figure 1-1). You tell iTunes what content from your desktop library you'd like to have on your device, and then iTunes does all the organizing and copying for you.

And when I say "always, always, *always*" of course I mean "not at all." But it's the only way to load up content into the iPhone's built-in music library. If you use an app like Air Sharing (praised in Chapter 20) or

TIDBIT

Creating playlists isn't absolutely necessary. Your iPhone does a fine job of allowing you to idly browse your content by artist, album title, etc. or search for what you want using the keyboard.

But as advanced as its technology is, your iPhone has no way of knowing that *these* 11 songs, played in *this* specific order, constitute the ultimate makeout mix tape. Without your guidance, *Tony Bennett and Bill Evans: Together Again* always begins with Track 1 and ends with Track 18, and doesn't skip over songs like "You Don't Know What Love Is," which I think you'll agree will totally destroy the romantic mood based on the title alone.

Figure 1-1
iTunes: the center of our iPhone passion play

attach virtual network storage using any of the resources in that same chapter, your iPhone can see and play individual media files that live outside its own media library.

So to go from "a file on your hard drive" to "something you can enjoy on your iPhone," we have to walk this path:

- Import the file into iTunes, which adds it to its huge and ever-increasing catalog of music and video.
- Organize your content into playlists.
- Tell iTunes which content should be automatically copied to your iPhone's media library whenever you sync.

Your iPhone will be updated with fresh content the next time you sync data between the phone and your desktop. If you select the Automatically Sync When

this iPhone is Connected option in iTunes's settings panel for your phone (check out Figure 1-5 later in this chapter if you want a visual): Click the name of your iPhone in the left column of the iTunes window, and then click the Summary tab to reveal your phone's options, then the promise made by that simple checkbox label will be fulfilled whenever you plug in your iPhone. Otherwise, you can explicitly tell iTunes to update your phone by clicking the Sync button at the bottom of that same Options pane.

IMPORTING FILES INTO ITUNES

iTunes isn't a simple music player. It isn't an app that just plays a file off your hard drive and then forgets that it ever existed.

TIDBIT

It's just a plain old folder on your hard drive. The idea is that if you learn not to mess around inside your Home ♦ Music ♦ iTunes folder or your My Documents ♦ My Music ♦ iTunes folder (depending on whether you have a Mac or a PC, naturally), you'll never accidentally move the Wendy O. Williams version of "Muskrat Love" where iTunes can't find it.

No, iTunes is grabby and ambitious: It's a Media Content Library Management System.

When you import a music or video file into iTunes, information about the file is added to a master database so that you can search for one song among thousands in an instant, just by providing a few details ("a seven-minute version of 'Anarchy in the U.K.,' recorded by Buddy Ebsen"). And unless you've explicitly told iTunes *not* to

TIP

When adding files to the library, you're not limited to just folders, either. If someone hands you a CD-R or a DVD-R loaded with media files, for instance, you can use your computer's file/folder browser to select the entire volume. iTunes scrounges every file from the disc.

organize your library for you, iTunes also copies the file into its own special music directory when you add it to the library, instead of keeping your files scattered all over Creation.

There are two different ways to add files to your iTunes library:

Method the First: the Add To Library Command

1. Choose File ♦ Add To Library.
   - ◻ In the Windows edition of iTunes, there are two Add To Library menu items. Add File allows you to select one specific file. If you select Add Folder, iTunes scans through the contents of a selected folder and automatically add any music or video files it's capable of playing.
   - ◻ In the Macintosh version of iTunes, a single command handles both tasks. Either way, you'll find yourself looking at your computer's standard file/folder browser.
2. Select a music or video file, or a folder containing music and videos.
3. Click the highlighted button. On a Mac, it'll be Choose. If you're selecting a file on a PC, it'll be OK, or Open if you're using the Add Folder command.

iTunes percolates for a minute. When it's done, all the selected files that iTunes knows how to deal with magically appear in the iTunes library.

Method the Second: Just Drag It

If you're in Windows Explorer or the Mac Finder and you can see the name or icon of the files you want to import into iTunes, you

Figure 1-2
A new playlist takes its first breath

---

can just drag the files straight into iTunes without any further ado. Drag them into the iTunes window, drag them into iTunes's desktop icon or its tile in the Windows taskbar or the Macintosh Dock. However you do it, if iTunes is equipped to handle that sort of file, a plus sign (+) appears next to your mouse pointer when you enter iTunes's airspace. Release the mouse button, and iTunes takes it from there.

CREATING PLAYLISTS

Using playlists brings two big boons. Yes, it's handy to be able to instantly access a collection of songs that are tailor-made for workouts, meditation, or piloting your souped-up Dodge Charger down rural backroads at breakneck speeds with Boss Hogg in close pursuit. But it also helps you manage the problem of having more music and video on your desktop than you have space on your iPhone.

After all, the explicit goal of this book is to help you stuff that device until it's ready to a-splode. If you work your way through this book all the way to the back cover and you have no need for playlists, then I'll somehow feel as though I haven't done my job.

No refunds. Seriously. I've already spent every penny this book could ever hope to make.

You can create as many different play-

TIDBIT

It's possible that a music or video file is compatible with iTunes and plays just fine inside the desktop app — but it isn't compatible with your iPhone or iPod Touch. When you try to sync it to the device, iTunes curtly informs you that it wants no part of this ridiculousness and has skipped over the file. iTunes can usually convert the media file into a compatible format if you ask it to (select the item, choose Advanced ▶ Create to convert an audio or video file to an iPhone-studly format). There are also a bunch of external tools for ensuring that you prepare an iPhone-compatible media file. I cover those apps later in the book.

---

lists as you like. iTunes offers two flavors of playlist: the plain-vanilla variety, through which you manually select specific music and video, and smart playlists, through which you simply describe the *sort* of music you'd like to hear, and trust iTunes to work out the specific details and fill the playlist on its own.

Plain Old Playlists

You can create a new playlist either by choosing File ▶ New Playlist or by clicking the plus (+) button at the bottom of the iTunes browser window. Either way, an untitled playlist appears in iTunes's list of music sources (see Figure 1-2); untitled playlist (the default playlist name) is highlighted and awaits your creative genius.

Type in something a little more memorable. "Just Drive" is my usual playlist of stuff I want to hear in the car.

And that's really all there is to it. Any songs I drag into Just Drive will be added to the playlist, viz:

1. In the iTunes window Sources list, select Library. A list of all the music and video in your iTunes library appears.
2. Select one or more items from your library.
3. Drag them over the playlist's name.

Incidentally, when you copy items into a playlist the only thing you're actually copying is the items' information. All your actual music and video files remain where they were in iTunes's library, which means that any individual music track or video can be in many different playlists at once.

I mean, honestly: What sort of life would it be if you could only enjoy "The Cockroach That Ate Cincinnati" in one playlist at a time?

If you click on the playlist's name, iTunes's browser window switches to a view of the list of tracks therein. You can change the play order of those items by just dragging them around, or remove items by selecting the track and then hitting the Backspace or Delete key on your keyboard.

Smart Playlists

There are certain features of certain apps that make me want to stick five bucks in an envelope and mail it to the company. Smart playlists definitely comprise one of those features.

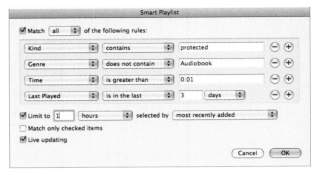

Figure 1-3
A smart playlist for my morning constitutional

Smart playlists allow you to create a playlist without being specific about its contents. You describe the *sort* of content you want and iTunes automatically fills the playlist with stuff that matches that description. iTunes stores a lot of information about all of the items in its library — including how frequently and recently you've played each and every track — which means that it's easy to get iTunes to make some fairly sophisticated choices on your behalf.

For instance: I buy lots of music through the iTunes Music Store, representing all kinds of artists and genres. And every time I take my hour-long constitutional (I'd *like* to call it a "morning jog" but that would imply an ability to run faster than the average man can walk on his hands) I want to listen to my latest tunes.

I could either religiously move tracks in and out of a manual playlist every time I buy new music, or I can just define a smart playlist by choosing File ▶ New Smart Playlist (see Figure 1-3):

Each line represents a different "rule" to apply when choosing songs; To add a new one, I click the + button at the end of any rule. This smart playlist says:

- Kind, Contains, Protected: Chooses only "protected" songs, meaning copy-protected songs, meaning songs purchased through the iTunes Store.

- Genre, Does Not Contain, Audiobook: Don't choose any spoken-word recordings, or books on tape. Neither my metabolism nor my enthusiasm for exercise are high enough to keep my legs moving during 45 minutes of Alan Greenspan's memoirs.

- Time, Is Greater Than, One Minute. Because sometimes you buy an album with a freak 30-second jingle track or something.

- Last Played, Is Not In The Last, 3, Days: If I've played this song any time in the last three days, don't bother playing it again. My attention span is a desperately short one.

After that list of rules, there's also a line where you specify how much music you'd like, and how you'd like iTunes to make the selection. One hour will do me just fine, though you can alternatively tell iTunes to limit by the number of songs or the amount of space the collection will take up. You might ask for 700 megabytes of music, which you can burn onto a CD and play in a rental car, for instance.

I've also told it to select the newest purchases. I could have asked iTunes to pick songs at random, songs that I haven't heard recently, or I could have chosen from an abundance of other options.

Once I click OK, the new playlist is automatically populated with items that match all of the rules I've

TIP

You can automatically create a new playlist from a group of selected tracks in one step. On a Mac, you can simply drag the group into any empty spot in the Sources section of the iTunes window. If you're not dragging 'em into an existing playlist, iTunes just assumes that you want to make a new playlist with these items inside it. In the Windows edition, select a group of items and then choose File ▶ New Playlist from Selection. The same menu item is also available on the Mac.

laid out (see Figure 1-4). If you don't like some of the tracks the smart playlist chose (note that the playlist in Figure 1-4 features a lot of classical tracks), you can just select the offending items and tap the Delete or Backspace key to remove them from the playlist. They'll be replaced with alternative selections automatically.

Figure 1-4

Presto! iTunes is a deejay, it am what you say.

Figure 1-5
The iPhone Options pane

And one of the (many) terrific features of smart playlists is that the list is "live." If for whatever reason a track inside a smart playlist no longer meets your list of rules, zap! It's removed from the playlist and replaced with one that does.

When I come home from my daily constitutional and re-dock my iPhone, iTunes discovers that all the tracks I listened to now fail the "hasn't been played in the past three days" test. So, by the time my iPhone is done syncing, those tracks in the Constitutional playlist have been replaced with all-new items. If I buy a few new tracks that evening, the three oldest tracks in the playlist are kicked out to make room for them.

(Exactly like the oldest contestants on *Survivor.*)

UPDATING YOUR IPHONE

When you connect your iPhone to your computer, it automatically appears in iTunes's list of available devices. What happens after that depends on the iPhone options you've set. You can open the iPhone Options window by clicking your iPhone's name in the Devices section of the iTunes window. You wind up with a pane like the one you see in Figure 1-5.

If you leave the Automatically Sync When This Phone Is Connected box checked, iTunes will update the iPhone's contents automatically every time you plug it in.

There's another tweak to all of this: The Sync Only Checked Songs and Videos checkbox. Each music track and every video in every iTunes pane has a checkbox next

Figure 1-6
Moving tunes from desktop to hiptop

to it. With this option enabled, any item that *does not* have its checkbox checked will not be synced to your iPhone. This makes it easy to "point and shoot" certain items that you never, ever, ever want to hear in the car.

Automatic updates take place only when you plug in your iPhone. You can also tell iTunes to "update this iPhone *right freaking now*" by clicking the Sync button. You'd do so if you've added new items or playlists to your iTunes library since plugging in your iPhone.

You'll note that the Options pane is organized into tabs. There's one for each different type of media that you can load up on your iPhone. Figure 1-6 shows you the Music tab.

Here's where you tell iTunes precisely which bits of your music (or video, or photo, or …) library should be copied to your iPhone.

Take this moment to observe the All Songs and Playlists Option. Take a goooooood long look at it.

Ha ha! Yes, we all enjoyed a good laugh over that one. Unless you've just had your computer for 40 minutes, you already have way more music and video on your machine than you have free space on your iPhone, most likely. That's why iTunes allows you to narrow down the library to just an easily managed subset of playlists.

Each pane is a little different, addressing the unique-ities of that kind of media. Video files tend to be humongous in their own right. An iPhone can handle a thousand songs, but a half a dozen movies can easily max out an 8-gigabyte model. So the Video tab lets you select individual shows or movies in addition to managing your content via playlists.

Automatic syncing is definitely the most whiz-bang approach. It makes you feel as though you're just days away from taking delivery on your own atomic-powered jetbelt.

But there's a second option for moving content onto your iPhone or iPod Touch. By clicking back onto the Summary tab of your iPhone's Options pane and then checking the Manually Manage Music and Video checkbox, you can tell iTunes to keep its mitts off your iPhone's library entirely. Nothing will land on that device unless you explicitly drag it onto your iPhone's icon in iTunes.

Yeah, that's definitely an option. Absolutely. I mean, speed, simplicity, and convenience are vastly overrated concepts. Besides, the automatic sync features burns as much fossil fuel in one year as an SUV does in an entire month.

(Source: Wikipedia, and I just added that fact a moment ago. So take it with a grain of salt.)

Managing content manually offers one pretty hefty advantage: It breaks the link between your iPhone and this *one* iTunes library. If you're visiting friends at their beach house and you're facing a two-hour drive home, you can simply plug your iPhone into your friend's computer and copy two hours' worth of fresh entertainment from your pals' iTunes library. Otherwise, only your "home" library has permission to add stuff to your iPhone.

WHAT ITUNES CAN'T DO

Even the third edition of the iPhone OS shines a spotlight on iTunes's limitations. As of this writing, iTunes really isn't a *universal* gatekeeper for putting information on your iPhone or iPod Touch: just music, video, calendars, contacts, and photos. iTunes does help you manage all that stuff. Everything else is your own problem.

And as you start installing third-party apps, that shortcoming becomes more and more glaring. I expound later on about installing electronic books on your iPhone, for example. It's a natural; e-books are just as popular and abundant a type of media as music and video. But iTunes will have none of it. Instead, if Tess of the D'Urbervilles is going to plant her dainty behind in your

phone, you'll need to acquire a third-party app to make it happen.

(Though by the time you read this, Apple might have added e-books to the iTunes Store. "Always in motion is the future," says Master Yoda.)

Apple has consistently bucked any possibility of allowing users and developers to use iTunes as a general concierge for *all* the data an iPhone user might want to manage. As a result, developers use all kinds of tricks to install user data.

If you're trying to put an MP3 of "Muskrat Ramble" on your phone, it travels along about three feet of USB cable strung between your computer and your iPhone. If you want a copy of a project outline, it doesn't matter that the same company made the desktop and iPhone also created the outline file and the iPhone app that reads it. It's possible that the file will have to travel out of your desktop, up across the Internet, into the software company's central server, and then from there back down to the iPhone that's sitting *right on the damned keyboard.*

Well, it works. Thank heavens. But there seems to be something punitive about such a complex answer to a simple question. I suppose I shouldn't complain. Problems like that are the reason why a book like this is necessary.

So that's the end of our first day of school. And now you see why we have all your little desks facing *me* instead of each other. This way, when the bell rings and you all flee into the hallways to whip out your phones and check in with Facebook, you can tell each other that this class was so *lame,* that you *totally* knew everything that Mr. Ihnatko discussed, that this is all so *easy.*

Meanwhile I'm the only one who saw the look on your face when I explained something elemental, and watched your eyes and ears go into full spread-spectrum capture mode. Funny, none of your *friends* seemed like they were learning something new. I bet they'd be really amused if they knew that you've had an iPhone since the very first day the first-generation hardware was available, and yet you didn't know how smart playlists worked.

To put it more simply: Those Hostess Cup Cakes your mom puts in your lunch come two to a pack. Send one my way from time to time and nobody ever needs to know about this. *Capice?*

How to Make 8 Gigabytes Seem Like 80, 32 Seem Like a Terabyte

The Skim

"What, exactly, does your media tangibly *become* when you rip a CD or a DVD into a digital media file?"

There was a time when that was a meaningless question suitable only for philosophy professors and the insane, who dress better. Now we know beyond any doubt: It turns into a gaseous substance. That's why the iPhone and other media devices are so tightly sealed. It's not so much keeping the moisture out as it is trying to keep the Oingo Boingo *in*.

A gas expands to occupy the full dimensions of whatever container you put it in. And so it is for your iPhone. The capacity of an iPhone or iPod Touch can be 64, 32, 16, 8, or even 4 gigabytes if you bought it in the very first month of release and went cheap and never bothered to upgrade. But the number couldn't matter less. When you upgraded your 8-gig first-generation iPhone to a 32-gig iPhone 3G S, the extra space felt glorious and expansive … until about a week later, when

Figure 2-1

Keeping content fresh automatically, thanks to smart playlists

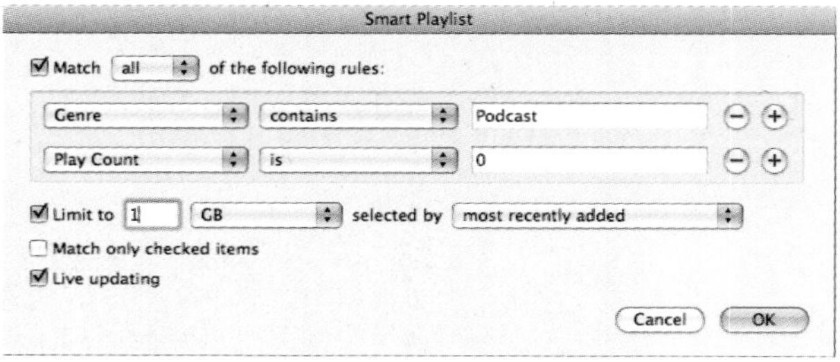

Figure 2-2

My daily dose of podcasts

after seven days of adding just *one* more movie, podcast, or playlist you were reintroduced to the "Some Files Could Not Be Copied" error.

Yes, if Apple were truly being square with you, instead of "16 gigabytes" the package would simply read "Capacity: not nearly enough." The iPhone doesn't have a card slot or any other way to physically add more memory, but iTunes and the iPhone contain enough powerful features that the physical capacity of the device can be rendered all but meaningless.

STRETCHING STORAGE WITH SMART PLAYLISTS

In fact, I have three different music players. My desktop iTunes library contains nearly a terabyte of movies and music. My iPod has its 160-gig drive, and it's packed to the gills. And then I have my 16-gig iPhone. Yet when it comes to a simple question of the breadth of content, the listening experience with the iPhone is just about the same as what I enjoy with any other.

Why? Because practically all the content on my iPhone is managed with smart playlists. Instead of assembling static lists of music and videos, I have merely described the *kind* of stuff that iTunes should maintain on my phone at all times. iTunes keeps churning the content with each night's sync. So while my iPhone only has 16 gigabytes of storage, the net effect is that iTunes is projecting a constantly moving 16-gig window of content from a media library that's more than 100 times larger.

I mean, think about it: It would take me *months* of nonstop listening to go through all the stuff on my iPod. Which is nice, if you have the sort of job where you can take that much time off for personal projects, but I rarely go more than, say, two days before I dock my iPhone back to my desktop. Every sync is another chance for iTunes to close the curtains and make sure there's a whole new scene in place by the time the curtains rise up on the next act.

Figure 2-1 shows you a typical example of one of these playlists.

It's dead simple but awesomely powerful. You can translate this playlist's mandate as "This playlist should only contain music that I really, really like and that I haven't played in more or less forever." It selects only music rated 4 or 5 stars, and puts the least recently played tracks into the playlist first.

It's the last bit that delivers the punch. Obviously, since this playlist contains only awesome music — I've titled it "Only Awesome Music" just to underscore the point — I use it a lot in the car. But as soon as I get home and dock my iPhone, every track that I listened to during the 20-minute drive to MIT, the 20-minute drive back home, and the 73 minutes spent orbiting Cambridge looking for a parking spot, is removed and replaced with *another* top-favorite track that I haven't played in ages.

Obediently and without demand for acknowledgement or reward, iTunes keeps digging through your library, looking for lost treasures.

That criterion is also useful when it's set to maintain a playlist of your library's freshest content. It's particularly good at maintaining a playlist of new podcasts (see Figure 2-2).

Another dead-simple playlist: It just looks for tracks whose genre is "podcast" and chooses the most recently added gigabyte's worth, from among those podcasts that I haven't heard yet.

This approach is actually more useful than relying on the iPhone music player app's built-in Podcasts button. I think Apple's feature is way too ... too — sorry, which side of the brain is it that handles all the Spock-like logical thinking? It's too *that* side of the brain. When I jump in my car or go for a walk, I'm not explicitly thinking, "I'd like to hear every unheard new episode

Figure 2-3
Seeing stars: rating the music on your iPhone

of *The Bugle*." I'm thinking, "Time to listen to today's new podcasts, whatever they are." I get *The Bugle*, followed by *Martini Shot*, followed by *SMODcast*, followed by ... etc.

I use these smart playlists to manage all my content. I do still have a handful of manual playlists — chiefly, a playlist of "must have" albums and videos that I always want to have handy — but everything else is selected and synced to my iPhone automatically.

I have about a dozen smart playlists covering every genre and situation, and by using the smart playlist's "Limit to X Gigabytes" feature, I can keep my iPhone partitioned. I always have 4 gigs of music I haven't heard in eons: 2 gigs of recently added movies, the latest 2 gigs of movies, 500 megs of jazz, 1 gig of classical, 1.5 gigs of rock, and a combined 500 gigs of country and bluegrass, leaving a healthy block of empty space.

THE RATING GAME

This technique becomes much more powerful once you've started applying personal ratings to *allll* your music. Most people never get around to doing this, even though it's pretty easy. In iTunes, you just click your mouse in the Rating column next to the track, and assign it from 1 to 5 stars. On your iPhone, you tap the album art twice while the track is playing, and then illuminate the appropriate number of stars with a second tap

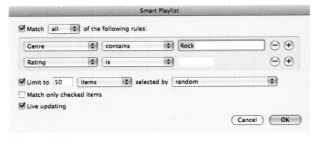

Figure 2-4

Hey now, you're a rock star. Or you will be, after putting this smart playlist into regular rotation.

(see Figure 2-3).

But it's a pain to go through all of that for hundreds or even thousands or tens of thousands of tracks. A smart playlist can actually automate the entire action, viz Figure 2-4.

This smart playlist hunts for rock music that I haven't gotten around to rating. If I get in the habit of listening to this playlist as I take my morning constitutional and noting my galvanic skin response as the first chords ring through my headphones, I'll eventually get every last one of my rock tracks duly starred.

It's like dog training, really. There's a positive reinforcement/reward for taking a moment to tap the screen and register my opinion. This is the only playlist I listen to for the whole hour, and if I want that unrated Neil Diamond song to *finally* go away, the *only* way to accomplish that is to assign it an inevitable one, lonely star so that iTunes replaces it with something that I *didn't* buy as a joke.

It really didn't take long before I'd tagged thousands of tracks. I'm still barely a third of the way toward rating my entire library, but I'm already reaping huge rewards: There

TIDBIT

I have nothing against Neil Diamond or his fine catalog of hit music. I made a Neil Diamond joke in print once and my big sister made the mistake of complaining about it, which of course triggered the genetic response that causes a little brother to automatically want to do something to annoy an elder sister.

That said, Neil Diamond fans, you really do have to finally confront the fact that *The Jazz Singer* was a wretched, *wretched* movie.

are times during a long ride when you want to be challenged with obscure tracks that shine a light on your preconceptions about art. But then there are those times when you just want to pump your fist in the air and yell, "She LOVES youuuu yeahhh, Yeahhh, YEAHH, *YEAHHHHH!!!!*"

You can't really make that happen without having some ratings in your library.

So honestly, I can't say that I've had any complaints whatsoever about the lack of a hard drive in my iPhone, or the lack of a card slot (which is something you find in most other smartphones). Even today, after the iPhone has become like the swine flu virus in terms of impact and global reach, there are still folks who complain that the iPhone has no card slot.

"Turn out your pockets," I said to one complainer, a Blackberry user who had really pushed me too far.

"What?"

"Right now. All of them. Let's see *everything* you have in your pockets. Because if the fact that the iPhone doesn't have a slot for an additional storage card really *is* a total deal-breaker for you, then you absolutely *must* be carrying more than 32 or 64 gigs' worth of memory cards on you. How I don't envy you, with an absolute need to have more than the massive amount of storage built into even the cheapest iPhone!

"And if you aren't carrying an iPhone's worth of memory cards," I finish with a condescending flourish, "then you're talking through your hat."

He wasn't carrying memory cards, thank heavens. If he was, I would have asked him if he *truly* preferred to swap out memory cards three times just to listen to *Quadrophenia* all the way through.

TIP

There's another great trick for making your iPhone appear to have much more storage than it actually does, particularly if you're frequently within reach of a Wi-Fi connection. Instead of syncing music and podcasts to your iPhone, why not just leave that stuff on your home hard drive or a remote server, and stream it through the Internet?

In Chapter 14, I talk about a neat little technique that I use all the time: I bookmark a favorite podcast's RSS feed in Safari, or in an iPhone feed reader app. The RSS feed is the podcast's invisible directory file, cataloging each available episode with a download link. Tap the link and the episode downloads, plays, and (unlike the iPod app's Download Podcast feature) is disposed of as soon as you're finished with it.

And Chapter 20! Boy, Chapter 20! There you'll find information on expanding the virtual storage of your iPhone! I told you about my hard drive full of music back in the office — the one with a full terabyte of media on it? Well, what if I could have all that media on my iPhone, available all at once, no matter where I am in the world? These things are possible. Read on.

PART II

Media from the Real World: Audio and Video

Ripping CDs

The Skim

promise you it's true: I held an actual CD in my hands. It was, well, two or three months ago. But I remember the experience clearly.

It was a little freaky. Kind of like that point in the guided tour of a zoo where you get to touch a boa constrictor. It's a little colder and stickier than you thought it would be. I didn't freak out or anything but still, it was an exciting enough moment that I couldn't stop talking about it to my friends for days afterward.

(And it actually had a little *book* inside the case! On paper and everything! With pictures, and lyrics. And Bono had, like, a *lot* of things to say about the situation in Costa Rica, but the text was teensy-tiny so I'm not really sure precisely what kind of trouble the folks down there are in. It still made me want to send the guy a lot of money, though.)

A whole generation is growing up without ever having had to remove the titanium shrink wrap and those sticky strips from the edges of a brand-new CD. Which is just another explanation for the older generations' envy and hatred of today's youth.

For all the benefits of buying music online or downloading it via podcast or directly from a band's Web site, the CD will still offer lots of practical advantages over any other method. I shall start you off by mentioning that at this writing, one and only one Stan Freberg track is available from the iTunes Store. I suppose there might be others, but really, do they matter?

iTunes makes it dead simple to convert CDs into digital music files. But there are subtleties that you ought to know about, particularly before you eye the 700 discs in your collection and begin a heroic monthlong ripping campaign.

Figure 3-1
Opening a CD in iTunes

RIPPING CDS

Okey-doke. Just stick a CD in the drive and after your machine has taken a moment to comprehend that it now has to deal with a copy of Howard Jones's *Greatest Hits*, iTunes opens the CD for playback and presents you with list of its tracks (see Figure 3-1), and (unless some little Norbert has unchecked this option) asks if you want to import the CD.

If you push iTunes's Play button, it'll play these tracks straight off the CD. But we're living in the exciting Pushbutton World of Tomorrow, not the leaden gaslight-and-spats era of the mid-Nineties: We want to make music files.

Turning all those tracks into digital music files is a complicated process consisting of:

1. Click the Yes button. If you skipped through it, just click the button marked Import CD, found in the lower-right corner of the iTunes window (see Figure 3-2).

2. (Optional) Go down to the kitchen and microwave yourself a Hot Pocket or something while the tracks are converted to music files and added to your iTunes library.

TIP

I'm your friend, so I'll take this moment to quietly tell you that *nobody* is impressed with the speed of your new computer. Honest. They're feigning interest while they scan the room for someone else to talk to. Your friends used to think this behavior was amusing, in a tragic sort of way, but now they say they can no longer sit by and watch you strike out time and time again talking about your new laptop, your hybrid car, the new watch you bought for marathon training, etc. "The best way to talk is to *listen*," they urge you. I concur heartily. They're not trying to embarrass you. They just don't want you to be so terribly *lonely*, that's all.

Figure 3-2
The Import button, a.k.a. All You Need to Know

Figure 3-3
The rip-in-progress

Because honestly, that's all there is to it.

All right, in truth, I desperately wanted to reduce it to one step, so I chose to gloss over the fact that if there are any tracks on this disc that you don't want to copy, you can just uncheck them by clicking the checkbox next to the tracks' names. I mean, on the off chance that the artists who created this CD failed to ensure that every single track was a timeless classic that plucks the soul strings of the zeitgeist and helps us all to coalesce into a more powerful understanding of our collective force of idealism as a society.

As you enjoy your Hot Pocket, you might want to pass the time by noting some of the things that are going on in the window (see Figure 3-3):

- The window's status display shows you which track is currently being imported, how far along the process has come, and, if you're the sort of person who likes to brag about how fast your computer is, the speed of the rip. Here, iTunes is pleased to report that it's converting the track 13 times faster than it'd take to play it.

- On the left side of the track list, next to the track numbers, you'll see little green checkmark icons that represent completed tracks, an orange one next to the track that's being ripped right

25

now, and colorful expanses of absolutely nothing next to tracks that have yet to be processed, glistening with the promise of digital files yet to come.

▢ There's a tiny X button on the right side of iTunes's status display. Click it to abort the rip-in-progress and cancel all the tracks due to be ripped.

▢ Unless you've turned off that particular feature in iTunes's Preferences dialog box, iTunes starts playing the ripped tracks as soon as the first one is complete. Click the Stop button to knock that off.

Once iTunes has finished ripping the disc, you can eject it from your computer by clicking the little Eject button next to the CD's name in the Devices list on the left side of the iTunes window (see Figure 3-4), or the big Eject button in the lower-right corner of the iTunes window. Pressing the Eject button on your keyboard or on your CD drive accomplishes the same thing.

Figure 3-4
Spitting out the disc

OH, THE TROUBLE

And I'm proud to say that here, 95 percent of my job as an instructationalist writer is done. Nothin' left for me to do here but clear up a few trims and ends, most of which orbit the theme of "Why Did This Go Wretchedly Wrong?"

But this world is a vale of tears, and even in a simple, flawless and foolproof process like iTunes CD ripping, a little rain must fall.

The Disc Doesn't Appear in iTunes

If the disc doesn't appear in iTunes, there are usually only two possible answers:

TIP

If you're settling down to rip dozens or hundreds of discs instead of a handful, iTunes has a hidden feature to speed things along. Open iTunes's Preferences dialog box (choose Edit ▶ Preferences in Windows, and iTunes ▶ Preferences in Mac OS). Click the Advanced tab, and then click the Importing sub-tab (see the figure).

Click the On CD Insert menu and you'll reveal a frisky item named Import Songs and Eject. It's tailor-made for processing CDs in bulk: Whenever it sees a disc, it rips all the tracks and then spits it out again, hungry for more. You can rip a 1,000-CD collection with little visible effort by merely keeping a stack of discs near the computer at all times and getting in the habit of sticking a new disc in there whenever a ripped disc seems to be sticking out of the drive.

- The disc is way too baffed up for your CD drive to recognize it. I mean, for heaven's sake, man, you felt your chair roll over it *twice*, and yet you rolled over it a third time before you picked it up. That's going to cost you a new copy of *Rubber Soul*, my friend.

- The disc isn't an audio CD. "Not an audio CD, eh?" Interesting. Usually, this means that the publisher chose to save you a little time by burning a CD-R or a DVD-R of digital music files. Open the disc in Windows Explorer or the Mac OS Finder and see what files are there. If it's loaded with documents with .mp3 or .aac or other music-ish filename extensions, then you can just drag those files straight into the iTunes window and they're added to your music library without any further ado.

Sometimes, though — and if you listen carefully, you can hear my teeth grinding as I type these words — it's because the CD has been intentionally corrupted by the publisher. Which is the more accurate way of describing a disc that's been monkeyed with to make its tracks harder to convert into digital music files.

The music industry once announced (quite haughtily) that copy protection was going to be the reality of CD publishing and if the public thought they had any recourse, well, then this is exactly why the music industry was right all along to treat us like the scum that we are.

But the whole thing turned out to be such a debacle that a "copy-protected" disc is about as hard to encounter as a person under the age of 60 who can name more than five Neil Sedaka hits. It's something to

> ## TIP
>
> Ripping your first disc is simple. It's the remaining 992 in your collection that are going to sting. Fortunately, there are lots of services out there that will rip all your CDs *for* you. You ship 'em the discs, they ship 'em all back accompanied buy a few DVDs filled with iTunes-compatible music files. These services are popping up all over the place, but if you want to check out pricing, RipTopia (www.riptopia.com) and MusicShifter (www.musicshifter.com) are good places to start.

keep in mind, though. These schemes have never stopped a Mac from ripping a disc. On Windows machines, holding down the Shift key while inserting the CD usually prevents whatever special satanic copy-protection technology is in place from working.

All the Tracks Are Untitled

Magically, iTunes fills in the title of the CD and the names and artists of each track for you. This particular mojo is powered by a massive online database containing info about very nearly (accent on "very nearly") every CD ever made. If you have an Internet connection, iTunes automatically connects to the database, asks, "Have you ever heard of this CD before?" and grabs the info it needs.

If something goes wrong, you'll see a huge window of tracks named Track, from a CD entitled Audio CD. This is an unhappy

27

Figure 3-5
Letting iTunes's fingers do the typing

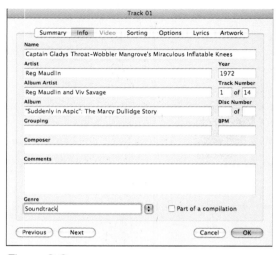

Figure 3-6
Pin the info in the track list, one by one.

state of affairs.

If you didn't have an Internet connection available when you ripped the disc, don't sweat it. The next time you're Net-study, select those tracks and then choose Advanced ▶ Get CD Track Names (see Figure 3-5).

It's possible, however, that you are the first human on this planet to ever purchase and rip this specific CD. In which case the database doesn't *have* any album, artist, or track info on file. You'll have to add that stuff yourself.

1. Select the first track in the album.
2. Choose File ▶ Get Info.
3. Click the Info tab of the window.

You'll be presented with the little form you see in Figure 3-6. Laboriously copy all that info from the back of the CD. When you finish one track, click the Next button to move on to the next track.

If you select more than one track before clicking Get Info, iTunes will (after a curt warning that this might be a bad idea) allow you to edit the info for all those tracks at once. The album, year, genre, and maybe even the artist and composer won't change from track to track, so it's a good way to save some time. But you're going to want to dismiss that window and then edit each track individually to add the specific track titles.

And this is your reward for supporting struggling independent artists. Because

honestly, the only CDs that aren't in the Gracenote Media Database are coffee shop performers who self-produce CDs in the dozens or hundreds at best. Every commercial CD is already in there, no matter how limited, rare, or bizarre. To produce an illustration of a CD with no track information available, I dug out my copy of *The Beatles on Panpipes*, a gag gift I bought for a pal of mine (and serious Beatles fan) but didn't have the courage to actually give him. No good; I found that even a disc of panpipe-based Beatle covers had already been processed and added to the central database.

(Stuck for a solution, I eventually realized that I could accomplish what I wanted if I simply turned off my notebook's Wi-Fi for a few minutes. Me Am #1 Clever Technology Writer of All.)

Once you've finished all that work, you *could* demonstrate that you're a responsible and contributing member of society by selecting the tracks and choosing Advanced ▶ Submit CD Track Names. This updates the CDDB with the info you've just added to iTunes, and potentially the rest of the world will benefit from your labors, in perpetuity. Not the best legacy that you can leave, but it's more than some people will ever contribute, I suppose.

THE FILE-FORMAT POLKA

Okey-doke. Just give me a moment to prepare a damp washcloth and clean all of that vitreous spittle off my screen so I can proceed.

There. That's better. We've come this far and we've only used a handful of acronyms. But they're all friendly and familiar ones: CD, PC, even LP, for the love of Mike.

Take a deep breath, because it's time to knock you down and pummel you with MP3, AAC, VBR, and other key players in the Obfuscation Hit Parade.

When you convert CD tracks into music files, there are a few different goals you want to achieve with the results:

- **You want the tracks to sound good.** We shall refer to this as the "Duh" Imperative.
- **You want files that don't take up a whole lot of space.** Because you only have a limited amount of space on your iPhone, and if iTunes is creating music files that are twice as big as they need to be, then your iPhone can only hold half as many tracks as it should.
- **You don't want to go through this bloody mess of ripping dozens, if not hundreds, of CDs all over again for any reason.** A subtler point, this, but nonetheless it's something that you ought to consider. You are a luminous

being, one of the Beloveds of the Universe, my child; your destiny is a long one and unless you're reading this book while driving a car, it's likely that you're going to be on this planet for many years to come.

"But wait," you're now thinking, after fully digesting the "Beloved of the Universe" line. "That means I really *shouldn't* go get the spaceship from *Battlestar Galactica* tattooed across my back, because although *right now* I think it's the most awesome show ever, and that it really sums up my outlook and philosophy of life, maybe I'll feel differently 10 years from now!" Indeed it does. Although that's not where I was going with that, I'm glad you're gleaning bits of incidental wisdom from this book.

So before you rip that Strokes CD, you ought to stop and picture yourself six months from now, when you've bought a doohickey that lets you plug your iPhone into your big home stereo system. Or a year from now, when you have an Apple TV or some other box that can wirelessly transmit music from your computer to any set of speakers anywhere in the house. Or some time in the far-off future, when something even better than iTunes has come along for managing and broadcasting all your family's music.

If you make the right choices today, you can create music files that will play on your iPhone or iPod Touch (good) and in iTunes (fab), but also nearly any sort of digital audio device or accessory that you might put your hands on in the next five or 10 years. It'll come down to:

- **File format.** You can't stick an 8-track into a CD drive, and with a similar sense of injustice not all devices and

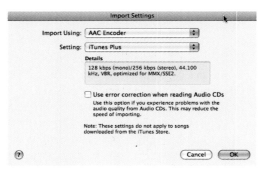

Figure 3-7

Modifying iTunes's default settings for ripping music

software can play every conceivable music file format. You want iTunes to use a file format that will work on the greatest range of stuff.

◻ **Sound quality.** "Hey, this file sounds great" is a relative term. Joan Rivers humming the score from *The Magnificent Seven* would sound great, too, through those crappy white earbuds that you got free with the iPhone. iTunes will always make certain sacrifices and trade-offs when converting a CD track into a music file, and often they're only apparent when you listen through a halfway decent set of home speakers. And look, if you've ripped a large CD collection into iTunes, one of the first things you're going to want to do is enjoy your music collection through your stereo. That's a bad time to discover that iTunes ripped all your tracks at the Joan Rivers setting.

The Settings I Think You Ought to Use

I'm betting that you're interested more in

immediate gratification than technical detail. So let's lead off with the tweaks I think you ought to make to iTunes's default music-ripping settings. You can access these settings by choosing Edit ▶ Preferences in Windows or iTunes ▶ Preferences on a Macintosh). Click the Advanced tab, and then click the Importing tab underneath.

You set the file format through the Import pop-up menu (see Figure 3-7). The default choice is AAC Encoder and you ought to leave it as is. But change the Setting pop-up menu to Higher Quality (256 Kbps).

There it is: Rip all of your tracks to the AAC file format, using a sample rate of 256 Kbps. I think that's the sweet spot that gives you terrific-sounding files that will play on a huge variety of devices but won't choke the capacity of your iPhone.

Now let's snap on a pair of latex gloves and get into a more exhaustive explanation.

File Formats

iTunes can rip music into a buttload of formats:

◻ **MP3.** MP3 is the Band-Aid of digital music. It's a specific format, but it's so old and so ubiquitous the world tends to use that word when it really is just referring to digital music files in general. And here you see the big advantage of MP3: Practically every piece of software and hardware created by anybody who breathes the customary human mixture of oxygen, carbon dioxide, and nitrogen gases can handle an MP3 file, whether it's a music player on a cell phone or a piece of software that lets you edit your home movies and create your own soundtracks.

- **AAC.** The Advanced Audio Coding format was what the industry created after digital music took off. It is the collective answer to the question "How can we make MP3 suck less?" Which is not to say that MP3 *sucks.* But it has a pretty shallow bag of tricks. AAC was developed a few years later and with a few years of additional experience in compressing music. The upshot is that AAC files sound better than MP3s and they take up less space. Well, generally-speaking, that is. Do keep in mind that there are wonks out there who absolutely insist that they can hear the difference between an LP and a CD. And ultra-ultra-wonks who claim that they can tell you what metal your speaker wires are made from. If you're at a party, you're meant to be dancing, not scrutinizing the music for time resolution and scale factor artifacts. You can indeed make an MP3 that sounds as good as an AAC file, but it'll still probably take up more space.

- **AIFF and Apple Lossless.** I'm grouping these two together because they fill the same function: to create the most perfect copy of the original CD track possible. Absolutely no sacrifices whatsoever will be made in the name of quality. This is a *good* thing if you're truly trying to archive your CDs permanently, creating a library of "masters" that you can burn duplicates from for years to come. This is a *bad* thing if you're truly trying to get more than, say, three songs to fit on your iPhone at once. Sacrifices have

to be made *somewhere,* and if you're not willing to sacrifice sound quality you're going to have to sacrifice file size to the max. Yes indeed, surely on this side of Jerusalem none suffer as you suffer. Just move on.

- **WAV.** The iPhone supports this format and so I suppose I'm begrudgingly required to report that yes, iTunes can rip to this format, too. But why on *earth* would you want to? WAV files are really big, they sound like a used coffee filter, and they're really only used by music producers who haven't bought new recording and mixing software in the past five years. Avoid.

Why I Choose AAC: It comes down to just AAC and MP3, and MP3's sole advantage is that it's a bit more widely supported. But it's a negligible advantage and even that minor gap continues to narrow. As a beloved industry columnist, I have dozens of devices here in my office that play digital music files, and the only thing I have that can play MP3s but not AAC files is a bizarre wristwatch music player that I got as a party favor.

Sound Quality

When we talk about sound quality, we're really talking about the bit rate iTunes uses when it converts a track into a music file. A higher bit rate translates into more detail. Think of it like this: a circle with two dots and a curvy line under it (what you humans call a "happy face") is a picture of your Uncle Sid if it were ripped at the lowest possible bit rate. A *moderate* bit rate is a cartoon that looks like him. Up the bit rate further, and it's a drawing that looks *exactly* like him. An image of Sid at the highest possible bit rate is a photo.

When you set the bit rate, you're telling iTunes, "Here's how much detail you can put into every second of the music file." As you might have guessed, though, when you increase the bit rate, all that extra detail amounts to a larger file. A track that was ripped with iTunes's default 128 Kbps bit rate won't sound as good as the same track ripped at 256 Kbps, but it'll take up half as much space on your iPhone and leave room for more music.

Bit rates are frustrating because they're so subjective. A drop in detail that one listener won't even notice will render a song unlistenable by another. And some songs are practically bulletproof. You can compress them down to nearly nothing without inflicting any damage on 'em.

Why I Choose 256 Kbps: Honestly? Because (a) I use smart playlists to replace the need to have the greatest possible quantity of music on my iPhone (you'll read about this in the next chapter), and (b) my new iPhone 3G S now has 32 gigabytes of storage instead of the 8 gigs in my original one. When you're using the AAC format, 128 Kbps is just fine for damned near every piece of music you throw at it. But if you rip a wide range of music styles (rock, folk, classical, skate-metal) and you listen to enough music, you will inevitably be lying there on the sofa, listening to (probably) a quiet piece played on acoustic instruments, and you'll realize that on *this* track and in *this* passage, a rich, thready violin sounds a bit … well, I dunno … mushy? I'd come up with a better word for it but the defect has already gone away, apparently, and it didn't really last long enough for me to focus in on it.

It's a problem of philosophy. You're going

to be ripping all your music into iTunes. If you're unhappy with the sound quality later on, there's nothing you can do about it except rip it all over again at a higher setting. I have over four terabytes of storage on my desktop Mac, and my iPhone can hold more music than I can possibly listen to in a whole month. I'm willing to put up with slightly larger music files if it means that a violin always sounds like a violin.

But because we're ripping with an iPhone or iPod Touch in mind — devices that don't have a beefy hard drive — be prepared to be flexible. I do think it's worth it to rip music at a higher bit rate, but if you find yourself ripping a book on tape, drop the bit rate down to 96 Kbps or even lower. It could be the difference between a three-hour file fitting on your device along with your other tracks, and having to leave it home. F. Murray Abraham has a fine voice and you don't need to hear it at maximum quality to follow all the plot points of the latest Danielle Steele bodice-ripper. So before you rip that *particular* disc, open up the Importing pane in the Preferences dialog box and choose Spoken Podcast from the Setting pop-up menu. Just remember to restore iTunes to its previous bit rate settings when you're done. Remember: These settings will apply to every track you rip.

Regard me as a member of the Sadder-But-Wiser club. The year I added my first truly humongous drive to my desktop was the year I determined to finally rip every last track of every last CD I owned into iTunes — nearly 800 in all.

Using that Import Songs and Eject setting I told you about earlier, I set up a laptop near the door to my office and kept a bin of CDs underneath. For a whole month, any time I crossed the threshold for any reason whatsoever, I would remove a "done" CD from the drive and replace it with a fresh one from the bin. At the end, the drive held a majestic 14,000 songs.

And then I had to do them all over again. Because I got this great little wireless box that streamed music files from iTunes any-where in the house. But it didn't like the file format I chose, and the bit rate was low enough that the difference was surprisingly noticeable when played through the good speakers downstairs.

Which is why my personal library has been ripped even more conservatively than I've advised you guys. Maximum possible bit rate, maximum possible compatibility. I've ripped 14,000 songs twice now and if I have to do it a third time, dammit, it's going to be done by a trained monkey in a little uniform.

Ripping DVDs

The Skim

'm not saying that the iTunes Store isn't a useful place to buy movies and TV shows. Just the other day, I was packing up after a week in San Francisco and wanted to download something to watch on my 6-hour flight home. So I got *Mon Oncle*, and …

Oh. No, that isn't in the iTunes Store. So I got *Mystery Science Theater 3000*, and …

Nope. *Columbo*? *Raiders of the Lost Ark*? *Shadow of the Thin Man*? *Paul Blart: Mall Cop*?

So I rented *Paul Blart: Mall Cop* and was mightily entertained for the first 14 minutes before I turned it off.

You see the problem. Thousands of movies and TV shows are available via iTunes. *Hundreds* of thousands of titles are available on DVD; more to the point, the movies and shows you actually want to watch on your iPhone are on DVD. Oh, and when you buy *The Big Lebowski* on DVD, you get all kinds of extras … and you'll be able to watch it in all kinds of places other than your iPhone and iTunes.

Yeah. I buy DVDs and rip them into movie files. It gives me access to a much larger library, I get all kinds of premium content (yes, iTunes now has "iTunes Extra" content but now we're talking about a range of offerings that's a subset *of* a subset of what's available on

DVD) and it's usually cheaper, besides.

BUT, IS THIS LEGAL?

Oh, legal, legal, *legal!* I swear! Is following the system of laws that keeps our democracy in place *all* that you care about?

It is?

Good. Just checking. My iPhone currently has three movies on it, and none of them

TIDBIT

I know that you're not here to feel sorry for me — though frankly, any pity you can throw my way is heartily appreciated — but it's probably worth pointing out how bloody difficult it is to write about DVD rippers that run on Windows.

In the several years I've been writing about this stuff, I've embraced and lost at least three different and terrific apps. One by one, like the crewmembers of the *USS Enterprise* who join Kirk, Spock, and the rest of the "name" cast on dangerous missions, these apps have been picked off by the movie industry's weasels. SlySoft actually makes a lovely little app called CloneDVD that does everything that HandBrake does. But it costs $40 and I can't really count on SlySoft selling it a year from now. It's Ensign McDonnell. It's wearing a red shirt, and it's just been sent off to investigate that strange noise coming from that rock that looks like it has a mouth and teeth.

are available for legal download anywhere. This leads some people to conclude that I in fact downloaded them *illegally,* from any one of hundreds of naughty file-sharing sites.

Nope. And I'll tell you why I didn't: Downloading copyrighted material without paying for it is just plain wrong. I say this without sarcasm, jokes, or subtle winks. If you want it, you have to buy it; in many cases, you can record a show off the TV.

Once you've obtained a legal copy of the movie (or TV show, or cartoon, or …), you have every right to make a copy that you can play on your iPhone. U.S. copyright law outlines several scenarios under which you can duplicate copyrighted material and it's right there in black and white: If you own it, you can copy it from one medium (such as a DVD) to another (such as a movie file). So it's all perfectly legal.

Pretty much.

As far as anyone can tell.

The only problem is that there's this *other* bit of the law, added in the Nineties, which says that if a publisher has put some sort of mojo on the recording to prevent copying, then it's illegal to break that copy protection. So on the one hand, the law says you have every right to copy that movie; on the other hand, it says that you're not really allowed to *exercise* that right.

So which part of the law wins? We dunno. A law hasn't received its official bar mitzvah until it's been tested in court, and either upheld or overturned. The very last thing the recording industry wants is for a judge to explicitly rule that a consumer has the right to copy a DVD onto an iPod and thus it's disinclined to truly test the extent of its legal protection.

Naturally, the very last thing that the entertainment industry wants is for a judge to explicitly underscore consumers' rights to copy movies regardless of the publisher's desire, so it's never dared do anything about any DVD copying done at the consumer level.

Instead, the entertainment industry has focused its legal efforts on preventing companies from *distributing* software that breaks the encryption on commercial discs. But where there's a will — or a world of people with empty iPhones, iPods, and other video players — there's a way.

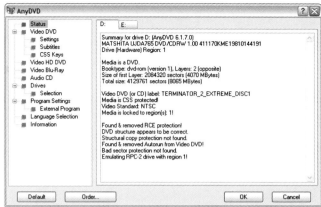

Figure 4-1

SlySoft's AnyDVD tames even the most savagely copy-protected commercial DVD.

WHAT A FRIEND WE HAVE IN HANDBRAKE

The great friend to the freedom-loving proletariat is a free app, available for both Windows *and* the Mac OS, known as HandBrake.

It's nearly impossible for the entertainment industry to shut this app down (as it has so successfully with so many other such apps) because — and get this — no one company owns it or profits from it. It's "open source" software, which means that it's built, maintained, updated, and distributed by the worldwide community of software developers. You might as well try to sue the stink off a donkey; it's everywhere and nowhere, so there's no real target.

You can download a copy of HandBrake for either Windows or Mac from the app's official site: http://handbrake.fr.

Both versions share the same user interface. And thanks to the entertainment industry's meddling, they share the same limitation: They can only rip DVDs that haven't been copy-protected. If you want to rip a DVD that you burned with a DVD recorder, HandBrake can convert the disc's contents to movie files unaided. If you want to rip the commercial movie you bought last week, you'll need a little helper app to handle the descrambling.

WINDOWS HELPER: ANYDVD

All righty. Good news, sensation-seekers, because SlySoft (www.slysoft.com) has come to the rescue with a rather simple and awesome little app: AnyDVD. It'll cost you €49 (at this writing) but it's a magical app and it's well-worth the dough, even if European dough has funny colors.

AnyDVD does one thing. It does it well, and it does it invisibly: It breaks the copy-

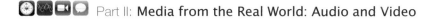

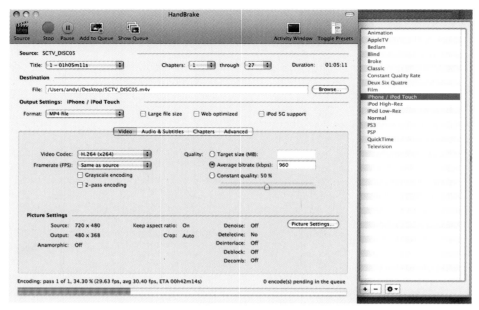

Figure 4-2
HandBrake in action

protection on commercial DVDs and bamboozles Windows into thinking it's just an ordinary, plane-Jane disc.

For the sake of completeness, and to take advantage of the lovely color layout of this book, I'll go ahead and show you what Any-DVD looks like. Take a gander at Figure 4-1.

This is the window that comes up if you click on the little cartoon fox that AnyDVD puts in your system tray. But honestly, it's just there to satisfy your curiosity and to confirm that it's working. Whenever you insert a DVD, AnyDVD grabs it before Windows or any other app ever sees it. It silently performs the mojo required to break the copy-protection on the disc, and *then* it presents it to the operating system.

From that point onward, any time any app makes a request for some of the data

on the DVD, it goes through AnyDVD. It decrypts the data and passes it along to the app that wanted it, without the app's knowledge. It's as though Pixar decided to actually, you know, *trust* you by selling you a copy of *The Incredibles* without any copy protection to begin with.

MAC HELPER: VLC

The Mac edition of HandBrake *used* to be an all-in-one solution. But its open-source developers chose to break out the DVD-ripping portion of the app, just to make it invulnerable to lawsuits.

The good news: The change amounts to a small inconvenience, nothing more. Whereas the Windows folks need to shell out €49 for a commercial tool, Mac users need only head to www.videolan.org/

vlc and download a free copy of VLC Player. It's an impressive video player in its own right but for our purposes, we love it because it contains a code library for decrypting DVDs. You don't even need to launch VLC Player; HandBrake knows where that code library is and loads it in when you ask it to rip a commercial DVD.

There's a second option and it's yet another open-source software project: Fairmount, a free download from www.metakine.com/products/fairmount. It works like AnyDVD. With Fairmount installed and running, any DVD you insert will be intercepted and then decrypted on the fly. The OS will then treat it like a normal, unencrypted DVD. You can even drag its contents to another hard drive, straight from the Finder.

OKAY, BACK TO HANDBRAKE

We're all now on the same page. We all have HandBrake running on our computers and have it capable of converting commercial discs. Figure 4-2 shows you the Mac version of HandBrake; I'm using it for all the examples that follow.

Converting a DVD just takes four steps:

1. Point HandBrake at the DVD. You do this by clicking the Browse button and then either selecting the disc in the file browser or navigating directly to the VIDEO_TS folder on the disc.

2. Tell HandBrake that you'd like the app to prepare a video file that's optimized for the iPhone. In Windows, you do this by choosing Presets ▶ iPhone or just selecting it from the panel of presets on the right side of the window. On the Mac, you'll find the presets in

TIP

One note about the Windows edition of HandBrake: it's what's called a ".Net" application. What that means to you is that you'll need to have Microsoft's free .Net framework installed on your PC.

Oh, a technical explanation of .Net? It's, er, a set of little software gremlins that helps .Net apps like HandBrake to run. It's likely that you already have .Net installed on your PC but if HandBrake complains when you launch it, you can download .Net for free from www.microsoft.com. The download URL is so long that it'd choke a giraffe, so I'll point you to www.microsoft.com/downloads and tell you to type ".Net framework" into the Search box. The first hit returned will probably be ".Net Framework Version (whatever) Redistributable Package." That's the baby.

the drawer on the right-hand side of the window, which you can open by clicking the Toggle Presets button if it isn't open already. HandBrake will choose all the settings that are appropriate for a video file playing on your iPhone.

3. Choose the content that you want to convert by making a selection from the Title pop-up menu. Note that a disc's content is chopped up into several different "titles." You don't normally see this organization because you usually navigate through the disc's

TROUBLE

In Chapter 3, I urge you to think about the world that exists outside your iPhone before you start ripping your entire 1,000-CD music library. Ripping is a hassle-filled, analog process — so you only want to do it once. So why not rip your music into a format that sounds great on your home stereo, not just through those cheap plastic earbuds?

Same deal with video. If you use the iPhone preset, your movie will be scaled down to the size of an iPhone screen: 480×256. But! If you select "iPod Hi-Rez," the resolution bumps up to 640×352. Go for broke? Sure! Select iPhone, and then click the Picture Settings button. A panel of controls opens and you can click the resolution all the way up to the DVD's maximum: 720×400.

Why *wouldn't* you want to encode the video at the highest possible quality? Er, because it'll create a gi-normous video file

and it *might* not sync to your iPhone or iPod Touch without an extra conversion. The ginormity problem is obvious. You'll wind up with a 1.5-gigabyte movie instead of a 1-gig version. Meaning: Your iPhone will lose three whole episodes of *The Simpsons* worth of storage. But the "won't play on the iPhone" bit is a hassle as well, sure. An iPhone video can't be wider than 640 pixels or taller than 480, and the bit rate — the amount of data that the device can be expected to throw up on the screen per second — can't exceed 1.5 megabits (given as: 1.5 Mbps). If you stick within those parameters, you'll be good. HandBrake's iPod Hi-Res setting should work fine.

On my most favoritest movies and TV shows, I work to get the best of both worlds. I ripped *The Conversation* twice. I made one compact version for my iPhone and a second, spare-no-horses version that will look great when I play it on the huge monitor in my living room.

content from that bouncy menu on your TV. Lurking underneath all that stuff, a DVD might have one title just for the main menu animation, a second for the actual movie, a third for a version of the movie with scenes restored from the director's first cut, that sort of thing. Usually the correct title just jumps right out at you. If you're converting *Terminator 2*, your eye's sort of drawn to that one title that says it's 2 hours and 32 minutes long, especially because you went on www.imdb.com and verified the film's running time.

4. Choose a destination for the video file. Give it a good name; HandBrake chooses one for you based on how the title is defined by the disc, but *Apocalypse Now — Redux Edition* is going to make more sense to you than ANOWR-99. But I suppose I shouldn't assume. Do whatever you want. You're an incorrigible movie pirate; you're a maverick who plays by your own rules! (Well, not really, but it's fun to pretend.)

5. And that's really it. Click Start.

And wait.

Lots.

If you've recently bought a 5,000-piece jigsaw puzzle, now's a good time to go back to the store and exchange it for a 10,000-piece one. Using HandBrake's default iPhone settings, converting a DVD to a movie file can take as long as two or three times the running time of the actual film. If you're running HandBrake on one of those ultra-affordable Windows notebooks with a CPU made from the same sort of stuff that goes into a Cheez-It cracker … well, suffice to say that the sequel to this movie will be in theaters by the time HandBrake is finished.

HandBrake will end the process by making a snarky comment about how long it took to finish the conversion. Pretend not to be annoyed and you're finished: Just drag the file into your iTunes library and presto, it can be synced to your iPhone without any further ado.

The neat thing about HandBrake's iPhone setting is that it's truly one-stop shopping. All the decisions have been made for you and the only thing you really need to do is figure out whether you'd prefer to pace fitfully or fretfully while your computer works on the problem.

But it has plenty of little tweaks, options, and settings, proving once again that life is a banquet and that we have but to take our seats and dig in:

◻ If you're converting a DVD that contains a dozen episodes of a TV series, you'll want to know about Hand-Brake's Queue feature. Repeat all of the steps above verbatim, and click Add To Queue instead of the button that starts the ripping process. Select

> **TIP**
>
> If you've got a plane to catch or something, you should instead choose MPEG-4 Video/AAC Audio from the popup list of codecs in the middle of the window. You'll have it in no time — about half the running time of the original movie. The quality won't be *quite* up to the same level, and it's *possible* that the video won't be compatible with all iPhones and iPods. But at least it leaves you with hope.

the next episode, give it a different name, and click the Add to Queue button. Repeat until you've added all the content you'd like to rip. When you click the start button, HandBrake will grind on each of these videos in turn, leaving you free to pursue those many humanitarian efforts that you've been putting off for way too long.

◻ HandBrake can include any audio track you want. If the movie has several audio tracks (a director's commentary, a foreign language track, etc.), you can select that track from HandBrake's Audio & Subtitles panel (see Figure 4-3). The only trick is that it's up to you to figure out which track is which. The first audio track is always the plain-vanilla one, but if there are three additional audio tracks you'll have to resort to a little bit of trial and error to figure out which one is the cast of *Reno: 911!* riffing on the movie in-character, and which one is

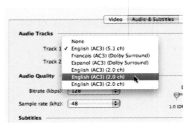

Figure 4-3
Choosing an alternative audio track

ranking executive with the Motion Picture Association of America.

Now if you'll excuse me, I have a four-hour train ride tomorrow, and HandBrake has just finished converting the original, *non*-hideous version of *All the King's Men*.

the actors commenting as themselves.

So if the movie industry has taken such great pains to prevent you from copying DVDs, why is it so bloody easy?

Oh, you'll love this: because the movie industry was way, *way* too secretive when its minions developed the encryption method.

The counterintuitive thing about developing a brand-new encryption scheme is that the very *last* thing you want to do is perform your work in secret. You want to share your efforts with the crypto community at every stage, and allow as many people as possible to peer at it from every conceivable angle. In short: You want people to *try* to break it early on, before you commit to this system and you've lost the ability to make it stronger.

But no, the same industry that thought that remaking the Oscar-winning *All the King's Men* was a good idea also thought that developing an encryption scheme behind closed doors would work gangbusters. And sure enough, within a year, weaknesses were found, published, and widely exploited.

If Wile E. Coyote had gone for his MBA instead of spending all that dough on Acme merchandise, then surely he'd be a high-

Ancient Analog Audio: LPs and Tapes

The Skim

Ah, the inherent superiority of vinyl! The added warmth ... the air around the notes ... the obvious parametric dimensionality at the top end of the spectrum!

What rubbish. What complete, cod-slapping *rubbish*. Good riddance to vinyl LPs. I suppose that if you have the sort of stereo system where each speaker costs roughly as much as a decent beach cottage and you're in a listening room built to the manufacturer's exact specifications, you can sense a superiority to analog recordings — if you're drunk enough. Only then could you fully appreciate the warmth, air, and dimensionality of every click and pop and skip of a 30-year-old LP.

LPs do have one advantage over CDs: The BBC has never issued an LP of *Not the 9 O'Clock News* on CD, nor has Amnesty International ever released *The Secret Policeman's Ball ...*

(searching ...)

Okay, it turns out that this album was released in 1992. But it's out of print and the cheapest copy I can find online is $99. I think you've caught up with me and my point anyway: There's a lot of material out there that never made it to CD, let alone the iTunes Store. If you ever want to enjoy one of these rare pressings again, you'll need to drag it clicking and screaming into the realm of digital by hand.

TIDBIT

I'm not kidding about having given up on converting commercial albums to digital. All the screen shots in this chapter show me converting Paul Shaffer's long-out-of-print first album *Coast to Coast* — you know, he's David Letterman's bandleader — to iTunes-studly files. By the time I was finished with the chapter, I'd probably devoted about a full week to recording, polishing, and importing all 11 tracks.

So am I now enjoying these tracks on my iPhone? Nope. Because on Day 2, I used the Best Technique Ever for converting out-of-print albums: I just went to Amazon.com. If an album is out of print, the store will hook you up with an independent store that can sell you a used copy. *Coast to Coast* is nearly 20 years old but it was indeed released on CD, and inside of five minutes I'd chosen a "Like New" copy from the list of 21 available sellers.

The cost: $8.30 including shipping. Best of all, I have an absolutely *perfect* copy of the extended *Late Night* theme and I ripped it in just under 40 seconds.

The lesson: *Don't be a hero.* I'm a professional. I get paid to do this.

On a more pressing note, there's plenty of family history on audiotape. Your parents or grandparents sure didn't record their kids' school holiday concert on a digital device; they had a cassette recorder from Sears.

MANAGING EXPECTATIONS

When you contemplate that stack of records, your goals should be Apollo 11 in scale. You'll get the astronauts there and you'll get them back alive. You'll emerge from the adventure with a cool box of moon rocks and some solid science and nobody can ever challenge your assertion that "Yes! I did that." What you *won't* wind up with is a profitable, self-sustaining 800-person permanent moon colony where Will Smith, the colony's military governor, off-planet for two months on R&R, returns to find a deadly conspiracy and two hours of action and adventure including a ten-minute lunar buggy chase in one-sixth Earth gravity.

Nope. Instead, you'll have audio files that sound nearly as good as the original. Even if these audio files are perfect — and as you can see, that might not even be possible — they'll dramatically underscore the limitations of LPs and cassettes as audio formats. You say the digital file has an annoying background hiss, and lacks a certain brightness and clarity? Well, congratulations: You've produced an MP3 that's *exactly* as good as the original tape. To bring it up to iTunes Store quality requires not only a good tape/record player and expensive, "prosumer" recording software, but a good ear and experience in producing audio … or a $100 utility and a bit of patience. And even then, luck needs to be on your side.

Over the past few years I've tried nearly

every combination of commercial hardware and software for converting old recordings to digital. And the experience has left me convinced that the only recordings that are truly worth all this effort are the ones that are never, ever going to be released on CD. Like tapes of family events, or conference and class lectures, and music that was lucky to ever win a commercial release to begin with.

Now that I've gotten you properly depressed about the feasibility of converting LPs and tapes to digital, onward to bright, optimistic solutions.

TECHNIQUE 1: TURN YOUR $2,000 PC INTO A $50 TAPE RECORDER

The easiest and cheapest solution? Go to Radio Shack, buy a stereo cable with a pair of RCA jacks on one end and a stereo headphone jack on the other, plug your audio component into the microphone jack of your PC or Mac, and then use desktop recording software to record each individual track or program the old fashioned way: Click the Record button on the software and then start the music playing from the other end.

This has the huge advantage of setting you back all of five bucks, tops. Even the software is free: Go to http://audacity.sourceforge.net and download Audacity. It's a powerful, open source, and free audio recording and editing app with editions for both PCs and Macs. Just be sure to download the MP3 plug-in. The main app can save files as AIFF audio, which iTunes can easily import and convert to AAC or MP3. But if you download the MP3 plug-in, Audacity saves the audio as an immediately

> **TIP**
>
> GarageBand is a nigh-professional audio recording app that comes with every Mac. You Windows folks might have something just as good on your PC, depending on where you bought it. And yet I'm recommending some Internet freebie?
>
> Indeed I am. We're just doing some very nuts-and-bolts audio recording and editing here and almost any alternative is overkill. You'll get the project finished more quickly and with far less fuss using Audacity than any other tool. I've tried 'em all and I keep coming back to this swift, elegant little app.

iPhone-friendly format — and you'll save a step.

(Yes, the iPhone can play AIFF. But it's gi-*nor*mous uncompressed audio, remember.)

Figure 5-1 shows you Audacity's basic editing window.

To record audio:

1. Plug the cable into your computer's microphone port, and select it as the source to record from. In Windows, go to the Sounds control panel and select the built-in line input in the Recording tab. On a Mac, open the Sound system preference, click the Input tab, and click on the built-in input.

2. Launch Audacity and choose Start Monitoring from the pop-up menu next to the microphone icon (see Figure 5-2). This will allow you to "watch" the sound coming in through

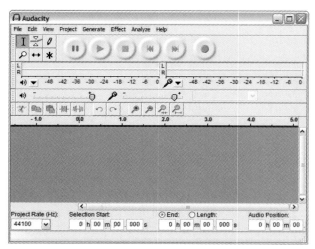

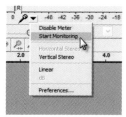

Figure 5-2
Turning on Audacity's input monitor

Figure 5-1
Audacity: basic, but effective, sound recording for both PC and Mac

Figure 5-3
Getting the levels just right

the microphone port and adjust the recording levels appropriately.

3. Play some music. It doesn't matter what; you're not recording yet. You just want to set the input level correctly. Start off by adjusting the output volume of your tape deck or the stereo your turntable is plugged into. Listen via a set of headphones plugged into your computer as you nudge the output volume of the component up, up, up. The moment you start to hear distortion, back off some. That's the right output level.

4. Once you're satisfied with the levels, click the Record button in Audacity and restart the playback from the beginning.

It's best to record an entire side of the album or cassette at once, and then use Audacity's simple cut-and-paste editing tools to slice each track into its own audio file afterward. Just highlight the section of the waveform that represents Dexy's Midnight Runners' "Come on, Eileen," click Copy, create a new file, and then click Paste.

This way, you don't need to babysit a whole album that (frankly) would have been issued on CD if it were any good to begin with. Dexy's Midnight Runners? Really? Oh, dear. I'm not here to judge you but still ... *oh, dear.*

TECHNIQUE 2: THROW SOME MONEY AT THE PROBLEM

Hooking up an old audio component with a $5 cable is a fine solution. But here I'm assuming that you still even own a working turntable. Even if you have one in the closet, is the needle in any sort of decent shape, or is it the same one that came with the player when your dad bought it in 1977?

Oh, and remember: Turntables tend to require a special input. If you run a cable straight from the player itself, the levels will probably be way too low, which is why you'd need to run it through an amp.

If you have *lots* of LPs to convert, you might want to make a small investment in a USB turntable. As the name implies, these are record players that use USB as their audio outputs instead of old-fashioned analog plugs. You plug it into any USB port and your PC or Mac sees it as a digital audio input device.

The upside? You wind up with solid, line-level audio that your computer can work with intimately. The medium is digital, so the hookup to your computer won't introduce any *more* problems with the audio. And these turntables are relatively cheap. Again, if you have plenty of LPs to convert, it simplifies things when you begin with a brand-new turntable with a brand-new needle.

Many companies make USB turntables — even big-names like Sony. I recommend turntables by Ion (www.ionaudio.com), which has a wide range of models; it's not just this one freak item in the product line.

Ion's TTUSB05 (shown in Figure 5-4) is sturdy, practical, and — at about $99 list — quite affordable; you won't feel like a dope for converting a dozen albums with it and then never using it ever again. For some extra scratch, you can avoid the computer middleman completely: The LP Dock model even has an iPhone-compatible dock, and via the iPhone's onboard stereo recording app, you can "play" albums directly into the device. The next time you sync your iPhone, the new recordings will be copied into your iTunes library as voice memos.

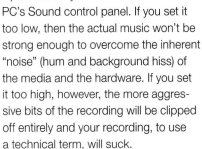

TIDBIT

Setting the *input* levels correctly is something of a black art. You set the input level via the microphone slider in Audacity, or via the master input level on your Mac or PC's Sound control panel. If you set it too low, then the actual music won't be strong enough to overcome the inherent "noise" (hum and background hiss) of the media and the hardware. If you set it too high, however, the more aggressive bits of the recording will be clipped off entirely and your recording, to use a technical term, will suck.

Figure 5-3 shows the input meter, displaying what Audacity is hearing at a given instant. It also shows you the input levels that I'm aiming for. 0 (zero) represents the strongest sound that the hardware can record cleanly. Any level above zero will be garbage. The blue lines in Figure 5-3 represent the "loudest" passages of the recording. The red lines represent the "recent" peaks.

Yes, it's sort of like a game of chicken. I want to have the input level high enough that the blue lines get *close* to zero without ever hitting it; that means I've chosen a nice, strong, clean, powerful level that won't distort. And if the power meter never gets anywhere near it, then I know I've set the volume level too low on the playback device.

Once you have the USB player hooked up, it's just another audio input; you can use

Figure 5-4

Ion modernizes the record player with USB.

Figure 5-5

Removing pops, hisses, and other nastiness with Audacity's built-in cleaner

Audacity (or any other audio recording app) as normal.

CLEANUP

I did set the standards low at the very top of the chapter, didn't I? Hiss, clicks, pops, buzzes ... they're impossible to avoid even with a brand-new LP fresh from wherever the hell people bought LPs from back when they were relevant.

If there's a pop or some other nastiness and it takes place during a *silent* passage, we can just select the offending blip and cover it with a little silence: Just choose Generate ▶ Silence in Audacity. Bang, it's gone.

It's more likely that you'll want to remove noise from actual music. Audacity has a tool for that as well in the form of a cleanup wizard. Choose Effect ▶ Noise Removal. The wizard appears, taking the spectral form of Figure 5-5.

Do not inquire as to the nature of the wizard's powers. In rough terms, you select a patch of the recording that represents "silence" and then the wizard uses that sampling to ask the question "if that section is meant to be silent, then I should 'clean' that sort of sound from the whole record-

ing?" You'll need to fiddle with the slider and experiment a little, but it usually offers some clear improvements.

If you're serious about this, buy a plug-in from Bias called SoundSoap (see Figure 5-6). Bias makes professional audio processing apps, and SoundSoap is the "consumer" edition of a pretty intense, heavy-duty tool. SoundSoap doesn't do everything that its Pro big brother can do, but the $79 edition can still perform wonders. Again, not a tool for the casual user but if you have a thick stack of important LPs and tapes to convert, it might be worth the investment. Go to http://bias-inc.com to download a free trial edition.

Gosh, that sounds like it was a lot of work. It almost seems as though it would have been simpler to get your favorite 1982 hair-metal band to reunite in your living room and re-record their one hit, directly into your PC's microphones.

(Maybe you should try that. They could probably use the gig.)

And we haven't even gotten to the steps

Figure 5-6
The professional hitman of audio noise:
SoundSoap by Bias

you need to perform after you import the
finished track into iTunes! None of these
tracks have the album, artist, and title information that you get automatically when you
rip a CD or purchase a track from iTunes.

All told, it's probably best to forget that
you ever cared about this band to begin
with.

I mean, take a look at those losers on the
album cover. I think the fewer people who
know that you were ever into this group, the
better.

Old Home Video

The Skim

This is a wonderful day, sensation-seekers: I am compelled, nay *commanded*, to come up with a reference to *The Prisoner*, the cult Sixties spy series. A secret agent played by Patrick McGoohan resigns from the Secret Agent Agency and returns to his apartment, which is flooded with knockout gas just as he's leafing through brochures for retirement destinations. He wakes up in The Village, a remote and not entirely unpleasant portside community. It's where spies are sent if they're in that itchy intersection of "no longer of any immediately relevant use" and "potentially too valuable to simply be allowed to run around free."

My version of The Village is a back corner of a basement closet. It contains (as of the last census): a VCR, an 8mm camcorder, and a LaserDisc player. Each of these items has long since been replaced by something far more digital and far less improbable. But like McGoohan's character (referred to in *The Village* only as "Number 6"), this obsolete gear must be held indefinitely. As long as there might be even just *one* 8mm cassette of a 17-year-old niece's third birthday party, or *one* VHS cassette containing the *Far Side Halloween Special* that aired just once, and as long as I know that I own *Let It Be* on LaserDisc and that The Beatles are so mortified by this movie that they'll never allow it to be released on DVD ... well, these devices will continue to enjoy a pleasant if marginal existence.

We won't be stuck with this stuff forever, though. I'm steadily converting those home movies, old TV shows, and extended sequences of Paul McCartney acting like a first-class noodge into digital video files so that I can enjoy them on my iPhone just as readily as anything I bought off the iTunes Store last night.

All this is possible because these old devices have standard analog video and audio connectors. Whether they're fat yellow RCA connectors or the higher-grade SVHS plugs, their outputs can be routed into devices that can transmogrify that content into ginchy, wonderful digital video. Some methods are more direct than others; the right choice depends on how much of this old content you have, and how serious you are about archiving it all into digital video.

Mind you, watching Chevy Chase's attempt at a late-night talk show will still suck. But at least it'll suck on an awesome smartphone, instead of via a big, clanky box.

THE MOST DIGITAL SOLUTION

At the top of the list is a video "bridge" that takes analog video and audio as input and converts it into digital video on the fly during playback. It squirts into your PC or Mac via a USB or FireWire port and desktop software takes it from there. The procedure, in broad strokes:

1. Hook the playback machine (the VHS deck, the old camcorder, the LaserDisc player) to your computer via a hardware interface.
2. Capture the video to your hard drive.
3. Edit the video and export it to an

iTunes-studly format.

This will cost you anything from (a) nothing to (b) hundreds of dollars, depending on what you already have lying around the house and how good you'd like the final results to be; the complexity of the process will depend on what software you use.

THE HARDWARE

If you're lucky, you already own a digital camcorder. You already know how well these things work with desktop computers. Unless you got the cheapest model in the store — the one they keep in stock just so the salesman can show off its shortcomings and help sell you the better ones — it has a built-in digital interface that lets you plug the camera right into your desktop. You can then "play" the video straight into your computer.

Many of these cameras also have an analog "pass through" feature. If you rummage deep down into the box, you'll find a cable with what appears to be a hyperthyroid headphone plug at one end and connectors at the other and that can accept standard analog RCA and SVHS video and audio. If so ... huzzah! You can connect the old analog video player into this plug, plug the camcorder into your computer, and use the camcorder as a capture device.

You'll have to operate the old player manually, but the camcorder will perform all the format conversions necessary and any standard video editing app (like Windows Movie Maker or the Mac's iMovie) will be able to record the incoming signal to your hard drive.

If you *don't* have a camcorder, you'll have to exercise the ancient martial art of MasterCard-Fu. You can buy simple USB-based analog-to-digital interfaces fairly cheap, though.

I really like the hardware made by Pinnacle Systems (www.pinnaclesys. com). The big-box stores are full of cheap and questionable products that promise to transfer your old videos to digital, but Pinnacle takes this sort of thing very seriously. Its Video Creator Plus is a solid, all-in-one solution. It captures video and also includes simple editing tools that can export video files directly into iTunes, all for $89.

Pinnacle's equivalent Mac offering is the Pinnacle Video Capture — another all-in-one hardware/software combo, but it'll cost you a full $99 smackers. Mac users might check out Elgato's own creatively named Video Capture, also $99 (www.elgato. com). As a Mac-only product, it's a little better thought-out than Pinnacle's box, which apparently is there in the product line just to cover all the bases.

All these devices capture high-quality video, and the digital conversion is handled by hardware inside the device instead of software running on your desktop — which means that you'll wind up with smooth, clean video with "as good as it's ever going to get" color and detail.

Cheaper gizmos rely on the processing power of your PC. At their worst, they're pretty damned bad. Many of them capture video at only half its original resolution and at a jerky 15 frames per second instead of 30.

If you're ambitious about converting and editing old video, you might want to upgrade to something like Canopus's ADVC-110. If you have any experience with technology, you know that when they give a product a name consisting of a random string of numbers and letters, it's going to cost you.

Yeah, this device isn't designed for random consumers who want to convert a few home movies and old TV shows. It's for people who want the highest level of performance (it captures gorgeous video) and greatest convenience (it doesn't require any special software or drivers; you plug it in and any consumer or professional video editing app that knows how to deal with digital video cameras can accept input from the box).

If you buy it online, it'll run you about $220. So yeah: The Pinnacle hardware is starting to look pretty good.

THE SOFTWARE

Onward to editing software. The software you get with the Pinnacle capture hardware (and other gear in its class) tends to be rather basic, like operating a VCR. If you want to do something more ambitious than deleting the commercials from a TV show, you might want to pop for a better app.

If you have a Mac, though, there's really no point in going any farther than the copy of iMovie that came installed on your computer. It's a simple, powerful, and fully mature editing app, and because it has an Apple logo on it you can be sure that when you tell it to export the final video to your iPhone or iPod Touch, the programmers knew what they were doing.

On the PC, there are two good choices. Pinnacle is actually a subsidiary of Avid Technologies, the company that makes the professional standard in TV and film editing systems. Its Pinnacle Studio app is dirt-cheap at $49 and can export finished video to iTunes for syncing.

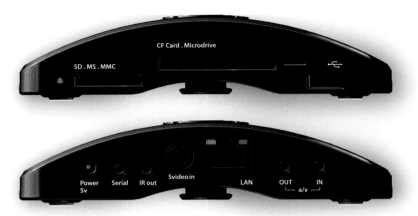

Figure 6-1
Neuros OSD: VCR for the Space Age

If you intend to do a lot of this sort of thing, you'll probably be happier giving Adobe $99 of your cash for a copy of Adobe Premiere Elements (www.adobe.com). It's filled with time-saving features and attractive little tweaks that let you turn two hours of boring soccer video into six minutes of terrific highlights, toot sweet.

INDIRECT SOLUTIONS WITH FRINGE BENEFITS

There's a certain satisfaction to buying a box that turns an old VCR into a desktop computer peripheral, more or less. But there are other ways of converting old video into digital, iPhone-studly formats. You might already have one or two of these things in your house. If you need to go out and *buy* a solution, you might prefer to buy something that will have a life outside of converting Aunt Mimsy's third bridal shower.

DVD Recorders

In Chapter 4, I talked about ripping DVDs into digital video. Well, then why

bother even hauling your VCR into your home office? Just hook it up to the DVD recorder's inputs, do a direct machine-to-machine copy, burn the disc and then slide it into your computer and rip it as normal.

The sole disadvantage of this method is that the video will be compressed as it's written to the disc. Ordinarily that'd be a drawback — when you're "remastering" content, you want it to arrive as clean as possible — but given the flaws in the original video source, you're not likely to lose much.

A DVD recorder is actually my favorite method of converting video. When I know I have something really important (like video of a newborn kid) I go all-out. But when I have a box of old TV shows — many of which are unlabeled — the recorder is a quick way to move those tapes from the garage into the trash. Put a 50-cent blank DVD in the machine, push Record on the recorder, push Play on the VCR, and walk away for two hours. By the time I remember doing that, the whole tape has been archived and I can toss the original, bulky cassette, saving the actual viewing and editing of its contents for later.

Neuros OSD

If you *really* want to be Captain Digital — or if you simply resist the concept of wholesale change — the Neuros OSD is an exciting piece of hardware (shown in Figure 6-1). It's a digital VCR. Really, that explanation is perfect. You plug it into the stack of video gear under your TV. Any time you're watching something and you think, "Oooh, I'd like to record that for my iPhone," you just pick up the Neuros's remote and press Record.

The video is automatically converted into a digital video file and stored on any storage device you've plugged into the Neuros's USB port, or any memory card you've popped into one of its exhaustive menagerie of card slots. When you unplug the hard drive or thumb drive or memory card from the OSD and plug it into your computer, you'll find it full of standard MP4 video files, which you can import directly into iTunes or edit using desktop video software.

Visit www.neurostechnology.com for more info. It costs $170 but man alive, it's a frightfully compelling video-to-digital solution that's right where you want it. Press a button, you've got MP4.

THE JOYS OF CONVERSION

What's the best thing about converting old videos? It removes irreplaceable family memories from decrepit media and puts them in a form where they can easily and flawlessly be duplicated and shared.

The second-best thing is that there's a great deal of fantastic creative work that simply dies because there's no way it'll ever be released on DVD or even re-aired. Either there's no financial incentive, or the rights are tangled up in a huge mess of companies that got bought by other companies which went bust, or it contains music that would be prohibitively expensive to license for home video distribution.

My usual example is a fantastic 1983 production of Shakespeare's *The Comedy of Errors*, starring the Flying Karamazov Brothers and two dozen other jugglers, rope walkers, and fellow New Vaudevillians. It was a successful stage show and PBS aired a performance on *Live from Lincoln Center*. It aired live. PBS stations were allowed to rebroadcast it once within the week, and then … that was it. Gone. It was an utterly brilliant show, but after the performers went their separate ways after the final performance, the show might as well never have happened in the first place.

But! Folks had taped it when it aired more than 25 years ago. I got a great tape duped from the collection of one of the original performers. After less than an afternoon, I had digital video on my iPhone and my desktop. I watch and enjoy it all over again every few months.

I was too young to appreciate the heyday of the telethon, but I still had to reflect that in the Seventies, you'd tune into the first couple of hours of this show and you'd see Frank Sinatra singing a duet with Ella Fitzgerald, followed by Sammy Davis Jr. backed by the Count Basie Orchestra.

Someone has that show on tape. If you do, let me know because I have a Neuros OSD and a desperate need to be entertained.

Glorious Television

The Skim

like the iTunes Store, I *use* the iTunes Store, and I want to *support* the iTunes Store. Those plucky Apple kids are showing a lot of spunk with their little garage startup, and if this is what they want to do after college instead of going on to law school like they've always said they wanted to, well, it breaks our hearts — mine and their poor mothers' — but we always *said* that we wanted to raise kids with enough confidence and self-reliance to choose their own paths in life.

But all too often, folks count on the iTunes Store as their sole means of acquiring content. It's like fast food. It's quick and it's easy and it's always available. But it's always more money than you need to spend, and it only offers a limited menu.

I'm pretty surprised, for instance, that folks pay $30 to $50 for season passes to their favorite shows. If you're willing to be a season behind at all times, that's more than the cost of that same season on DVD. And you don't get a DVD's higher video quality or its huge quantity of extras.

And if you *don't* want to wait, then hell, you can buy simple TV tuner hardware that plugs into a USB port. A USB TV tuner is afford-able. It's a tiny and simple piece of hardware, usually no larger than

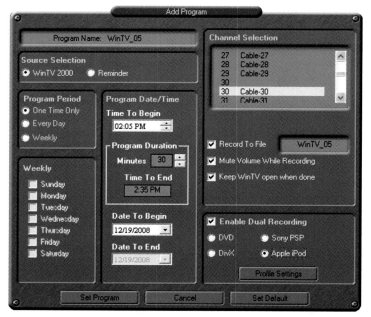

Figure 7-1

Recording WinTV shows to your iPhone on a Wing

TV TO PC TO IPHONE

On the Mac, there's really only one choice for TV-recording hardware and software. But on a PC, there's ... let's see ...

(Ihnatko shoves the edge of his desk and sends self and his chair to the other side of the office; retrieves a big plastic tub full of hardware; crab-walks chair back to desk.)

... at least seven. But my favorite continues to be the broad line of choices available from Hauppage (www.hauppage.com).

You can buy a dirt-cheap, $55 card that installs inside your desktop PC, a little $80 USB box, a just-as-cheap thing the size of a USB thumb drive that you can easily take with you when you travel ... even big $200 cards that can record digital satellite TV and features dual tuners so that it can record more than one show at a time.

They all include Hauppage's WinTV tuner/PVR (personal video recorder) software, which is a treat to use. WinTV is available in both conventional analog and bleeding-edge digital TV editions.

Unfortunately, the WinTV software doesn't support iTunes directly. But the company offers Wing, a $25 add-on app that can record TV shows directly to your

a USB thumb drive.

Whether over-the-air (ATSC) or clear-QAM cable programming, it records pure digital signals that are every bit as good as anything you'd get from the iTunes Store — and the shows you record can be added to your iTunes library and synced to your iPhone automatically, shortly after the show's end-credits have been squished off the side of the screen.

If you were going to buy two or three season passes, you've more than covered the cost of the hardware. And remember, *Late Show with David Letterman* isn't coming to the iTunes Store anytime soon.

So it's a choice of either the infinite possibilities of cooking your own TV content or spending more money and having a limited range of options. It's a no-brainer.

iPhone or iPod Touch by simply clicking a checkbox (see Figure 7-1).

WINDOWS MEDIA CENTER

I can tell just by the way you're holding this book that you're a person of wealth and taste. It's possible that you already *own* a machine that records TV shows digitally.

If you happen to use the Media Center features available in Windows Vista or Windows 7, there's a fab little app that can take its programming, convert them to MP4 files, and add them to your iTunes library: iPodifier, a free download from www. ipodifier.com.

Figure 7-2 shows the app in action. After a few moments of pointing and clicking, the shows you've recorded will be transcoded into an iPhone-studly format and squirted into your iTunes library.

TV TO MAC TO IPHONE

In the grand tradition that's been kept alive by everyone who's ever gotten a tattoo on an impulse, I'm going to pretend that something bad is actually exactly the *perfect thing*. Watch me:

"Hey, isn't it terrific that there's pretty much only *one* solution for recording TV on a Mac? Those poor bastards with PCs have to make a decision after looking at almost a *dozen* different options!"

Okay, well, it's not like there's *really* only one piece of tuner hardware and PVR software available. For the Mac there are as many as ... um ... okay, two.

But the only one I'll tell you about is the EyeTV from Elgato. The hardware and software are head-and-shoulders above anything else. They have a whole line of external boxes that work on nearly all Macs,

TIDBIT

I honestly don't get why *all* the TV tuner cards available for PCs don't directly support iTunes export. I *understand* it — it's a little bit of extra work, plus they're wimping out to pressure from TV networks, who would rather that everybody *purchased* their shows in digital format, rather than transcoding them for free as is their right — but still, I don't get it. Nonetheless, every PC TV tuner card or USB device I've seen records your TV shows in either MPEG-1 or MPEG-2 format. And both of these can be converted to an iPhone or iPod Touch-compatible MP4 file easily with Applian's $29 Replay Converter (www.applian. com). Just locate the file (it might be buried inside the app's Program directory), choose the preset iPod or iPhone configuration, and click.

including conventional and HDTV options.

Check out products and prices at www. elgato.com. I use the $149 EyeTV Hybrid, seen in Figure 7-3, for both my desktop and my MacBook. It's compact enough to travel with me and silently keep me up to date with the irresponsible self-absorbed recreational drug use of Dr. Gregory House while I travel.

As a Mac-only product, the EyeTV software is aggressive in its support for iPhones and iPods (see Figure 7-4). Any recorded show can be transcoded to the correct specs and added to your iTunes library with

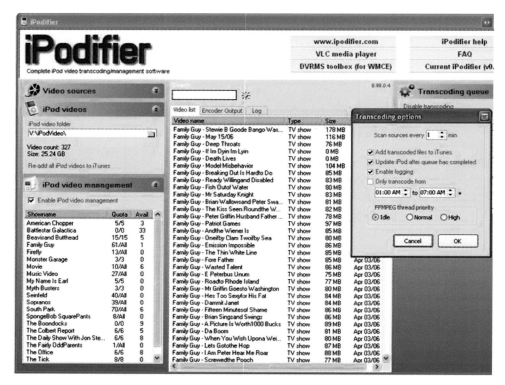

Figure 7-2
Adding iPod support to Windows Media Center with iPodifier

just one click.

As with almost any transcoding process, it'll take a while before the file's finished (even on an Intel-based Mac, it can take two times the running length of the show). But if you've set EyeTV to record your favorite shows, you can have the app convert the programs to iPod the moment recording is finished. Just choose the iPhone option from the Export To pop-up menu in either the show's schedule detail view (see Figure 7-5) or in the schedule list itself.

With the iPhone export option enabled, by the time you wake up in the morning all of the nights' recordings will be waiting

for you in your library and ready to sync to your iPhone or your iPod Touch. Just don't watch them while you drive; it's very rude to the person you're talking to on the phone in your other hand.

STREAMING LIVE TV TO THE IPHONE

Recording TV to a hard drive and then syncing it to your iPhone is lovely. But when you're being dragged to a cousin's daughter's dance recital on the evening of a possibly deciding World Series game, "record, then watch" technologies fail you.

There are in fact a couple of slick ways

to stream live TV from your home to your iPhone. The slickest is Orb, a streaming service available only for Windows PCs. Go to www.orb.com, download the free app, and set up a free account. Then download the $9.99 OrbLive app from the iTunes store. The software, which you must leave running on your desktop, maintains a connection between your tuner and Orb's central server; the iPhone app connects to the server and offers a range of live features (see Figure 7-6).

And Elgato's EyeTV also has a brand-new, $4.99 iPhone app — so new, in fact, that I am hastily adding this paragraph to the book just a couple of days before the book goes to press — that will stream live or recorded TV from your Mac to your iPhone, provided that you have your EyeTV tuner plugged in and the software is running.

There are just two problems with Orb and EyeTV for iPhone. You do need to keep your PC or Mac up and running 24/7 (or at least during the whole evening you're going to be at the recital, hoping to see the Red Sox win their third Series), and you do need to have a computer.

The Slingbox, from Sling Media (www. slingmedia.com), is a far more ambitious, aggressive, useful, and *expensive* way to make your cable TV follow you wherever you go. It's actually a box that you interpose between your cable box and your TV. You plug it into your wired home network, stick an infrared transmitter in front of the cable box, and then you magically have the ability to "project" your cable box wherever you want it to go. Launch Slingbox's app on your PC or Mac and the software will automatically "find" your Slingbox no matter where you are in the world. Seconds later, you're

Figure 7-3
The EyeTV Hybrid

Figure 7-4
TV to iPhone PDQ with EyeTV

Figure 7-5
iPhone Conversion: the zero-click method

Figure 7-6
Watching live television via Orb

watching whatever the cable box is pumping out, live as it happens.

Bonus: There's an onscreen remote control. Click the Next Channel button and the Slingbox sends the appropriate remote control signal to the cable box. You can change channels, search through your cable system's show guide, watch shows on your DVR, delete shows and schedule new recordings, ... It's exactly like sitting on your living room sofa, only way more complicated.

And there's an iPhone app, which you can peep out in Figure 7-7.

The bad news: It's a $29 app from the iTunes Store.

The *worse* news: It requires a Wi-Fi con-

nection. You can't watch via the 3G cellular network.

A RADICAL APPROACH: THE DVD METHOD

I have sort of a genetic attraction toward the "record TV on a computer, have the computer transcode the show to an iPhone-compatible format" solution. When the computer handles everything from start to finish, you feel as secure and at peace as you do when you see the lady at Dunkin' Donuts box your half-dozen with a set of tongs.

But if you're going to go around buying hardware, you probably ought to consider the option of just buying yourself a stand-alone DVD recorder. It can make a timed recording the output of your cable box just like a VCR, and after you've burned the disc you can pop it into your PC or Mac and use any DVD-ripper software to convert the shows therein to video files. (Read all about that in Chapter 4.)

And because that DVD isn't copy-protected, you won't even need any of the extra decoding software that the PC apps usually require. It's more complicated than recording shows directly to your hard drive, but maybe you *wanted* to buy a DVD recorder anyway. It's up to you, all right? I'm just a man, here.

WHERE DID ALL THOSE GIGABYTES GO?

In a few weeks, I'll be taking a five-hour Amtrak ride from Boston to Baltimore. The night before I go it'll be very, very important that I check my EyeTV schedules and make sure that it's going to record and transcode about six hours' worth of overnight programming.

Which is in itself a double-edged thing. I was upfront with you about the nature of this book: If there's even 100K of unused space on your iPhone or iPod Touch, then you just aren't trying hard enough. But man alive, once you start using your desktop computer as a DVR, your goal stops being "I want to fill this 32-gigabyte device to

Figure 7-7

Your cable box, to go: Slingbox for the iPhone

TIP

The SlingPlayer app is one of those long-standing legends of iPhone app development. Sling wanted to sell this app. Desperately so. But Apple must approve all apps before they're placed in the store, and it was hopelessly stalled.

Rumors abounded that Apple was bowing to pressure from TV networks, or maybe AT&T (which didn't want its 3G network to get clobbered by thousands of people streaming bandwidth-hungry video). Maybe the Illuminati were involved.

As the months ticked by, and more people (like me) were personally shown a demo of the app and how well it worked and tongues continued to wag, the conspiracy theories became more baroque. It's probably significant that when it finally appeared in the App Store, it was limited to just Wi-Fi connections.

But there's a way around that limitation. Instead of getting your Internet connection from your carrier's 3G system, and instead of trying to locate a nearby Wi-Fi hot spot, get the best of both worlds with a MiFi. This gadget (made by Novatel) is available from Verizon and Sprint on a monthly subscription plan; it's a pocket-sized Wi-Fi base station that connects to the Internet via the carrier's 3G network. Press the button. After a few seconds, it appears to the iPhone (or any other Wi-Fi-enabled machine) as an Internet hot spot.

Presto, you can stream your Slingbox. It won't be anywhere near as fast as a conventional base station (remember, it's still just a connection to a 3G network) and your $60 a month only gets you a limited amount of data transmission before you start racking up overcharges. But it's a solution.

full capacity" and starts being "Er … you know, I now have less than 20 megabytes of storage on an internal hard drive that had about 200 gigs free last month, before I hooked up the TV tuner box."

As I write this, the lack of free space has made my Mac slow and sluggish. I tell it, "You know what you should do? You should open Photoshop and help me edit these 320 photos I took at the MIT Flea Market last weekend." The computer takes a few moments to acknowledge me and even then, it clearly would just like to remain inert.

So in the end, a TV tuner box adds an extra level of sophistication to the home-video experience. It's often been said that the purpose of DVR is to monitor hundreds of hours of TV programming so you don't have to. With the advent of a little USB peripheral, now your PC or Mac can dupli-cate the *physical* effects of so much TV watching as well.

Radio

The Skim

The RadioShark ◦ Recording Radio Shows ◦
Importing Shows into iTunes ◦ Reports of Radio's Death, …

For many people, an AM/FM radio is an object that gets pressed into service only when (a) there's a baseball or hockey game on, or (b) you're reminded that you're *not* at the tippy-top of that list of Most Smartest Land Mammals. A higher lifeform than yourself would have thought, "Gosh, it's a four-hour drive to Flagstaff; I'd better double-check to make extra sure that I packed my iPhone car adapter or else I'll be at the mercy of the car radio for entertainment the whole way."

But don't scoff at radio. It's only at those long, lonely forsaken moments that you come to appreciate the value of radio. Well, yeah, corporate stations I can take or leave (and that first option doesn't count). But local radio is wonderful. We may pride ourselves on being Thoroughly Modern Millies, but there's still something fundamental about interactive community-based call-in shows that a message board will never duplicate.

Besides, radio is a swell source of free content for your iPhone or iPod Touch. You can't switch on a $12 radio and think, "I'm sticking it to The Man!" But the fact that you're listening to copyrighted music without paying for it has *got* to have the Recording Industry Association of America upset for *some* bloody reason.

And isn't that enough reason to buy the hardware you need to

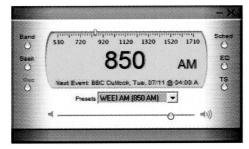

Figure 8-2
The main tuner window (in Windows)

Figure 8-1
The RadioShark: instant awesome

record radio shows and automatically load them on your iPhone?

THE RADIOSHARK

There are a bunch of PC and Mac radio receivers on the market, but I believe that all discussion of what to buy begins and ends with the $49 RadioShark 2 by Griffin Technology (www.griffintechnology. com). My argument, which I promise you is quite ironclad:

◻ It's an external USB device, and installs as easily as a mouse, whether you're using a desktop or a notebook.

◻ It lives up to its marketing tagline as "TiVo for radio." The software makes it dead-simple to schedule regular recordings, and to automatically save those programs as files that can slurp

straight into iTunes without any further ado.

◻ It's both PC- and Mac-compatible, which means you can move it from system to system, cackling with glee.

And that's all very, very true. But the trump card, the feature that closed down the competition before it ever really started is this:

◻ It looks like a jet-black shark fin, and is studded with colored lights (see Figure 8-1).

Game, set, and match. There is no piece of office equipment that cannot be immeasurably improved by having a light-up electronic shark fin placed atop it or on a nearby shelf.

I mean, come *on*. To be honest, I might have recommended it even if it didn't actually do anything.

Conveniently, it works exactly as advertised. Installation takes less than five minutes and leaves you with a radio tuner window on your desktop (see Figure 8-2).

You spins the radio dial (or just use the Seek button for auto-tuning), you enjoy the sounds as they float down through the air, and if you like what you're hearing, you punch the Record button.

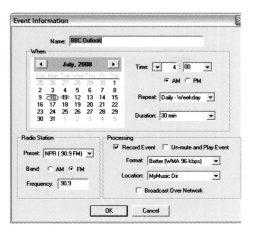

Figure 8-3
Setting up a scheduled recording (in Windows)

Simple, but not simple enough: I want to make every episode of Boston's local radio newscast or just next Thursday's Red Sox game as easy to load into my iTunes library as a podcast. RadioShark has a full compliment of scheduled-recording features to do just that (see Figure 8-3).

You can schedule an event days or even months in advance, and if it's a regular show you can specify that it's a "repeating" show that should be recorded every Sunday, or every weekday, or on whatever schedule you specify. And there's no limit to how many items you can add to the schedule.

As much as I like the RadioShark, I *should* point out that most radio stations are all too aware that you kids today are into flared trousers, Beatles haircuts, and digital music players, and offer alternative delivery methods. So before you go the RadioShark route, Google the call letters of your local stations and see what's available via their Web sites.

Oftentimes, their most popular shows are posted as podcasts shortly after transmission. Search through the iTunes Store for those call letters. Or, maybe they simulcast all their programming via streaming audio. In Chapter 13, you can read about software that will allow you to schedule and automatically capture these feeds to audio files. Either way, you might get a cleaner reception through a download than from over the air.

The RadioShark isn't expensive, but it costs more than a copy of *People* magazine, so it's not like it's dirt-cheap. Still, a pal of mine bought one to record one thing and one thing only: the morning traffic report, which is never on precisely when she wants to hear it. No kidding. This one five-minute recording that she plays while the car's warming up saves her so much annoyance and time that she says she would have paid double what Griffin asks for the device.

As for a custom little script that automatically creates a brand-new iTunes playlist of podcasts and music, with the traffic report always inserted into the No, 1 position — *that,* she was more than happy to let me write for free. Yes, it still stings.

RECORDING RADIO SHOWS

Whether you punch Record manually or allow RadioShark to record shows for you automatically, the app will stash the recording inside your default music folder. That's My Music if you're using Windows, Music if you're on a Mac.

RadioShark for Windows

By default, the Windows edition chooses Windows Media as the audio format, with conservative settings that result in tight, compact files. You can downgrade the quality (and get smaller files) by choosing a lower bit rate from the Format pop-up menu when you schedule the recording.

To use these files in iTunes, just drag them into your iTunes library window. iTunes will automatically convert them to AAC.

TIDBIT

This chapter is all about pulling in content from actual radio stations. It's still a neat topic — chiefly because the RadioShark is such a neat accessory, but also because the most valuable content is the most *local* content. And smaller, local stations aren't as likely to be streaming their content over the Web.

But if the station and the show you want to record *is* available via streaming, you're probably better off using a technique I explain in Chapter 18. Here you'll find the tools and techniques for taking any audio stream coming through your computer and capturing it to disk automatically. No $50 shark fin required.

And by now, I bet you've been looking through the iTunes App Store and discovered the hundreds of little radio tuner apps available. Many large-ish stations have commissioned and released an iPhone app that does nothing more than tune into the station's online stream

Removing the filthy analog aspect entirely: listening to live radio through an iPhone app

and play it live (try searching for the call letters of your favorite station; you're likely to find a tuner for it).

Because the stream is highly-compressed audio, no Wi-Fi connection is necessary; your iPhone's 3G data connection is plenty fast enough to tune it "live," even when you're driving. The figure above shows you but one example: Public Radio Tuner is a single app that can tune just about every public radio station, coast to coast.

Figure 8-4
Putting last night's hockey game onto
your iPhone automagically

RadioShark for Macintosh

RadioShark's Mac app has a little bonus
feature: If you select the Add Recordings to
iTunes checkbox in the app's Record & Playback preferences, RadioShark automatically
sends the recordings it creates straight into
your iTunes library ... and right into the
playlist you specify (see Figure 8-4). By your
telling iTunes to keep this playlist synced
to your iPhone, your device will always
contain the local morning news and traffic
when you plug it into your car stereo and
begin that brutal, soul-wrenching commute
morning after morning.

Otherwise, just locate the files inside your
Music folder and drag 'em into your iTunes
library window.

REPORTS OF RADIO'S DEATH, ...

There are times when I'm convinced that
radio is doomed to die a deathly death.
When I listen to certain sports phone-in
shows, there are times when I avidly wish
for it to die.

But there are also times when I wonder
if it's commercial music radio whose days
are numbered. We all have iPhones and
iPods and other digital music players and
there are a million ways to cause hours
and hours of free programming to arrive
each and every day and fill up their storage
space. And services like Pandora and Last.

fm, which stream free music based on your
personal preferences straight to your iPhone
through their own custom iPhone apps,
make the idea of bee-bopping to AM or FM
seem even more quaint.

To be honest, iTunes already downloads
more podcasts every day than I can possibly
play. With the addition of the RadioShark,
which grabs hours and hours' worth of
music and copyrighted sports broadcasts
... well, my interest in purchasing the new
American Idol holiday ballads CD continues
to decline. And it ain't like I was all that
interested to begin with.

PART III

The Death of Print

Books and Huge-ish Documents

The Skim

Yes, indeed, Apple has missed the boat. It could not have possibly missed the boat any worse if it were standing at a bus stop. In a city where there's no bus system. Y'see, a book reader is every bit as key to the iPhone and iPod Touch experience as almost any other kind of media reader. Yet there's no built-in support for it.

The iPhone is designed to be the computer and the media library that you carry with you when you don't think you'll need 'em. Is Apple suggesting that America's transportation system is now running at such stellar peak efficiency that we're *never* stuck somewhere waiting for either (a) a departure announcement or (b) the cold, sweet kiss of death, whichever comes first?

(In case someone from Apple is reading I should make it clear: This is most assuredly not the case.)

The iPhone has a brilliant big crisp screen and the ability to turn pages with just a flick of the finger. It's a natural for reading books. True, if I'm going to be reading for a few hours, I'd rather curl up on the sofa with a thick paperback than a slim iPhone. But when I have 20 minutes to kill in a dentist's waiting room, or I want to proofread a long report on the train ride to work, the iPhone is an ideal tool.

Well, Apple might not be interested in making money by selling books for the iPhone. But others are certainly eager to stick their hands in the till. And it's easy to convert both the free books you can download online, as well as the big documents you have on your hard drive, into formats that can be read in the cushy comfort of an iPhone book reader.

COMMERCIAL BOOKS

Electronic book distribution hasn't achieved even a fraction of the escape velocity of online music sales. It's sort of a famous uncracked nut of marketing, although apparently *every* media and tech company worth mentioning is striding toward it purposefully with a freakishly big hammer.

Electronic publishing is the obvious

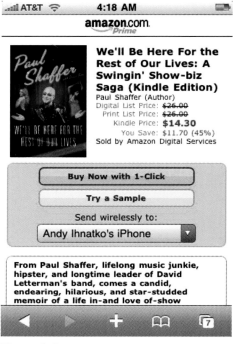

Figure 9-1
Finding books for sale in Amazon.com's Kindle Store

future of the business and plenty of companies have convinced themselves that they've found the right combination of pricing, convenience, technology, and marketing to finally convince consumers that dead trees are best left dead. But so far ... well, the huddled masses must be afraid of dropping their BlackBerries and Palms and laptops in the tub or something. Or maybe they just don't want to spend $250 for an electronic device that will allow them to spend $14 for a downloadable version of a $22 Danielle Steele hardback.

So will Apple *ever* start selling e-books via the iTunes Store?

Mmmmmaybe. Possibly. Who knows?

TIP

Amazon.com isn't the least bit shy about taking full advantage of its power and reach. Sure, you can shop for books on the iPhone, but you can also make purchases from any Web browser. Your Amazon.com store account knows that you have a copy of the Kindle app. Any time you view a Kindle e-book from your desktop Web browser, the item's Web page gives you the option of purchasing the e-book and sending it to your iPhone. It'll be downloaded directly to the device once you launch the Kindle app and tap the app's Refresh button.

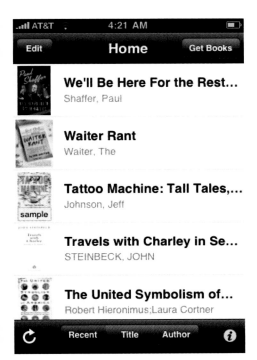

Figure 9-2
The Kindle Bookshelf: a wide variety of gore and stimulation

For now, it isn't, and Steve Jobs is on record as pooh-poohing the entire market. Which natcherly leaves the market wide open to other players.

Amazon Kindle e-Book Reader

Amazon.com has made the showiest attempt at creating "the iTunes Store of e-books." It started off by creating "the iPod of e-book devices" — the Kindle — and over the past three years it's sold so many of them that if you *ask* the folks at Amazon.com how many they've sold, they mutter something into their shoes and finally say that it's not *important* how many they've sold, really.

Still, Amazon.com is by far the strongest mover in this market. It's a natural extension of its business, and the Kindle e-book reader has an advantage that no reader from Sony or any other company has: It's the pet project of the company's crazy billionaire CEO, Jeff Bezos.

(Bezos is also bankrolling the research, development, and construction of his own private space fleet. You tell *me* if he's going to run out of funding, or bull-headed determination.)

The Kindle app is a free download from the App Store. It acts both as a tool for finding and buying e-books from Amazon.com, and as a reader. Tap on the Get Books button to open the front door to the online bookstore. You can browse on any datum you desire: title, subject, author, the works.

When you find a title you like (see Figure 9-1) you can either buy the book immediately, or tap the Try a Sample button to download a free taste (usually the book's intro, and then the first chapter or two).

Either way, the title will appear in the Kindle app's bookshelf, shown in Figure 9-2. Amazon has a very friendly attitude toward your purchases. You can remove titles from your iPhone once you've finished reading them, but the app and Amazon never forget what you've purchased. If you get a hankering to re-read this book in a few months, you can re-download it right from the app itself.

Tap on any title to start reading. It's a fairly muscular reader that works in either portrait or landscape mode, and it allows you set bookmarks and take notes as you go. Kindle presents you with a clean, uncluttered screen of resizable text. Figure 9-3 shows you what you'll see if you give the screen a tap to expose its function buttons.

I buy all of my e-books from Amazon.com for a simple reason: I also own an actual hardware Kindle reader. An iPhone makes a marvelous companion to this (yoiks — $259) reader. I bring the Kindle with me on trips, or when I know I'm going to be hanging around somewhere waiting for a good while. And when I launch my Kindle app on the iPhone, not only can I download an iPhone copy of the book I'm reading on the "real" Kindle, but the app is also smart enough to pick up at the page where I left off on the other device.

eReader.com

But despite Amazon.com's brand-name and its crazy billionaire CEO's commitment to The Cause, it's hard to label one company an outright winner in the e-book market. Amazon.com does have the largest e-book library (about 300,000 titles) but that's a little like being the best surfer in Minnesota; 300,000 e-books are a mere bookbag compared with the millions of current and out-of-print paperbacks and hardcovers you can order from Amazon.com.

So eReader (made by Fictionwise) is still worth a mention. It's another free app that encourages you to spend money at an external service. In this case, (you guessed it) the online store at www.ereader.com (see Figure 9-4).

The store attracts top books by top authors, often selling the e-book edition on day-and-date with their hardcover release. If you *do* enjoy the Long-Since Lapsed Into Public Domain genre — I suppose this Dickens fellow sort of knew what he was doing — there are also plenty of free and cheap-as-free public domain titles available.

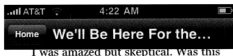

I was amazed but skeptical. Was this a joke?

"Mr. Shaffer, I'm calling for Mr. Spector. He would like you to meet him at the Plaza Hotel this evening and wonders if you have any suggestions about going to hear jazz."

I couldn't believe it. Phil Spector wanted to hang out.

That night, bonding over big-band jazz, we became friends. That's when I learned that, as far as raconteurs go, Phil is in a class with Kirshner and Ertegun. He had endless stories about the mono days. He also has great knowledge of music of all kinds, and I was thrilled to go along for the ride. The ride went on for years. Whenever Phil came to town, we were off to another evening of conversation.

Location 3585-3594

Figure 9-3
The Kindle app provides all the essential tools for Paul Shaffer scholars.

---

eReader.com works just like the main Amazon.com store page. Click, search, browse, click, buy, after you've created a free account on the site, of course. As with the Kindle app, your books are delivered in the form of DRM'd (copy-protected) files that can be read only by eReader-compatible reader apps. There are versions for just about every desktop and mobile OS out there.

After you've bought your books from eReader, you can install them on your iPhone directly from the device.

1. Launch the eReader app and tap the + (plus) button on the Bookshelf page. Tell eReader you want to download

Figure 9-4
eReader.com sells current, commercial books for iPhones and other devices.

Figure 9-5
Adding new books to your eReader bookshelf

books from eReader.com by tapping the eReader Sites button.

2. Enter your eReader.com login information. A list of your purchased books appears.

3. Tap the name of the book you'd like to download and eReader confirms that you really want to grab it (see Figure 9-5).

The download begins automatically. When finished, the new book appears with the rest of the titles in your Bookshelf.

The first time you open a purchased book, eReader confirms that you bought it legitimately by asking for the credit-card number you used to purchase it. Which seems squirrely, I know, but if eReader were out to commit card fraud, it hasn't made its move yet — I bought my first title from them a year or more ago, with no nefarious

results.

The reading experience is nice. You're presented with a full and flush page of text, and the eReader app's buttons and user-interface elements don't appear unless you tap the screen to call them into view (see Figure 9-6). You can adjust font sizes and page flow, and make other adjustments to make the experience more comfortable.

Otherwise, you turn pages with a careless flick of your finger. Like all friendly iPhone apps, the screen rotates as the iPhone does.

I like the overall eReader experience. Its prices are no bargain (I've no idea why an electronic edition should cost the same as the "dead trees" edition) and usually aren't competitive with what you'll find in the Kindle Store. But unlike Amazon.com, eReader.com often offers pretty hefty store-wide sales.

I do wish its library of titles was as large as the Kindle's. But both the Kindle app and eReader offer you a much, much wider range of titles than most corner bookstores do. You're likely to find any book of note published in the past five or so years, all new bestsellers, and any book by a prominent author.

Which frankly is the best that we can hope for before Apple enters the e-book market, partners with Amazon.com, and utterly crushes eReader and all other competitors. (Fingers crossed on that one.)

FINDING (AND MAKING) YOUR OWN FREE BOOKS

These online stores bring a friendly, iTunes-ish (well, more like "iTunes-ish-y") face to the e-book experience. But as indicated above, there are hundreds of thousands of books out on the Internet that are free for the downloading. To say nothing about all the documents that you come across in your professional and personal life that begs for a more luxurious reading experience than the bare-bones Microsoft Office reader that's baked into the iPhone OS.

LexCycle (www.lexcycle.com) seems to have applied both lobes of their collective brain to the problem of iPhone e-book reading because they've come up with a total slam-dunk of a solution: Stanza, a commercial desktop e-book reader app (available for both PC and Mac) and a free iPhone edition that complement each other wonderfully. It's such a killer desktop and iPhone app

— Ben Franklin, Poor Richard's Almanack

Three cold days passed. The thermometer never made it up to the zero mark, not even at midday. Shadow wondered how people had survived this weather in the days before electricity, before thermal face masks and lightweight thermal underwear, before easy travel.

He was down at the video, tanning, bait and tackle store, being shown Hinzelmann's hand-tied trout flies. They

Figure 9-6
Reading with eReader

that (get this) Amazon.com bought the company.

Figure 9-7 shows the Mac edition. The desktop edition is itself a stirring testimonial to the credibility of electronic books. It can open just about any kind of text document imaginable — including all the popular e-book formats floating around. It can read the books you bought from eReader.com and can also directly download free e-books from a number of online libraries. But for now, let's look at its ability to convert desktop e-books and docs.

"What formats are those?"

Great. Just great. Okay, you asked for it: "Open e-Book, Amazon Kindle, Mobipocket, HTML, PDF, Microsoft LIT,

PalmDoc, plain text, RTF, Microsoft Word, and Fiction-Book."

Yes, even Amazon.com Kindle-formatted books! Alas, it can't open or read Kindle books that are protected by digital rights management, but both the desktop and iPhone editions of Stanza can read any unlocked and unprotected file.

But my little book isn't here to sell desktop book readers. You only care about the iPhone angle, don't you?

Copying an e-book or any other document from your desktop to the iPhone edition of Stanza is so simple, I actually found it confusing at first. And it was my fault, not the app's: I kept expecting there to be extra steps!

In truth, there's almost nothing to it:

1. In the desktop app, open all the books and documents you'd like to load up on your iPhone.
2. Go to the Tools menu and make sure Enable Sharing has been checked.
3. Open the iPhone edition of Stanza. From the Library page, tap the Shared Books button (shown in Figure 9-8). Stanza shows you a list of every computer it can see on the local Wi-Fi network running a Sharing-enabled copy of Desktop Stanza.
4. Tap the name of your computer. Stanza shows you a list of every document that the app has open.
5. Tap the document you'd like to download. After a quick confirmation (see Figure 9-9), it's sent to your iPhone.

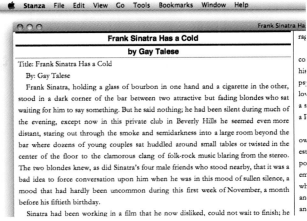

Figure 9-7

Desktop book reading and management with Stanza

You're finished. The new book appears in your iPhone's library, ready to be read (see Figure 9-10).

You'll find the reading experience is similar to eReader's. Screen space is at a premium, so the user interface only shimmers

TIP

The magical bit where the iPhone simply "senses" the presence of Stanza running on a nearby desktop won't work on your PC unless your desktop has a special system enhancement installed. If the machine doesn't appear on your iPhone, visit the following URL on your PC and download a free installer: `www.apple.com/support/downloads/bonjourforwindows.html`.

into visibility when you tap the screen. But Stanza's developers have made some very good design choices. Stanza's screen is notably more clean and elegant than that of any other book reader I've seen.

The iPhone edition of Stanza contains links to more than a dozen online sources of free and commercial e-books. If you're in the mood for a little Mikhail Aleksandrovich Sholokhov and can spell his name correctly using the iPhone's virtual keyboard, you can be reading *Oni Srazhalis*

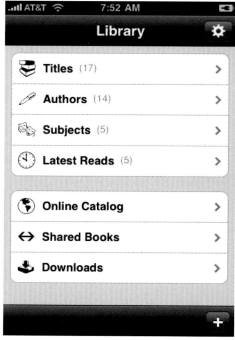

Figure 9-8
Stanza's Library page: the app's main dashboard

---

za Rodinu mere moments after the whim strikes you.

The desktop edition of Stanza also can download books. But there's no online store; You need to know the URL of a specific e-book. It's actually much simpler to visit an online book site in your desktop browser, search for titles of interest, and then download them manually. Then you can open them in the desktop Stanza and sync 'em to your iPhone.

WHERE TO FIND FREE BOOKS

Authors all over the world are doing their part for culture and scholarship each

---

TIDBIT

It's a little-known bit of history trivia: The purpose of the copyright system, as Thomas Jefferson envisioned it, was *not* to protect the rights of authors. It was to make works of art and scholarship available to the widest audience possible.

Authors and creators want to be able to make money from their work without it being stolen and reproduced without their permission. But society benefits from the ability to simply distribute creative works without restriction. So society and creators made a deal: As an author, I get legal protection for my work for my whole life plus the lives of my kids and grandkids. After 70 or 80 years, it stops making money for people and belongs to the public as a whole.

Not a bad compromise. I bet my great-great-grandkids would just spend my royalty checks on novelty pens and cheap gin, anyway.

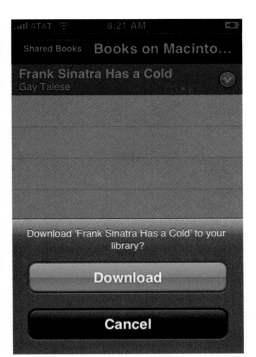

Figure 9-9
Grabbing a doc or e-book from the desktop Stanza

Figure 9-10
Reading a book with Stanza

and every day, by writing something brilliant and then dying. Wait seven or eight decades and presto: You have a brand-new public domain book that you can install on your iPhone without paying a single corn-whistling cent.

Your go-to sites, as a skinflint literary aesthete:

- **Project Gutenberg** (www. gutenberg.org). The granddaddy of public-domain book depositories. If it isn't here, the author prolly ain't even dead yet. Most popular titles are available in multiple formats, in fact.

- **Wowio** (www.wowio.com). This contains the usual old suspects but

also a large library of modern titles by authors who either are forward-thinking enough to see the commercial value in giving away their work or can't get their trash published any other way. But it's always worth a browse.

- **Tor Books** (www.tor.com). Many major publishers offer "promotional" copies of commercial books in their catalogs; the month when H. Mark Veryfamousauthor releases his newest book, the publisher releases a title from his back catalog as a free download for a limited time. Tor is a reliable source for these things, and it's a leading publisher of science fiction. Just enter "download," "e-book," or "ebook" into the site's search box.

- **Memoware** (www.memoware.com). Largely a public-domain archive, this site has a twist: Most of these titles are formatted for mobile readers. So the reading experience might be superior.
- **Webscription** (www.webscription.net). This is a library of books by authors who support the free-publishing movement, and publishers who think it's a great marketing tool. If you like the overall library here, there's a free iPhone app that browses, downloads, and reads these books without the need to grab 'em on a desktop machine first. Visit www.iphonebookshelf.com for more details.
- **Google Books** (http://books.google.com). This is a great URL to find and download free books, but actually it merits its own little section of this book.

GOOGLE BOOKS

Google does wonderful things for users, by virtue of the fact that it has all the money and manpower in the world and it can afford to create and give away fantastic services. Even if in doing so, it sort of wrecks things for little companies that *don't* have any money and are trying to build a business from a neat idea.

Like distributing books online. Google has undertaken the Herculean task of converting entire university and public libraries into e-books; It even converts hundreds of thousands of copyrighted materials, in the interest of allowing Google users to, at the very least, search through every book

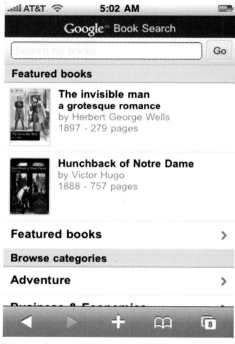

Figure 9-11
Google Books' online iPhone library and reader

ever written. If "Apple Pie Hubbub" turns up in an obscure religious tract from 1302, Google Books allows you to read the book online and even download it to your desktop. If it's a copyrighted book, it helps you find a store that sells it.

Google Books' main portal is indeed at http://books.google.com. But there is a spiffy mobile-studly edition as well: http://books.google.com/googlebooks/mobile. Figure 9-11 shows you the front door. As you can see, it practically rivals the Kindle Store in sophistication, with quick links by subject, new and notable titles — the works.

Ah. But there's one hitch to the mobile

experience: It's not a sophisticated, purpose-built iPhone app. Whereas Kindle and eReader offer you tidy formatting and a quasi-luxurious page-turning experience, Google's online-only book reader gives you a slightly funky-looking mobile Web page.

Good for browsing, fine for when you're caught outside your house with nothing to read and no money to spend on a download from Kindle or eReader.com, but otherwise the best use of this resources is to visit `http://books.google.com` from your desktop, download books to your hard drive, and then add them to your Stanza library.

You can tell that the makers of Stanza aren't too worried about the threat posed by Google Books: The Stanza iPhone app will take you directly to Google Books' mobile page straight from the app.

RIPPING A PHYSICAL BOOK: PRACTICAL?

I can't end this chapter without at least addressing the idea of converting an actual, physical book into an e-book. Here we go:

"You'll probably want to forget the idea."

There. I've addressed it.

Which seems like a pretty glib and dismissive response, considering that I've actually converted many of my favorite titles into e-books. But it's a determination that comes from experience. Digitizing a 300-page book is a hugely labor-intensive process and there are no opportunities for labor-saving shortcuts.

You have two big challenges ahead of you:

Challenge 1: Scan the whole damned book. If it's a 342-page book then, well son, you're going to have to scan allllll 342 pages.

And this actually isn't quite so bad. It's like crocheting an afghan. Its busy-work for your hands while your eyes and your brain can be focused on the TV. I find that I can scan a 300-page book in just two or three two-hour sessions.

The only labor-saving tip I offer is this: Pull the book completely apart and cut the pages free of their binding, so you have nice, clean, flat pages that your scanner can image perfectly from margin to margin. Don't even try laying the whole book flat on your scanner.

Challenge 2: Hand these 342 scanned images off to an OCR program — and fine-tune every damned page by hand. OCR software has made great leaps in the past 10 years but converting these images to text still involves a lot of manual labor. Figure 9-12 shows my favorite consumer OCR app: Abbyy's FineReader Express (`http://finereader.abbyy.com`). It's available in both PC and Mac editions at a price that will scare off the punters (roughly $130), but is still within reach of people with a real need to convert printed text into e-books.

You open your entire folder of sequentially-numbered page scans in the app, and it proceeds to munch through the pile. FineReader must do more than just figure out that this word here is "antediluvian"; it also has to get a sense of the layout of the page, and omit things like page numbers, headers, and footers.

I like FineReader Express because it's very, very smart. Still, you do need to go through every page to ensure that the app guessed right. The green boxes in Figure 9-12 denote regions of text. If the app accidentally tried to OCR a little fidgety graphic, I'd have to use a tool to exclude that area of the page. Sometimes I need to

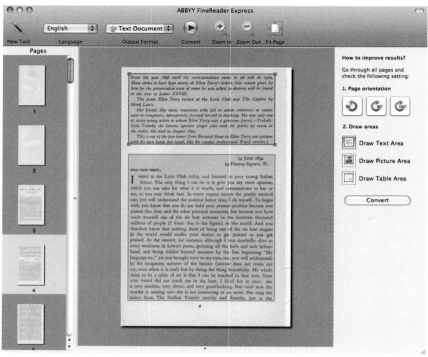

Figure 9-12
Abbyy's FineReader Express converts books into e-books.

expand one of these boxes to include a line of text that got cut off.

It's a very fiddly, complicated process. However, we all have that collection of *absolute* favorite books. You know: the ones we seem to re-read once a year or even more *and* which, you reckon, are so far out of print that they'll never ever be made into commercial e-books that you can buy for 10 bucks.

It was worth my time and trouble to convert (say) Steven Bach's incredible *Final Cut* into an e-book. I'll be re-reading it another 30 or 40 times over the course of my life, I bet; I might as well put in the effort to convert it to a more convenient format. The

scanning cost me a couple of afternoons of working the flatbed while I watched TV. The actual conversion and fine-tuning was performed in hourlong chunks spread out over the course of a week or so. OCR'ing another chapter was a task I performed when I had nothing better to do.

Naturally, I've bought a second copy of every book I OCR'd; I wasn't about to cut apart my only copy of something precious … and please do take me at my word when I remind you that the only way to get the pages to lay completely flat on the scanner is to cut them free from their binding.

But once again: I include this section more as a cautionary tale than as an encouragement.

The case in favor of putting e-books on an iPhone is made by the presence of a battered and tattered but beloved paperback of P.G. Wodehouse's *The Code of the Woosters* in my satchel. It's never left that bag.

Why? Because I'm a reader and I get nervous if I leave the house without anything to read. With that book in tow, I know that I always have an emergency book on hand.

When you use your iPhone as a book reader, you can always have dozens of books with you wherever you go. You never leave the house without your iPhone and thus you'll never find an idle moment when you can't be reading something. *Whew.*

I can do without companionship for weeks, food for days, and water for hours. But honestly: My definition of Hell is being stuck in an airport and facing a three-hour flight delay with nothing to read.

10

Comic Books

The Skim

Comic books remain one of the Holy Grails for electronic publishing. Music, video, and even books are good fits for digital distribution: An iPhone screen is nicely sized for movies and TV shows, and text, like water, can flow to fit the limited bounds of whatever display contains it.

As you will see in Chapter 11, an iPhone makes a great reader for comic strips. But things get tougher for comic *books*. A comic book page is a rigid field that can have any number of panels of any size and shape ... and your eyes can take just about any path through them, at the artist's or your own discretion.

In fact, the iPhone's touch interface makes it a very credible comic reader. Any iPhone user considers it to be second nature to pinch to zoom out, stretch to zoom in, and flick a finger to slide around the page. Pages that are too detailed to really read when shrunk down to the size of an iPhone screen (admittedly, that includes most of them) can easily be "surfed" with a minimum of hassle.

The real difficulty? Comix publishers aren't really getting their acts together. There's one service on the immediate horizon that aims to change that (more on that in a bit) but for the most part, digital comics are a big leaky bag of Fail. The publishers that do digital comics at all publish just a fraction of their print output, usually months after the comic has hit the comic shops. And then you can't simply load them onto your iPhone and read them like a regular comic.

Wrong: comics that can only be read online. Wrong: comics that are only promotional in nature … just the first six pages of an issue that will be released next week, as opposed to the whole comic. Wrong: comics that are transmogrified into cartoons with motion and sound. A comic book is a *comic book*. Why can't Marvel and DC understand that?

Oh, well. Onward.

The comix industry is still figuring out how to deal with the digital world. Small, independent publishers with little to lose have started to package their comics inside self-contained little viewer apps and are making them available for purchase on the App Store's Books page. DC and Marvel, however, have yet to really figure out how to separate an iPhone owner from his or her money.

(Admittedly: more likely "his.")

So when we talk about reading comic books on the iPhone, we're generally talking about three hurdles: finding the bloody things in the first place, downloading a whole comic in a format that the iPhone can handle, and then actually viewing it.

FINDING FREE COMICS ONLINE

Despite publishers' inability to truly get their act together, free and legal digital comics are out there to be found. One of the Big Two publishers swore to me that it didn't have any of its titles available for download. But sure enough, after poking around on its site I found a couple dozen of its most well-known titles in complete editions as free promotional giveaways.

Publishers' sites are always good places to look, and comix aficionados are always scanning out-of-copyright and public-domain books and making them available.

I used to have a hefty list of URLs for free comics but then I found someone else's list that was (a) much heftier and (b) already online. Visit www.lorencollins.net/freecomic for a thrillingly comprehensive catalog of legal freebies.

Most of these files will be in one of three formats:

- **PDF**. Our good old friend, Portable Document Format. We don't even need a formal reader app for this, really. Just copy the file onto the iPhone using any of the methods explained in Chapter 20, tap it to open, and the iPhone's build-in PDF reader will display the multipage book.

- **CBR and CBZ**. These are the Internet comic-community's open standards for collecting a couple of dozen scanned JPEGs of comics pages and bundling them together in a format that a standalone comic reader can understand. Both CBR and CBZ files work using the same concept. The only difference is the archiving standard that was used to compress all those JPEGs into a single file. All you need on your iPhone is a decent CBR/CBZ reader, and you're off and running. More on this later.

Given that you know what *kinds* of files you're looking for, you can use a Google search technique I explain in greater detail in Chapter 17. It's possible to use Google to search for files of a specific type.

No, you can't just type "free cbr comics" into Google and get racks and racks of free comics. You'll get way too many hits, thanks mostly to the fact that there's a great site that covers the comix industry called Comic Book Resources. But you *can* use some of Google's power tools to broadly say "Please search for .cbr and .cbz files located on public Web servers."

Take a deep breath and type this search string into Google's search box, all in one line:

```
www.google.com/search?hl=en
&q=-inurl%3Ahtm+-inurl%3A
html+intitle%3A%22index+of
%22+%22Last+modified%22+
comics+cbr+cbz&btnG=Google+
Search
```

(Oh, that's cruel. No, I've gone to the Bit.ly URL-shortening service and tightened that baby up for you. Try `http://bit.ly/searchforcomics` instead; it'll automatically redirect to that huge URL.)

You'll get back a lonnnng list of links to individual files with no descriptions, but in addition to the links you'll get some clues of individual sites that host small collections of comics. Replace "comic" with a more specific search term (like "horror") if you like.

Kudos to `www.tech-recipes.com`, which is full of little tidbits like this. I was about to build this string myself but hey, cool, they had it all ready to go.

You'll find lots of independent comics and "portfolio" work from talented artists … though of course it's a bit of a firehose.

Comics creators often use the RapidShare file-distribution service to post these big comix files without racking up big hosting fees. RapidShare has no search function of its own, but services like `www.filecrop.com` act as a search front-end. Enter a couple of search terms including "cbz" and "cbr"

and you'll turn up plenty of hits.

And social bookmarking services that can help you out as well. If someone was traipsing through the Web like Hansel or Gretel and came across a free comic he liked, he might have posted the link to Delicious.com or Digg.com. So try these two sets of URLs on for size, the first two for Delicious.com and the second two for Digg.com (*don't* break the two Digg.com URLs in your browser to match how they break below to fit the column width):

```
http://delicious.com/tag/cbr
http://delicious.com/tag/cbz
http://digg.com/
search?section=all&s=cbr+comic
http://digg.com/
search?section=all&s=cbz+comic
```

These URLs are a bit more scattershot than the other techniques. But hey, the hunt is part of the fun.

One obvious word of warning: Any of these searches might also turn up illegal digital copies of copyrighted comics that were posted without the copyright holders' consent. Every time this sort of topic comes up, I'm careful to remind you of something that I think is very, very important: *Do not* download pirated copyrighted material. I'm telling you about these search techniques because they're a legitimate and handy way to find legal content.

But I also know of specific blog URLs and techniques that will unerringly lead you to illegal copies of just about every major new comic published the previous week. Why do you think I'm not including *that* information?

Right: because downloading pirated material is tantamount to stealing. It's like kicking good, honest creators in the guts. Nice people don't do that sort of thing.

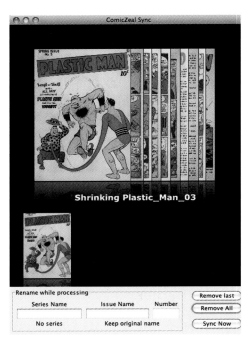

Figure 10-1
Transmogrifying comics files with ComicZeal Sync

Figure 10-2
ComicZeal's onboard iPhone comic-book library

LOADING COMICS ONTO YOUR IPHONE

If your digital comic is a PDF, your work is done: Skip to Chapter 20 and use any of the fine methods delineated therein to copy the file to your iPhone, where the OS's built-in reader will open and display the comic without any further ado.

For CBR and CBZ files, you'll want a copy of ComicZeal, by Bitolithic. It's a five-buck reader app that peachily handles the file transfer and library functions.

Once you've purchased and installed the iPhone app, go to www.bitolithic.com on your desktop browser and download the free ComicZeal Sync app (available in both PC and Mac editions). The app will take any

CBR, CBZ, or even PDF file, transmogrify the comic into the Zeal format, and move it over via Wi-Fi.

To copy comics to your iPhone:

1. Drag the files into the ComicZeal Sync window (see Figure 10-1). The files automatically begin processing. You can keep dragging in more as you go, just like with a garbage disposal.

2. When the files are finished processing, launch ComicZeal on your iPhone. Click the Sync Now button on the desktop Sync app. In ComicZeal on your iPhone, tap the Featured button at the bottom of the screen and then the wide Connect to ComicZeal Sync

Figure 10-3
Reading a comic with ComicZeal

button.

3. The iPhone app searches the local Wi-Fi network for your computer. If it presents you with a list of choices, click the item named SyncDocs. After a few minutes of percolation, the comics will be available in ComicZeal's iPhone library (see Figure 10-2). Give a title a tap, and you'll be in the app's tidy little reader.

Figure 10-3 shows off what I like about ComicZeal. These onscreen controls vanish with a tap, and the app truly stays out of your way as you skate from panel to panel.

ComicZeal has a second side as well: It's linked to its own sources of free comics and is a healthy source of golden-age titles.

LONGBOX DIGITAL: AT LONG LAST, LOVE?

There are other sources of iPhoneable comix that I haven't mentioned. Lots of smaller publishers have packaged individual titles as self-contained e-books and placed them in the App Store. A few small publishers have banded together and created puny, ineffective "iTunes Store" type of kiosk apps for their digital comics.

You can find these yourselves. Though you might wonder why you bothered. It's all very poorly organized and the quality of the content is generally poor, given the amount of effort you needed to get it. There's no ability to "browse" comics before committing to a purchase, as you can do with Kindle books.

But there's a bright spot on the near horizon. A new company called Longbox Digital (http://longboxinc.com) aims to truly be the first and only useful store for digital comics, and at this moment, it's also frustrating the *hell* out of me (see Figure 10-4).

This is one of the very last chapters I've written for this book. Why? Because I knew this online comic service was coming and I was hoping very hard that it'd open its virtual doors before my final deadline. I've had a lengthy private briefing with the CEO and seen tantalizing glimpses of what Longbox promises to be. I suspect it could be *great.*

Hence my frustration: It's just weeks away from release but it might as well be 50 years because I need to hand in this last chapter.

Here's what I know, and why I'm excited:

- **It's inclusive of all publishers**. I have no use for 19 different iPhone apps, each offering the comics from one or two teensy-tiny publishers and each publisher offering two comics — neither one of which seems interesting.

Figure 10-4
Longbox Digital: Will it be the perfect answer for digital comics on the iPhone?

Longbox endeavors to be like Amazon.com, selling all titles from all comix publishers. It's not here to be the darling cash-cow of any one company.

▢ **It offers a shopping experience that's consumer-friendly**. You can buy individual issues or subscriptions. Your purchases are downloaded; you don't need to have Internet access to read your comics. Rather than a scattershot approach of a title here, an issue there, you'll be able to buy entire runs of monthly comics via Longbox.

▢ **It's *real* comics**. I asked the CEO if the service would be selling those weird cartoonish movie-like "motion comics."

He responded in the negative, using an obscene gerund to underscore his passionate opinion on this point.

▢ **Longbox digital comics will work on anything**. It's not just an iPhone app. It'll be desktop apps for PC and Mac, and then apps for iPhone, Windows Mobile, Android, and any other flavor that's on the menu.

▢ **Publishers can create Longbox digital comics themselves**. So many of these kinds of initiatives have been hamstrung by the need to send files to an outside service to have some sort of voodoo done to them. If a publisher is distributing comics via Longbox, it simply adds a plug-in to its current publishing software. Putting a comic in the correct file format and sending it to Longbox's servers is about as complicated as doing a Save As of the file.

Suffice to say that I had a long list of reasons why a service like Longbox will probably fail and I wound up drawing a line through every last one of them.

So, keep an eye out for this service and visit `http://longboxinc.com`. I suspect that if any company manages to crack this impenetrable nut — if any company manages to build an alliance with Apple to become the official purveyor of comic books to iPhone users — it'll be this one.

IN DEFENSE OF THE COMIX READER

When you first picked up this book and looked at my photo on the back, you probably thought, "Good God … now *here's* the sort of grown man who still reads comic books."

You know, prejudice, bigotry, and snap judgments are ugly, useless things that jam a potato in the tailpipe of the engines of the progress of society.

(And there's nothing wrong with reading comic books in your thirties. *Nothing wrong.* Shut up!!!)

Well, gee, who's the bigger loser? The loser, or the loser who just spent a half an hour *reading* about what the loser does? Huh?

Let's just put this whole incident behind us and move on. Friends?

Okay, well, I *still* have your money. So there.

Comic Strips

The Skim

Stripping for Fun ◘ The Newspaper with Great Comics ◘
Comic Envi ◘ Dark Gate Comic Slurper

had a great childhood. The clearest sign of this is the fact that one of my chief sources of heartbreak was the fact that *Peanuts* was my favorite comic strip and our house subscribed to *The Boston Globe*. The *Herald* carried *Peanuts*. I'd have to go to the Periodicals room of the local library and catch up on a week's worth of Charlie Brown and Snoopy in one sitting and if I got there too late, the papers had already been thrown away and I was stuck.

So. I'm grateful to the world of technology for providing me with, you know, a career. But I'm just as pleased that it's now possible for me to access every strip I like from every source possible. It's a keen concept on the desktop but it's well-suited to the iPhone as well, a device geared toward acquiring fresh, timely media and allowing you to enjoy it wherever you are.

STRIPPING FOR FUN

There's a difficulty getting your comic strips digitally: The landscape is even more fragmented today than it was when I was a kid, reading strips via mashed treeware. In addition to the separate old-fashioned newspaper syndicates, each independent Web comic creator hosts his or her strip on a separate site.

And it goes without saying that all of these separate sources haven't

Figure 11-1
Scrolling through the funny pages on the SeattlePi's site

TIP

For the single most exhaustive list of comic strips available on the Web, visit www.thewebcomiclist.com/latest. Here, my friends, is the true firehose listing: The site lists hundreds upon hundreds of strips. Internationally beloved strips that appeared in 2,500 newspapers (back when there were 2,500 newspapers) are listed here, as are one-off bits of idiocy written and drown through the green smoke of a late-night dorm room … and every level of proficiency and non-proficiency in between.

I just wish it had a decent reader component. This list is designed to serve as a directory and not as an actual, readable comics page.

THE NEWSPAPER WITH GREAT COMICS

The Web sites of many Great Metropolitan Newspapers have decent digital versions of their comic's pages. I particularly like the Comics & Games page of *The Seattle Post-Intelligencer*: www.seattlepi.com/fun. It's a double win because it hosts a great many strips, and it's laid out in a way that's helpful to iTunes users. The complete list of strips is a pop-up list, making it easy to navigate to the strips you want to see, both by title and by date (see Figure 11-1).

Nice. But it's hardly exhaustive, and it's still just a Web page.

COMIC ENVI

I would have *hoped* that a truly great comic-strip aggregator app would have shown up in the App Store by now … but alas, the quest continues.

And yes, an "aggregator" is what we desperately want. I want an app that knows where each one of my favorite strips is hosted on the Web and can download them all into one seamless, cohesive viewing experience.

banded together to create standards for downloading strips, or create an "iTunes Store"-like experience. So: You can't simply download and sync strips from your desktop.

Okay, that's no big loss. Strips are a perishable commodity. As soon as you've read the morning pile, you're done with them. The bigger problem is collecting these dozen, perhaps even *many dozens* of different hosts and sites into a single, unified experience akin to a traditional comics page: You want one-click access, with classic *Peanuts* strips alongside fresh *Pearls before Swine* offerings alongside the little Web comic from some high-school kid with a graphics tablet, a blog, and a dream.

.ııll AT&T 📶   7:32 AM   🔋

◀ Back | Comic strip collections

A

Archie

Arlo & Janis

Ask Shagg

B

B.C.

Baby Blues

Bad Reporter

Baldo

Figure 11-2

Comic Envi: a dedicated iPhone app for downloading and reading comic strips

Comic Envi (a cheap-as-anything $0.99 app from Open Door Networks) comes *close* to the ideal. It's a special edition of the company's Envision app, which is designed to grab and display images from the Web, such as those fantastic space photos from NASA's Astronomy Picture of the Day site.

Comic Envi comes pre-loaded with dozens and dozens of strips. The list scrolls endlessly (see Figure 11-2). Tap the name of a strip, and you're reading the latest one. By swiping left or right, you can work your way backwards and forwards through the dailies.

Nice *and* good; it's a great app that tries to collect every strip from every source in just one or two handy, scrolling lists. And it's dirt-cheap.

Envi's only fault is in the presentation. It's spiffy for reading a week's worth of *Dilbert*s, but not very helpful when you want to read all of today's new strips. You can't simply scroll from today's *Doonesbury* to today's *Dilbert*. You can only scroll from today's to yesterday's.

DARK GATE COMIC SLURPER

My favorite tool for reading daily comics is a fantastic Web app created and hosted on DarkGate.net: the Dark Gate Comic Slurper (`http://darkgate.net/comic`). Darkgate.net maintains a huge list of comics available on the Net. It doesn't offer *every* strip, but it's a mix of newspaper and Web comics — and of the strips you can't access through the Slurper, there are very few that are really worth reading.

The Slurper keeps adding new strips as they appear and when existing strips move to other servers, Dark Gate makes a note of the change. Set it and forget it.

The first time you open the Web page, you spend what will probably be several minutes clicking the checkboxes of the strips you like. DarkGate.net drops a cookie file into your browser with your choices. From that point onward, every time you visit the site, it will build a custom comics page.

Here's how to set things up:

1. Open the URL in any desktop browser. It's a standard Web page and opens even in the iPhone browser. But for reasons that shall become clear soon, you'll want to open it in a big, desktop window.

Figure 11-3
Choosing your favorite comic strips in Dark Gate

2. Click the Choose button on the left side of the page. Dark Gate presents the Dark Gate Slurper Configuration device: a cluttered list of every strip it's ever heard of (see Figure 11-3).

3. Click the checkboxes of every strip you'd like to see.

4. Click the Subscribe button at the very bottom of the Web page when you're finished.

The Slurper is now locked and loaded. Immediately, it redraws the page with the freshest editions of all your chosen strips, in one smooth scrolling window (see Figure 11-4).

This is, in fact, how I read my comics

every single morning. But how is this relevant, in a book about iPhones?

Ah. Scroll to the very, very, *very* bottom of the window. What do you see? Aha! a link marked PDA Friendly Version. This is a special articulation of this Web page with no-frills formatting, designed for phones and other small screens.

It actually works a little bit differently from the desktop edition of the Web page. The desktop Web page deposits a cookie in your browser with a list of all the strips you've subscribed to. The PDA edition embeds that list right in the URL. Here's the URL to my personal PDA-friendly version of the Slurper:

Figure 11-4
The very model of a modern desktop comics page

```
http://darkgate.net/comic/?
showme=adamhome:applegeeks:
applegeekslite:arloandjanis:
basicinstructions:bc:bizarro:b
londie:calvin:crankshaft:
curtis:dieselsweeties:dilbert:
doonesbury:dorktower:fbow:
foxtrot:funkywinkerbean:
garfieldminusgarfield:
getfuzzy:girlswithslingshots:
luann:maryworth:monty:nonseq:
peanuts:pearls:pvp:redmeat:
sallyforth:tomtoles:unshelved:
xkcd:zippy:zits:pennyarcade:
```

When I open this URL (as one line) in Safari, I get Figure 11-5: a beautiful, clean, all-in-one color comics page.

And because it's a standard, simple Web page, I can rotate the screen, zoom in on individual strips, and scroll from panel to panel (see Figure 11-6). Comic strips are actually perfect for iPhone viewing. Unlike a complex comic book page, a strip is a fixed-height graphic that you read by simply scrolling from left to right.

All you need to do now is to move that URL into your iPhone's Safari browser. It's a piece of cake if you've turned on book-

103

Figure 11-5
The Dark Gate Slurper on iPhone:
That's more like it!

Figure 11-6
Reading a Slurped strip

mark syncing. Bookmark it in your desktop browser (Safari or Internet Explorer) and it'll show up in iPhone Safari on your next sync.

I don't use that feature. Here's what I do:

5. Right-click (or, on a Mac, Control+click) on the PDA-Friendly Version link to bring up your browser's contextual menu.

6. Choose Copy Link from the contextual menu to copy the link to the Clipboard.

7. Go to your desktop mail client. Create a new message, paste the link in the body of the message, and send it to any mail account your iPhone can access.

8. Pick up your iPhone, fetch new mail, open the message, and tap the link to open it in Safari. You're then free to bookmark it in Safari, or bookmark it as a new button for your Home screen so you can launch it like an app.

I do love the Dark Gate Comic Slurper. It's simple, it's free, it's exhaustive, and it delivers that single, unified comics page of my childhood dreams. And it's been around for 10 years, as of this writing, so it's a reliable part of the landscape.

I often think of the purchase price of my iPhone in terms of individual contributions it makes to my day. I wouldn't spend $199 on a device that just downloads comic strips. But bloody hell. Every time I'm stuck in a line somewhere

TIP

Be sure to check out Chapter
14, which is all about RSS.
RSS is a humongously pow-
erful and mercifully invisible
Internet standard that makes it
easy to keep track of sites that
publish new content on a regular basis.
Many online comics have these RSS
feeds; you can "subscribe" to individual
strips using an iPhone or desktop news-
reading app. New strips will be located
and downloaded for you automatically
every time you ask your iPhone "What's
new in the world?"

Dark Gate proves that it's the greatest comics aggregator in the world by
including RSS support. Look for the
RSS link button on the left-side of the
desktop Web page. It's a link to this
magical RSS feed. Copy and paste this
link into your desktop or iPhone RSS
newsreader and your entire Dark Gate
comics page will be included in your
news download.

and I can tap one button and get dozens of
the day's freshest comics on my phone, I feel
like I've earned back at least a dollar of the
purchase price.

Comic strips are bite-sized nuggets of art,
entertainment, humor, and social commentary. It's possibly the most personal of art-
forms. Thus, it's a perfect medium for this
most personal of consumer devices.

12

Crosswords

The Skim

This book is largely my gift to humanity, but I can't deny that it has selfish undertones. I'm cashing the advance checks, for one. For another, I'm slinging in a chapter on crosswords because I'm interpreting my self-imposed mandate "take everything from your personal and professional life and put it on your iPhone" and doing a simple swap of personal pronouns.

I love crosswords. I try to do several a week. It gives me all the benefits of a game (procrastination, spending money on a lonely, isolating activity) with the expectation that the brain cells I fry will be outweighed by the number of new synaptic pathways I form while trying to figure out a three-letter word for "Shovels can be these, blankly" that starts with a Q.

Solutions for putting crossword puzzles on an iPhone settle into two options: a single iPhone app that's a great puzzle downloader for many difference puzzle sources, and the dedicated apps pushed out by the publishers of certain blue-chip and quasi-blue-chip daily crosswords.

JUST CROSSWORDS

Crosswords by Stand Alone (www.standalone.com) is my favorite crossword app for the iPhone. It's truly one-stop shopping. It

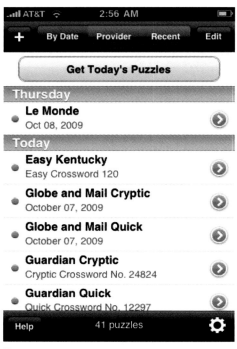

Figure 12-1
Downloading puzzles in Stand Alone's Crosswords

Figure 12-2
Sumptuous gameplay makes Crosswords a big winner.

connects to several online sources of free, daily and weekly crosswords, and can keep you rolling in brain-wranglers indefinitely. Just tap on a puzzle and it arrives on your iPhone in moments (see Figure 12-1). If you have a specific favorite provider, you can simply "subscribe" to those puzzles and they'll automatically be downloaded every time the app launches.

Stand Alone really gets how an app like this should function. At launch, it checks the Net and shows me all the new puzzles of which it's aware. Alternatively, I can sort the list by source.

The second Big Win is the glorious gameplay. The puzzle works in either vertical or horizontal orientation. And when you tilt the iPhone on its side you get a rather majestic view that combines clues, puzzle grid, and keyboard (see Figure 12-2).

Every user control you'd expect in an iPhone app is available. Pinch and stretch the puzzle to zoom in and out, hold down a finger to call up a magnifying glass, scroll all over creation if you like. A Sunday crossword is a bit of a trial for any small screen like the iPhone's, but Stand Alone's Crosswords manages this set of problems with far greater elegance and creativity than any other handheld app. It even lets you dispense with the grid entirely, and work the puzzle as a simple set of linear clues (as shown in Figure 12-3).

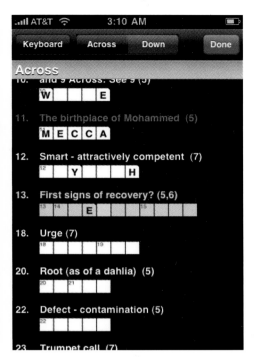

Figure 12-3
Slightly kinky: solving puzzles as a one-dimensional list

And it truly respects players of all skill levels. Those of us who have never bothered to memorize all the tributaries of the Rhone can get hints (either the entire answer to a stumper, of just an individual letter). Those of us who sneered at the concept of "hints" and now need to wipe the inevitable ejected fury-fueled spittle off this page will be encouraged to find that there's formal scorekeeping and timing, and the ability to compare your times against your previous performances and those of other users across the world.

Finally, it's the only app that allows you to load up arbitrary puzzles. There's only one popular file format for digital crossword puzzles: Across Lite (.puz) format. Crosswords can download any arbitrary .puz file. Just tap the + (plus) button to add puzzles, click the Browse for Puzzles button, and type in the URL of the puzzle file.

The *New York Times* offers its famous crossword puzzles online via subscription. Crosswords can access your account and use this subscription material alongside all of the app's "free" puzzle sources. Just add your *New York Times* account name and password (for the *Times* and certain other subscription services) via the app's Settings page.

PUZZLING DIRECTLY FROM THE NEWSPAPER OF RECORD

Some of you *might* be puzzle snobs. You've tried Stand Alone's app but as soon as you noticed that the *People* magazine crossword was among the app's offerings ("3. *Who's the Boss* star Tony _____") your nose hairs curled, and you bailed.

The *New York Times* has licensed Magmic to create an official daily puzzle app for the iPhone. It features many of the same features as Stand Alone's Crosswords but isn't nearly as full-featured, overall (see Figure 12-4). It does offer a logistical advantage in that it allows for in-app purchases of new puzzles.

In 2010, in fact, the app is going to an all-subscription model. The app itself is just a buck or two, but to get real puzzles, you'll need to buy a subscription pass for a month, a year, of half a year's worth of regular content. Plus, it plugs you into a social community of (specifically) *New York Times* puzzle solvers. If you're such a metropolitan egghead that you hire a neighborhood kid who comes around the house once a week

Figure 12-4
The *New York Times's* officially blessed puzzle app

TIDBIT

The Crossword category of iPhone apps suffers from the same sometimes-exasperating problem as books, comics, and other categories of creative content: It's a little cluttered with "also-ran" apps that pull together a collection of puzzle content that isn't very good, which you play using software that's even more Not Very Good. Between Stand Alone's Crosswords (the best all-around app) and the *New York Times's* crossword app (good for fans of that specific community of puzzle solvers), I think this category is well and truly taken care of, and if Apple were to accept no new apps in this category, I think it could save countless lives.

to replace the leather elbow patches on your tweed jackets, this might be the right app for you.

There's science out there that claims that solving crossword puzzles is in fact a positive daily exercise for your brain. It keeps the juices flowing to both the penthouse and low-rent districts of both lobes and thus can help to stave off a multitude of hugely-scary progressive disorders.

I dunno. I suppose if I solved as many puzzles as I abandoned, I might be in a position to evaluate the science from a rational perspective. As is, I stack up my experience with Crosswords against the three racing games I own and I must confess that I've benefited far more from the former than the

latter. I know, for example that a montane is the region of a mountain below the treeline. All I learned from Real Racing is that if in real life I'd bought myself a Lamborghini Gallardo five years ago instead of a four-door Mercury Sable, I probably would have killed myself and countless others within 40 yards of the dealer's lot.

PART IV

The Internet

13

News, Blogs, and Bookmarks

The Skim

What's Going on Right Now ◌ Blogs and Newsreaders ◌ Bookmarks

I f the only thing the iPhone did for you was deliver online information, it'd still be cheap at double the price.

Well, okay … it'd still be worth paying full retail.

Oh, I've forgotten about the two-year cell phone contract. Okay: The *iPod Touch* would definitely be worth paying full retail if all it did was deliver online information.

(I seem to be getting sidetracked again.)

The secret is the power and ambition of the Safari browser. It's absolutely tops in mobile. But you'll be missing a number of neat tricks and conveniences if you lock yourself in to the standard mode of bookmarking sites and visiting them. The shortest distance between your eyeballs and the information you want to be reading is usually along the line of a brilliant online service — or a dedicated iPhone application.

WHAT'S GOING ON RIGHT NOW

The Firehose Effect is a big problem with the Internet in general, but it's an operatic-scale lament when you just want your iPhone to deliver the convenience and browsability of a simple 50-cent newspaper. There's just way too much data out there, scattered across way too

Figure 13-1
Digg.com: The world reads the Web so
you don't have to.

Figure 13-2
Digg lets you try before you buy.

many resources.

So when you want to fill 20 minutes of
waiting time at your dentist's office with
a quick look at what's going on in the world
right this very moment, you don't reach for
the Internet's full firehose. You should let
others do the filtering and aggregating for
you.

Digg.com

Digg.com is like a big Internet funnel. The
short way of explaining this site is that it
contains all of the articles and stories that
millions of people consider to be interesting, today.

Folks all across the Internet reach for

a browser button marked "Digg This!"
whenever they come across a page or an
article that's so interesting they feel it's
deserving of wider attention. Their recom-
mendation winds up at Digg.com and if
hundreds or even thousands of users made
the same choice, it lands on Digg's top
pages. Digg factors in not just the number
of recommendations but their velocity and
other factors.

Digg is a great resource for instant, fast-
moving information, sorted by topic and
subcategory. And it has a wonderful iPhone
interface. Just point Safari to http://m.
digg.com.

Figure 13-1 shows the top page of world
news. If one of these headlines leaps out at

Figure 13-3

Google News assembles one massive newspaper from every online edition on the planet.

you, give it a tap and you're taken to a page that describes the content (see Figure 13-2). Tapping on the headline takes you to the actual article on the actual Web page.

I like Digg because it casts a wide net. The top page will link to a PDF file of a David Hasselhoff paper doll. But the next item in the listing will be a *Wall Street Journal* story about furious lobbying to overturn a key piece of legislation that will keep the lights turned on for the whole Eastern Seaboard. Then a YouTube of some kid trying to play "Radar Love" on a cheap guitar using only his feet, a revealing interview with a presidential appointee, …

But if that's a bit to firehose-y for your liking, you can drill down to just the topics that interest you (politics, national news, sports, etc.) by tapping the Topics button.

Digg is the perfect answer to the question "What are people interested in and talking about right now?" In olden days you'd hear people scurrying around and you'd rush to switch on the TV to find out what's going on. Now, you'd turn to Digg.com.

Google News

If thousands of human hearts beat at the core of Digg's news page, Google News's choices are cold and calculating, a pure and perfect killing machine of targeted information. Remorseless; it has no soul, so, so …

Er, what I mean is that Google's servers simply make a whole bunch of calculations about what news items are receiving the most coverage and attention. And it has a purty iPhone interface too: `http://news.google.com`.

Figure 13-3 tells the story. Google News is the interactive resource you turn to when you want to have a conventional newsprint experience. The stories that the News Terminator T-10000 selects for these pages are from some of the most trusted sources in journalism. Yahoo News (`http://m.yahoo.com`) goes for the same sort of approach, though it seems to cull from fewer sources but is much easier to navigate and read.

News Apps

Many news agencies have built their own iPhone apps for delivering content from their own services. I'm not a huge fan. When I want to read news, I'm generally connected to the Internet and thus I prefer

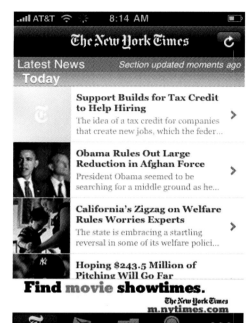

Figure 13-4
Yahoo News: a tidier presentation than Google News, though it casts a narrower net

Figure 13-5
Read all over: the *New York Times* iPhone app

not to acquire a large collection of individual news apps.

But I do like the *New York Times*'s app. The Gray Lady has always put lots of its dough into moving beyond the concept of mashed-up soybeans smeared on top of mashed-up tree pulp, and its iPhone app shows its enthusiasm for new media and new ideas (shown in Figure 13-5). It's probably the closest to the true experience of reading a newspaper. It's very, very easy to "graze" through the electronic edition and discover news items that you never would have actively searched for but which you're glad you found. Items of particular inter-

est can be saved for offline reading later on. And it's free, free, free (at least when this book went to press; the Gray Lady has been making noises that a subscription plan is in the works).

Of course, all of this presumes that you want to sit down and ingest the news as a destination in and of itself. But there's a *lot* of information out there in the world and some great tools to help you soak it all up in one big gooey porridge.

So, hmmm. Maybe a dedicated news source isn't the right answer for you. With the newsreader services and apps in the next section, you can tell a separate app to track, sort, and update your favorite news

Figure 13-6
This symbol in a browser's address bar means the site has an RSS feed.

sources *for* you — and present it in the same wobbly list of content that's showing you what photos your pals have posted to a photo site, what your favorite author is blogging about, and what surf conditions are like in Wisconsin right about now.

(Actually, I can tell you that right now: Calm. Very, very calm.)

BLOGS AND NEWSREADERS

Everyone brings his or her own specific needs to a smartphone. Some want killer e-mail, others want to manage blazing furies of incoming and outgoing calls, while others really want a great media player that can also be used to call out for pizza.

I've had smartphones for several years now and to me, the killer feature of an Internet-enabled phone is its ability to use a news aggregator (usually referred to as a *newsreader*). These apps act practically like a TiVo for the Web. You tell it what sites and blogs you're interested in — from newspapers with international reputations to your friend's MySpace page with his habit of posting florid videos of hockey fights — and it'll keep an eye on 'em for you. And when you're in the mood for a little readin', the newsreader directs you to all the pieces that interest you.

The next time you wander through the

> **TIP**
>
> For more info about RSS and the awesome things your iPhone or iPod Touch can do with it, check out Chapter 14, which is a series of tricks and techniques for exploiting RSS. Many of my most favoritest shortcuts for the iPhone are in that chapter.

Web using Internet Explorer or Firefox or the desktop edition of Safari, keep an eye peeled on the right side of the browser window's address bar. On most sites, you'll see a little icon like the one in Figure 13-6. In Safari, it's a little blue pill marked RSS.

These are great things to see. And it's not that sort of mixed-blessing reaction you have when you peek into the kitchen of your favorite restaurant and spot three full rattraps. "Maybe this means they got 'em all," you think, hopefully. No, a Web site with syndicated content is *incontrovertible* good news for you, the home viewer.

Because it means that the Web site contains a little invisible file that maintains an up-to-the-second catalog that records and summarizes the entire site's content. That file (known as a "syndication feed") isn't designed to be read by humans. It's there to be read and examined by a newsreader app that can use that data to decide what's new and interesting on the site. The software can even determine which articles you've already read and what's been posted just since your last visit.

The upshot is that instead of hitting hundreds of sites just to see if they've been

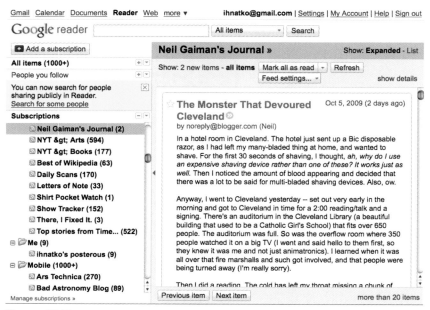

Figure 13-7
Google Reader: all the news stuff from all your favorite sites

updated recently, and *then* hoping that some of the content is actually interesting, the newsreader will do that work *for* you.

Of all these news aggregators — local app or Web service, desktop or mobile — Google Reader is by far my favorite. It's the most sophisticated. It works great on any computer or device you have handy. And when a desktop reader has the ability to share its subscriptions with an iPhone or with an online service, it's Google Reader that usually acts as the glue.

Plug `http://reader.google.com` into your desktop browser to take a look at Google Reader. Figure 13-7 shows you what my world looked like a moment ago. It ain't the iPhone edition but it'll show you what I mean. The column on the left contains some of the hundreds of blogs and news

sites that I've told Reader to keep an eye on. The fact that they're showing up in the list at all means there are articles there that I haven't read; The number to the right of the name tells me how many.

This is the top page: It's showing me a reverse-chronological list of all the latest items posted to all my favorite sites. I can read most of them right in Google Reader, without even visiting the sites directly. Some sites only make article summaries available to services like Reader. It's enough to get a sense of the piece, and if I'm interested, one click takes me to the page itself.

Naturally, Google Reader has a very slick iPhone edition of its service (shown in Figure 13-8), which can be accessed from the same URL as the desktop edition.

As if the desktop edition weren't good

enough! With *this* version, I can eat a quick sandwich with my right hand while keeping up with all my news sites with the other. A long list shows me just the sites that have been updated. In Figure 13-8, I'm looking at the "top" of my subscription list. This is a list of every blog I've subscribed to and the new articles on each one. I can drill down by subject or by individual blog. If I just want to see what's new on the *Bad Astronomy* blog, I can make a couple of taps and get a nice tidy list of the latest astronomy news.

Or I can tap on one of my "collections" of subscriptions. You can organize a collection for news, one for your friends' blogs, one for online comic strips … each one cutting your enormous toilet-paper-like scroll of subscriptions down to just the handful you want to focus on at any given moment.

The fact that this one, centralized service keeps track of your reading means that you can have a seamless experience as you move from location to location. Let's say you've spent an hour reading your favorite blogs on Google Reader via your desktop browser in your office. At 4:20, you put on your coat, sign "5:12 PM" on your timesheet, and knock off work for the day. You head for the park, crack open a Yoo-Hoo, and envy the squirrels, wondering what it must be like to experience that sense of total, naked freedom for once in your life.

Then you fish your iPhone out of your pocket and open Google Reader in Safari. Presto: Reader is exactly as you left it back in the office. It knows which articles you've read already, and automatically removes them from the list. Oh, some new articles has been posted in the past half an hour? Cool, they've been placed at the very top of the list.

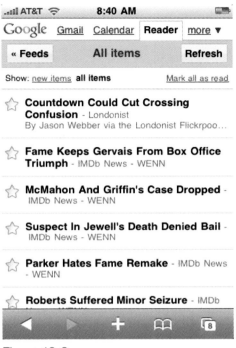

Figure 13-8
Google Reader: the iPhone experience

Adding Blog Subscriptions to Google Reader

Google Reader becomes more and more useful as you keep bookmarking more and more sites from your desktop browser. To track and read a site in Reader, all you need to do is click the Add a Subscription button in the Reader window and then paste its URL into the pop-up form. Reader will "discover" that site's RSS feed and add a new subscription.

(And "subscribe" doesn't mean what it does in the magazine world. There's no fee for subscribing to a site's syndication feed. Nor are there any of those annoying little subscription cards that fall in your lap when you're trying to find out what's the deal with

Figure 13-9
You add subscriptions to Reader from any browser window, via a bookmarklet you install yourself.

Angelina Jolie's husband. Geez, it's no wonder that print is a dying medium.)

Google Reader offers an even quicker subscription mechanism: a Subscribe to this Web Page bookmarklet that you simply add

TIP

Google Reader has an extra little feature: It allows you to search blog postings for a specific term or phrase. That's damned handy, particularly when you're trying to find opinions of the general public or trying to get a bead on a story that's so new that the major news organizations have yet to really pick up on it.

I'm not ashamed to admit it — I mean, I'm ashamed that I *do* this, but not to admit it to you nice folks — but after I give a talk to a large audience or make an appearance on TV ... well, yeah, I do a blog search to see what people might have said about it on their blogs. It's not so much an ego thing so much as a desire to know if people were creeped out by the way I was staring offscreen halfway through. Look, I was distracted by a duck.

to your browser's bookmarks bar (see Figure 13-9). With this bookmarklet installed, just click on the bookmarklet and a subscription to whatever blog or news site you happen to be eyeing at the moment will automatically be added.

You can find Google Reader's bookmarklets by clicking on the service's Settings tab in the browser window, and then clicking on Goodies. Just drag it *straight* off the Web page and into your browser's Bookmarks bar, below the address bar. Once it's in place, just click it whenever you're visiting a site you'd like to track.

Finally, many browsers are so hip about RSS that merely clicking on the RSS symbol that appears next to the site's URL in the window's address bar will open a window that lets you bookmark the page in your favorite newsreader. Check the Preferences dialog box of your favorite browser for more details.

Native Newsreader Apps

So. Reader. I love it. But! It has a key weakness: ...

(You have 30 seconds to buzz in. Remember, this is for that pair of Rally mountain bikes ... Yes! Well done.)

"It might *look* like an application, but it's actually a Web page being accessed via the iPhone's Internet connection."

(Your response wasn't in the form of a question but hey, I'm easy.)

Which means, of course, that these services are no good to you when you're *sans* network. As in: in the middle of a four-hour flight, sitting in that bit of my house separated from the rest of the house by a Wi-Fi-blocking brick wall, or (to my enduring annoyance) anywhere in the state of Vermont.

The ideal here would be a piece of software that slurps down all those news articles when there's an Internet connection presence, and stores and sorts them on your iPhone where you can read them at your leisure. And what great news: There are many such apps available at the App Store.

Figure 13-10 shows my favorite newsreader app is RSS Runner (www.golden-apps.com).

Why? Whereas most iPhone newsreader apps work great with a couple of dozen sites, RSS Runner works great even with a few *hundred* sites. And believe me, after a year of using Google Reader, you'll have that many sites bookmarked.

Speaking of Google Reader, wait'll you see how well RSS Runner works with the service. Less than a minute after purchasing the app, I had pointed Runner at my Google Reader account and within seconds, pop! All my Reader subscriptions were imported into RSS Runner subscriptions.

But the big win of Runner is that it's simply the most iPhone-like newsreader available. It was conceived with taps and finger-flicks in mind. Figure 13-10 shows my usual view of the app after I've launched it. It's showing me an aggregated list of every RSS feed with unread content, with the number of unread articles listed in the little balloon to the left.

If a story sounds interesting, I tap and I'm reading it. Runner checked every blog and downloaded the text of every new article when I tapped the Refresh button, so I know that a huge amount of new news and info is tucked away safely on my iPhone.

I love the flexibility of the app. When I'm at the burrito place with the free Wi-Fi,

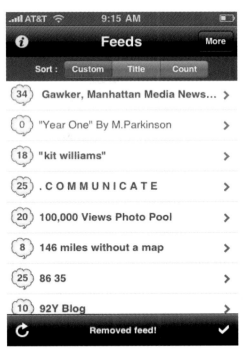

Figure 13-10
The whole world, downloaded to your iPhone, thanks to RSS Runner

I don't bother downloading articles. I'm just grazing for info. I scroll through the list of new articles and tap on any interesting headline to read the article immediately. At the other extreme, if I'm strapped in to Seat 14A waiting for everybody to board, I know that I'm going to have to switch to Airplane Mode in about 10 minutes and then I'll lose the Internet for six whole hours. Who cares? I'm carrying the Internet *with* me!

And sometimes I just want to know the latest Apple news. So I can flip to the Feeds tab and tap on Macworld.com directly. If I want to see the actual Web page, I tap a button and the original page opens.

That sort of freedom of choice is very

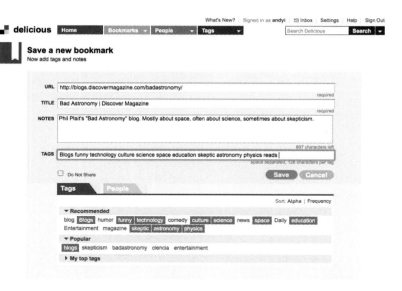

Figure 13-11
Bookmarking a Web page using the Delicious service

valuable. I typically have only a couple of gigabytes free, thanks to all the movies and music I keep on my iPhone. So I appreciate how Runner allows me to "travel light."

There are other creature comforts as well. Every newsreader should have a handy feature for e-mailing articles to people; I often e-mail articles to myself when I'm reading RSS Runner at the burrito place. This way, I know that a certain news item that I need for an upcoming column will be safe and sound in my desktop inbox when I get back to the office.

I mean, if the app is *this* good as a Version 1.0, I can't wait to see what the future holds. A big, big win. It's one hell of a bargain. And it's a free app!

Honorable mention: Manifesto (`www.manifestoapp.com`) is very nearly tied for first place. My only difficulty is that it starts to choke as you add more and more

feeds to it. I *know* that RSS Runner will have downloaded all my news before I board my plane; with Manifesto, it's possible that by the time I'm being told to switch off my phone, the app has only just begun. But if you've subscribed to dozens of feeds instead of hundreds (like me), it's probably not a problem.

BOOKMARKS

The syncing of bookmarks between your desktop browser and your iPhone's browser is a fundamental feature and it couldn't be easier. Check Sync Bookmarks in iTunes and it's done.

But I don't like it. The feature tanks. First, it only works with Safari and Internet Explorer. My favorite desktop browser is Firefox.

And despite my aforementioned "if I love it so much, why don't I marry it?" relation-

Figure 13-12
Retrieving a bookmark using Delicious's
Firefox plug-in

ship with Google, I do indeed have lots and lots of sites bookmarked on my desktop but very few have *any* relevance to what I do on my iPhone. So when I'm on the go, the site I actually want is quickly lost in that big soup. I can create a separate desktop folder for the sites I use on my iPhone, but that fails, too.

See, I need to actually *think* in order to use that method. That's the weak point in any plan, I find.

My goal is to have access to the sites and services that I find memorable, without cluttering up the Bookmarks page of either my desktop or iPhone browser. The solution: Use a bookmarking service that stores your bookmarks in a central location where they can be accessed by any Internet device you own … including the iPhone.

The most popular standard is the free online service Delicious (`http://delicious.com`). It has much the same ginchiness as Google Reader. You can "bookmark" a site to Delicious by either pasting the URL into a form on the site, or just clicking a familiar bookmarklet that handles the job automatically.

You can also install Delicious plug-ins

for all popular browsers. With the plug-in installed, you just click a Delicious button in your browser, and your current page will be bookmarked at the service.

In Figure 13-11, I'm bookmarking a site using the form on Delicious's Web site. As you can see, you're recording way more than just a name and a URL. You can also add a description, as well as Delicious's most powerful feature: tags that organize the site under as many categories as you want.

So you really don't *need* to organize your bookmarks into folders. Once you've logged in to Delicious.com, you can see a reverse-chronological list of your bookmarks. Want to see a list of all your science blogs? No sweat. Whether you're using Delicious via Delicious.com or a plug-in, just click the Science tag. Figure 13-12 shows you how easy it is to use Delicious via the Firefox plug-in. Presto: There are all my science bookmarks in one handy list, with the freshest ones listed first.

Hmmm. It seems like this whole section is just a promo for the *desktop* editions of Delicious.

Trust me: We're about to get into the iPhone thing. The service offers two things that make it the essential iPhone bookmarking utility. First, thanks to its tagging feature, it's very, very easy to have bookmarked hundreds or thousands of sites and retrieve the one you want at a moment's notice. Or even just get an overview of all bookmarked pages with the same general topic.

Second, because the bookmarks are stored in a central location, you never need to worry about synchronizing bookmarks between your desktop and your iPhone. Hell, or your office PC and your home Mac. It's all the same pool.

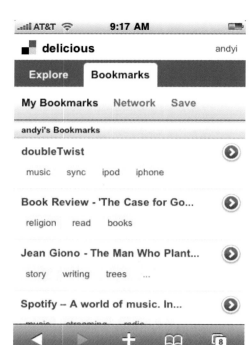

Figure 13-13
Accessing your stored bookmarks via
Delicious's iPhone Web interface.

As with other big online services, Delicious.com offers a neat iPhone-specific interface. You don't need a special iPhone app ... just plug `http://m.delicious.com` into your browser and sign in to access all your Delicious bookmarks (see Figure 13-13).

The regular Delicious Web page opens just fine on your iPhone in Safari. The main site will allow you to access some of Delicious's bigger features, like being able to search your bookmarks for specific tags and descriptions.

Let's revisit one important detail of how bookmarks arrive on Delicious: *Someone thought this Web page was so valuable that*

they didn't want to forget it.

That's a pretty solid endorsement, wouldn't you say?

That's why when I'm hoping to find something *specific* on the Web, my first weapon isn't Google. It's Delicious. If I'm looking for a good free antispyware utility, a Google search will turn up dozens if not hundreds of online ads from companies trying to sell me something. But if I plug "antispyware" "utility" and "free" into Delicious's search box, the gems are immediately apparent. Sure, there will be some duds, but hey, willya look at that: There's one link that's been saved by more than 3,200 users. I'm guessing this is a terrific resource.

Similarly, you should make use of Delicious's Popular and Recent links, for a look at what the world seems to be interested in all of a sudden. For your convenience, you can even bookmark direct links to those lists: `http://delicious.com/popular` and `http://delicious.com/recent`. Those are great links; they help you to find wonderful articles and resources even when you have no idea what you want to look for.

It really is marvelous, the way Delicious is organized. You can bookmark searches for *any* tag in plain English. If you're interested in the Red Sox, for example, bookmark `http://delicious.com/tag/redsox`. It'll always take you to Delicious's newest Red Sox-related tags.

And! All these Delicious searched pages are wired with syndication feeds. So go right ahead! Go to `http://delicious.com`, search for "space elevator," and bookmark that results page in Google Reader. Every time someone reads an article about developments on the technology for moving satellites and people into orbit on a 100-

mile long carbon fiber ribbon (don't laugh; it's being tried) and he or she bookmarks it in Delicious, it'll appear alongside all the other online info you're tracking.

I'm sitting back in my chair now and trying to figure out if I've done a good thing or not.

Bookmarks are dead-simple. They're effective, they're handy, and they do the job they were designed to do. Couldn't be easier to use, either.

But somehow … *that's just not enough.*

Some of us — yes, mainly I'm thinking "me" — have to pervert this Zen-like perfection by introducing new twists that add new power and functionality. That's fine, but now I have you people thinking "This page is Delicious, I think."

Well, if I can't resist the urge to muck things up, I'm following in some fairly illustrious footsteps. God created the egg. Smooth, round, meditatively beautiful. He *could* have left well enough alone, but what did he go and do?

He had a platypus break out of it. Go figure.

What a Friend We Have in RSS

The Skim

RSS Has a Wonderful Plan ◘ Bookmark Your Favorite Sites ◘
Bookmark Your Most Useful Web Searches as RSS Feeds ◘
Building Your Own Feeds ◘ One of the Best Tips in This Whole Damned Book

I n Chapter 13, I give y'all a quick sell on the concept of RSS — the mechanism that nearly every site and service uses to inform the world of its latest content — and what a powerful tool it is. But the point of Chapter 13 is to talk about slick ways of accessing news, blogs, and Internet bookmarks.

In this chapter (Chapter 14), I want to focus more on the subject because the more you understand how pervasive site syndication is, the more powerful your iPhone becomes. The App Store has been a boon and a burden. There are a million apps out there (well, tens of thousands, but that's more than enough). The temptation is to download an eBay app to manage your eBay information, and a Twitter client to keep track of your favorite Twitterers, and a Flickr app to find out if your friends have posted new photos from their vacation.

But in truth, it's possible to use just *one* application — a third-party newsreader app such as RSS Runner (my fave), or even just the powerful RSS reader functions built in to your iPhone's Safari browser — to manage your whole life. True one-stop shopping: This single screen can give you a view on everything in the whole world that interests you.

So here are some elaborations about RSS and some of my favorite ways of exploiting it.

RSS HAS A WONDERFUL PLAN

RSS stands for Really Simple Syndication. Colloquially, it refers to the "newsfeed" of a Web site. There's the site itself, with all of the words and pictures laid out so nicely in pages for the benefit of the humans, but then there's a little file tucked away on the server that contains all that information in a nice, structured database-y sort of format.

So while the humans read the Web pages, *software* can examine the feed. "Forget the ads and the pictures of the blog's author doing rude things next to the wax statue of Brad Pitt near Times Square," a news aggregator service like Google Reader commands. "This guy last visited your site 21 hours ago. Just show me the articles that have been posted since then. I'll format it nicely along with little summaries so he can pick and choose the articles he actually wants to see."

RSS actually delivers two kinds of flexibility because it pretty much hands off the site's raw data to the software of your choice. This software can search, sort, and filter it any way you choose, and it also has complete control over how that data is formatted and displayed, too. A Web page is concrete; a Web site's

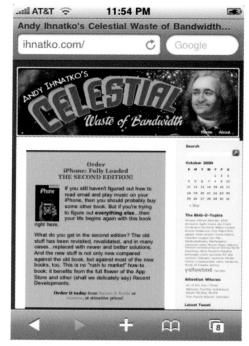

Figure 14-1
My humble blog

Figure 14-2
When you see a symbol like this on a Web page, it's usually a link to the site's RSS feed.

feed is clay.

Chapter 13 talks about some great news "aggregators" — Web-based and native apps that deliver all the fresh content from all your favorite sites in a unified, tidy, scrolling interface.

But Safari has its own built-in RSS reader. If you visit my blog at http://ihnatko.com, you'll see it as a regular Web page (as in Figure 14-1). But if you scrolllllllll down to the bottom of the blog, you'll notice a funny-looking blue XML logo shown in Figure 14-2. That's one of the universal symbols meaning "this button is a link to the site's RSS feed." Tap the button, and Safari

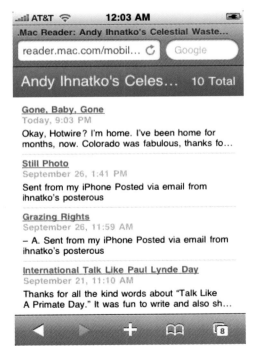

Figure 14-3
My blog re-interpreted by Safari as just a pile of streamlined iPhone-screen-filling content.

reads and processes the feed, then presents my blog as a nice, tidy summary, as shown in Figure 14-3. Safari opens the actual Web site only when I tap on the headline of an article I want to read ... and it'll open the page on that specific article.

If you tap the New Bookmark button at this point, Safari generates a bookmark to this RSS feed and not to the Web page itself. So every time you open this bookmark, you'll open the site in its RSS view.

Gosh, my blog looks purty in Figure 14-3. This brings us nicely to the first thing I use Safari's RSS reader for.

BOOKMARK YOUR FAVORITE SITES

If I'm about to bookmark a page that I'm apt to visit often, I'll bookmark the page's RSS feed instead of bookmarking the page directly. Because it's *always* faster and more convenient to see all of a site's content in one slick, scrolling list of plain text than as a Web page — especially on a small screen like the iPhone's. I use it all the time when I bookmark icons directly to the application launcher. I need to know the latest traffic alerts for my county. Tap one button and bang: here's a tidy, summarized list.

It's particularly handy when you don't have a high-speed Wi-Fi connection to the Internet. When you access a site's RSS feed, your iPhone only has to download a small amount of text. When you access the page itself, Safari has to download every article, every photo, every ad, every *everything*.

Even when you're dealing with an RSS feed with complicated content, RSS simplifies your life by integrating it into your newsreader. Think about comics as a prime example. I think the best way to read your

131

daily comic strips on the iPhone isn't via a purpose-built app from the App Store. It's through an RSS newsreader and a Web site that mashes all your favorite strips into a single RSS feed.

But RSS isn't just a way of reading Web pages. Syndication is such a powerful, flexible, and ubiquitous concept on the Web that it tends to turn up in the strangest places.

BOOKMARK YOUR MOST USEFUL WEB SEARCHES AS RSS FEEDS

No kiddin'. Many sites not only let you do searches, but their servers will deliver the results of that search as an RSS feed that they build for you on the fly. Some examples:

▫ **eBay**. Do a search from your desktop browser and then examine the results closely. Aha! Look at the bottom of the search results: There's that familiar orange syndication logo. This is a link to this same search, with the results delivered as an RSS feed. If you bookmark this search in your RSS newsreader (like Google Reader), it's added to your master list of Everything on the Whole Web You're Interested In. You'll be informed every time new items appear on eBay. Every item will be neatly listed, as in Figure 14-4, which is my usual search for Chewbacca licensed merchandise. And if you tap an individual auction item, you'll note that eBay's search feed actually returns a pretty rich experience. You can see pretty much everything you'd see if you were looking at the actual Web page (see Figure 14-5).

▫ **Technorati blog search**. Yes, I know. You *never* search for your own name

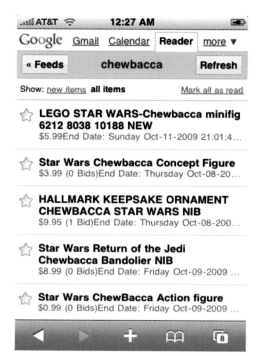

Figure 14-4

An eBay search, bookmarked in Google Reader as a nice, efficient RSS feed

to see if people are talking about you. Never ever ever. But conceptually, if you *were* ever that full of yourself, you could bookmark it and any time the whim struck, you could see what those lying jerks are doing while your back is turned.

▫ **Digg.com user-recommended Web sites**. As I explain in Chapter 13, Digg.com has a nice iPhone-specific Web app for browsing what's hot on the Web; sites that have been recommended and posted to the service by the community of Digg users. But you don't need to use it, really — because each section and search is backed by

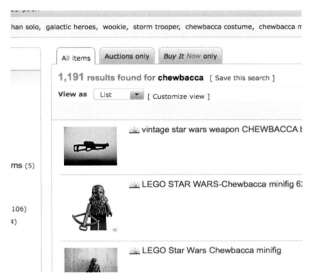

han solo, galactic heroes, wookie, storm trooper, chewbacca costume, chewbacca m

| All items | Auctions only | Buy It Now only |

1,191 results found for **chewbacca** [Save this search]

View as [List ▼] [Customize view]

ms (5)

⚡ vintage star wars weapon CHEWBACCA t

106)
4)

⚡ LEGO STAR WARS-Chewbacca minifig 6:

⚡ LEGO Star Wars Chewbacca minifig

Figure 14-5
RSS search results show you all the info you'd get if you were actually looking at eBay's Web page.

RSS, and if you're specifically interested in news and sites about the Boston Red Sox, you can bookmark an RSS feed that always contains the most recently recommended sites about the Sox.

Indeed, nearly every service you can name is wired up with RSS. Open http://delicious.com/tag/iphone to see the latest hot iPhone pages and apps posted to the Delicious service. Then click on the RSS badge on the page and bookmark it. Presto: You'll never be more than a step away from breaking events in the iPhone world.

I swear, your eyes will become so keenly tuned to spotting RSS badges on Web pages as a hawk's are for spotting small, scared scampering things in a meadow. Whether you use Google Reader or a standalone iPhone app as your newsreader, it'll quickly

become the center of your iPhone world.

BUILDING YOUR OWN FEEDS

Most sites have a syndication feed attached. It's a feature delivered by the software that the owner uses to publish content. But there are still a few holdouts.

If you encounter a great site with no syndication feed, try plugging its URL into http://feedity.com. Feedity is a service that analyzes the content on a page and builds an RSS feed for the content therein. It spits out a URL to a custom RSS feed that you can then give to Google Reader or any other newsreader.

And sometimes, no single RSS feed can collect the info you want. Take online comic strips, for example. They're usually published online by their creators. These strips are wonderful but do I really want to click on 40 separate links each and every morning while I eat my Froot Loops?

Fortunately, there are some simple tools that allow you to build your *own* RSS feeds. My favorite tool is hosted by Yahoo, and it's called Yahoo Pipes (http://pipes.yahoo.com).

On your desktop browser, you literally sketch out what you'd like your new RSS feed to look like. It's really very simple. Figure 14-6 shows you one of my pipes. "The Ethicist" is a great column on the *New York Times*'s site that answers questions about ethics sent in by readers. Snarky site Gawker.com published a funny parody of it called the "*Un*-Ethicist" that answers the

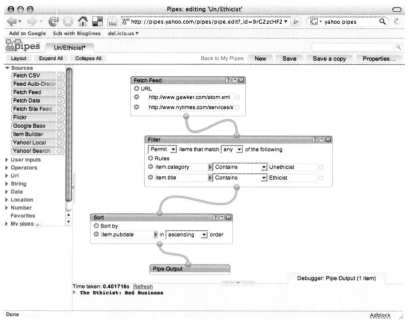

Figure 14-6
Yahoo Pipes lets you build RSS feeds that don't already exist, but should.

same questions, but from a slightly different point of view.

I like both columns, and this pipe mashes them together into a single feed. It's actually doing two tricky things. Neither column has its own separate RSS feed, so this pipe searches www.nytimes.com's and www.gawker.com's RSS feeds, culls out only the articles that match those two column titles, and then combines them into a single new feed that I can subscribe to in Safari.

And Yahoo Pipes does far more than simply mash together multiple RSS feeds. Maybe you're not interested in *all* of *The Washington Post*'s political stories. If you only want to read the ones that mention the secretary of agriculture, have Yahoo Pipes filter the *Post*'s feed for mentions of "Vilsack."

Better: If you're spending a week at a big consumer electronics conference, and you want to make bloody sure you don't miss any news about Nintendo's new Blrgf gaming console, Yahoo Pipes can quickly build you an RSS feed that contains every article on Gizmodo and Engadget that contains a mention of that product, plus any mentions of "Nintendo," or "Blrgf," or "Nasally-Fitted Game Controller," on Twitter, along with any similarly tagged photos on Flickr. One simple feed gives you a comprehensive periscope.

There are tons of ways to exploit this ... which you'll quickly grok once you start combing through Yahoo Pipes to look at the pipes that other users have already built and which are available for you to modify and exploit.

Oh, and I certainly can't let you go before telling you

ONE OF THE BEST TIPS IN THIS WHOLE DAMNED BOOK

Because wouldn't you know it? It takes advantage of Safari's RSS reader.

Observe the following points:

1. The iPhone and the iPod Touch both have wicked-fast Wi-Fi connections to the Internet, baked right in.

2. The iPhone has a wicked-fast 3G connection to the Internet, from nearly anywhere in the country.

3. It's damned-near impossible to listen to anything on your iPhone or iPod Touch unless you have access to a Mac or PC and a sync cable and can sync the media file to your phone via iTunes.

4. A lot of the stuff you like to listen to — like podcasts — are disposable entertainment. You listen to the newscast and you're done with it; from that point onward, the podcast is just taking up valuable space.

5. The iPod app can look for and download new editions of your favorite podcasts, but if you want to listen to *any* past show, or if you haven't already subscribed to the podcast in iTunes, you're generally out of luck.

And now consider the ongoing disappointments that points 3, 4. and 5 engender. You're in a waiting room somewhere. Your dentist is running late. If you knew that you'd be stuck here for two hours instead of 20 minutes, you'd have brought a book. As it is, you have your iPhone. But you forgot to sync it this morning and you've already heard all of yesterday's podcasts.

Figure 14-7

Tracking down the podcast's RSS feed

Ah! But you know that there's a brand-new episode of *Fanboy Radio* up on the podcast's Web server. Just sitting there waiting for you.

You can't sync it to your iPhone from here. But you *can* play that episode "live," streaming it directly from the server.

Or! You're having lunch with a friend and he simply cannot stop talking about *The Bugle*, his absolute favorite weekly podcast. You bicker over the splitting of the check and part, leaving you to face a 50-minute drive home. You'd love to check out *The Bugle* but you haven't subscribed to it in iTunes, obviously. Well, you can still stream it live, directly from the server.

How?

A podcast exists on the server as two components. There's the audio or video file that iTunes downloads, and then there's (yes indeed) the RSS feed file that describes the content and helps iTunes (or any other podcatcher app) figure out that a new show has been uploaded.

So if you bookmark this podcast feed *directly* — either directly in Safari, or via Google Reader, Manifesto, or any other RSS newsreader — you'll be able to play any podcast you want *whenever* you want ... so long as you have a live Internet connection. The bookmark will eventually lead you to a list of

Figure 14-8
Your podcast, shown as a list of RSS
show descriptions

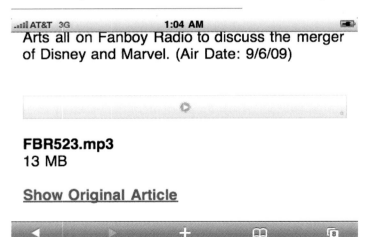

Figure 14-9
A link to the actual online MP3 file is embedded in the episode description.

new episodes, and to a link that downloads
and plays the MP3 episode you want to hear.

All you need to do is find the podcast or
video podcast's RSS file or direct Web site,
and open or bookmark it in Safari or your
newsreader. That's simple enough.

1. Find the show in your list of subscribed podcasts. Just click on the
Podcasts item under Library in your
iTunes window.

2. Right-click (or, on the Mac,
Control+click) on the title to bring up
the item's pop-up menu. Make sure you
click on the title of the overall podcast,
not on any individual episode.

3. Choose Show Description from the
pop-up menu. iTunes opens a little
window describing the show. The URL
for the podcast's RSS feed is right at
the top (see Figure 14-7).

If you want to use a podcast that you
haven't subscribed to in iTunes, you'll have
to do a Google search for the podcast's Web
page. If you examine
the Web page, you
should be able to spot
an orange RSS button
that links to the feed.

Open this feed
URL in Safari on your
iPhone, and look at
what happens: You
wind up with a nice,
RSS-y list of all the
shows in the podcast
(as shown in Figure
14-8). Just choose an
episode that seems
interesting. And sure,
you can subscribe to
this feed in Google

Figure 14-10
Streaming live geekery without syncing your iPhone or iPod Touch via iTunes

Reader, RSS Runner, or any other RSS app on your iPhone.

But let's focus on Safari's RSS reader. So we can stop to curse Apple, just a little bit.

In previous editions of Safari for iPhone and iPod Touch, the built-in Safari reader was more than happy to play a linked media file directly from the Safari reader. Thrilled to, in fact. "Aren't you clever for figuring out this trick?" The Safari reader seemed to say.

But today? Nothing doing. You have to tap the item to open it in the podcast's Web page, where you will find a link to the episode's actual MP3 audio file (see Figure 14-9). Tap the little bar that represents the actual file, and your iPhone happily starts

streaming the audio or video in the standard iPhone player (see Figure 14-10). If it's a media type that the iPhone or iPod Touch can handle (but that's almost a certainty).

It works flawlessly. If you have a Wi-Fi connection to the Internet you can stream audio or video. But even a mere 3G connection can keep up with streaming audio just fine.

RSS, whether experienced through Safari, Google Reader, or a newsreader app, is truly my kind of feature. It's nice to have something as muscular and well-articulated as the iPhone's iPod application, but it never does more for you than what Apple intended it to do. A feature like RSS is so broad and powerful that it invites you to keep coming up with new ways to exploit it.

And so long as developers of Web sites and services keep coming up with new ways to incorporate feeds into the online world, Safari will continue to become more and more powerful and flexible. RSS works great with a newsreader app — again I urge you to (re-)read Chapter 13 — but like a nice ripe banana, it's even good raw.

15

The Web, for Keeps

The Skim

This chapter is *allllll* about viewing Web pages on your iPhone or iPod Touch.

"The most brilliant and valuable chapter in the whole damned book," you sneer. "Sure, the presence of a Web browser on my iPhone sort of *implies* that I could open Web pages quite easily, but for the past year, I've been too terrified to click it, suspecting that there was some sort of sorcery involved. Bless you, Andy Ihnatko. You are surely the prominent genius of the iPhone community."

You know, you're a thousand miles away and several months in the future as I write this. Yet your sarcasm still hurts. You know? *It still hurts.*

Onward. No, of *course* I'm not talking about just opening Web pages in a browser. I'm talking about *keeping* the Web pages you want and need, so that you can still read 'em when you're away from an Internet connection. This chapter reveals tools and techniques that take a Web page in your desktop browser and preserves it inside a technological Mason jar on your iPhone, safe from the ravages of Murphy's Law.

You think you don't need these techniques? You've never tried to catch a train at the Amtrak station near my house. The waiting room is a black hole for cell coverage and I need to write down the confirmation number of my reservation in order to use the little self-service kiosk and print my tickets. If it's information that you truly need, then you truly need to save it to your iPhone in some way. The Internet will

.ıll CHN-... ○   12:17 PM   🔋

雅秀市场

◄   ►   +   📖   🗐

Figure 15-1
The iPhone screen shot trick got me to Yashow Market safe and sound.

TIDBIT

There's an additional advantage to *saving* a Web page instead of merely bookmarking it: You've no idea what's going to happen to that site in the next three weeks to 40 years. It's *exactly* the information you need to properly prepare the pufferfish for your dinner party without killing anybody who doesn't deserve it. But sure enough, a week later, "law enforcement" (whatever *that* means) has forced the site to take the page down.

When you download the page to your hard drive, nobody can take it away from ya.

fail you at the damnedest times.

There are plenty of pages that beg for that sort of treatment. Like the map to the location of your corporate retreat, or an electronic receipt. Hell, you've been to parts of the Web that made you think, "I wish I could stick this page in a Mason jar. With an inch or two of chloroform in it. And then bury it somewhere so that the page couldn't disturb another human being the way that it's just disturbed me."

Well, I can't help you with *those* kinds of pages. But with the *useful* kinds ... read on.

THE UNIVERSAL "KEEP THIS INFO, PLEASE!" FEATURE

This chapter features one indispensable app for storing Web pages on your iPhone permanently. But there's a cheap little trick that you can use to achieve much the same result — and it exploits a feature that comes with your phone.

Much of the time, you don't actually want

to save an entire Web page. You're looking at your travel itinerary, and you want to make sure you "keep" the address of your hotel and your confirmation number. You're looking at the train schedules and you want to "keep" the schedule of outbound trains leaving Boston on the Franklin/Forge Park Line. Or maybe it's a quick online bio of the person you'll be meeting with later today, or a section of a Google Map pinpointing the cross-street of your meeting location.

One *simple* solution is to use the Cut and Paste features that arrived with iPhone OS 3.0. Select the info you want to preserve, copy it, and then paste it into a new note in the Note Pad app.

Good to know. But it's a lot of steps when really, all you want is that seven-digit confirmation number.

The next time you're looking at a screen full of information that you want to preserve, just hold down your iPhone's Home button and then immediately press the Power button.

You'll hear the sound of a camera shutter and the screen will flash. Congratulations: You've just discovered your iPhone's hidden screen-capture mode. A picture of your screen has been deposited in your iPhone's "camera roll." Just launch the Photos app to view it.

It's instantaneous and it gets the job done — and you'll find a million ways to use this trick.

I spent a couple of weeks in Asia over the summer. Natcherly, I don't speak much Japanese or Mandarin, and the pictograms of those languages are utter gibberish to me. But when some Beijing friends suggested that we meet at Yashow Marketplace for lunch, I just Googled for the name. When

I found a Web page with the name of the place written in Mandarin, I zoomed in real nice and took the screen shot.

A day later, I hailed a cab, opened the Photos app, and then showed Figure 15-1 to the cabbie — who took me right there without any ado. In Japan, I used Google Maps to pinpoint my current location. I zoomed in, took a screen shot, and then at the end of the day simply showed my iPhone to the driver I hailed. Because Google Maps always uses the local language, he was able to "read" my marked destination and he brought me right back to the park I had departed from.

SAVING A WEB PAGE TO AN IPHONE-STUDLY FILE

Chapter 20 talks about how to install document files on an iPhone. So the first and obvious solution for keeping Web pages permanently is to export the Web page to a file format that the iPhone can read natively. If you can move that file onto your iPhone or iPod Touch using any of the techniques in Chapter 20 — using Dropbox, Air Sharing, or some other utility — the iPhone's built-in reader will open the Web page with just a tap, whether you're online or not.

You're sitting pretty if you use the PC or Mac version of Safari as your desktop browser. This app can export the current Web page in Apple's Web Archive format (choose File ▶ Save As, then choose Web Archive in the Export pop-up menu). The result is a single file that bundles the Web page with all its associated graphics and other resources. Natcherly, the iPhone can open and display this file with its built-in Safari browser just about as well as it can

Figure 15-2
A saved Web page exported from Safari on a Mac or PC

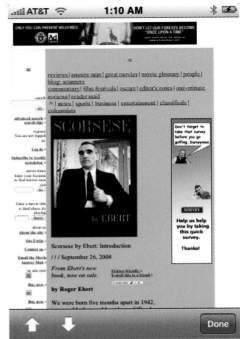

Figure 15-3
A saved Web page exported from Firefox

display the original page (see Figure 15-2).

If you're using Firefox or Internet Explorer, you can still export the page as HTML. In Firefox, choose File ▶ Save Page As and then choose Web Page, Complete in the Save As pop-up menu; in IE, choose Page ▶ Save As and then choose Webpage, Complete in the Save as Type pop-up menu. The resulting page (see Figure 15-3) won't be *quite* so pretty as the one in Figure 15-2, but it'll have all of the text and most of the pictures and formatting.

Figures 15-2 and 15-3 show the same Web page copied to the iPhone using the Air Sharing utility and viewed with the phone's built-in viewer.

Exporting in *some* sort of Web-native format is the most convenient solution to the problem. If utter perfect reproduction is required regardless of the browser, export the Web page as a PDF.

Instead of saving a Web page as a Web Archive or as complete HTML files, you can simply use a Print-to-PDF utility to transmogrify the contents of your browser window into a PDF file. All Macs have print-to-PDF hard-wired right into the standard printer driver. Just select Save as PDF from the PDF pop-up menu in the Print dialog box.

Windows machines acquire this sorcerous feature when you make the correct incantation to your Web browser. The incantation is unpronounceable by human lips but when the runes of its bizarre shape are cast, the lines look remarkably like a URL: `http://en.pdfforge.org/pdfcreator`, to be specific.

Translated: Download PDFCreator, a utility that creates a new Print to PDF printer driver.

Yes? I see a hand up at the back?

"Can't I just do a select-all on the page, copy the text, paste it into a text document, and then put *that* on my iPhone?"

Yes.

Yes, you could.

You could also wear a plastic clip-on bow tie to a job interview with the FBI.

(A *text file!* Of all the …)

THE CO-BEST ANSWER: INSTAPAPER

Turning a Web page into a file works just fine, but there are multiple steps to creating the file and then you have to undertake additional steps to move it onto your iPhone.

A free iPhone app (available from the App Store, naturally) is the grateful solution to those problems. Instapaper is a free online service that lets you "save" Web pages of interest to a centralized server at `www.instapaper.com` and then view them later, online or off, at your leisure. Visit the site, sign up for a free account, and then install the Read Later bookmarklet in your bookmarks bar. This bookmarklet is available for all desktop browsers. There's even a version for the iPhone's own Safari browser.

This bookmarklet is the "desktop" half of the magic. Once it's installed, you can copy

> **TIP**
>
> Yet another advantage of "saving" Web pages onto your iPhone so that you can read them without an Internet connection: Internet access can cost a bloody fortune when you take your iPhone across international borders. By collating and saving all the Web information you'd typically rely on while touring Barcelona, you'll avoid either the $100 that 100 megabytes of data will cost on an international roaming plan, or the much, much, *much* higher costs that you incur if you use your iPhone overseas without signing up for an international plan in advance.

any Web page to your iPhone by clicking the bookmarklet. The bookmarklet simply

> **TIP**
>
> No matter which method you use to export a Web page for use on an iPhone, click on the Web page's View on One Page or Printable Version link if there is one. The site will reformat the page so that it prints well; that is to say it'll reformat it so that it looks great when reformatted for the iPhone screen. Plus, you won't have to download a sequence of eight pages to get the whole page or article.

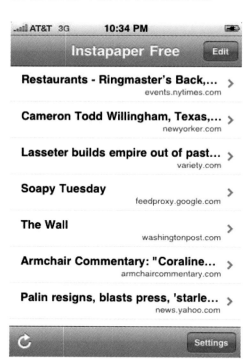

Figure 15-4

A collection of saved and downloaded Web pages on my iPhone, thanks to Instapaper

Figure 15-5

Instapaper creates a nice, comfy reading experience.

passes the URL of the Web page you're viewing over to Instapaper.com, where its contents are preserved.

To download your saved Web pages on your iPhone, launch the Instapaper app and then tap the Update button (see Figure 15-4). All those pages are slurped down into the phone's storage ... safe, sound, and viewable in the app's own text reader (see the example in Figure 15-5).

I love Instapaper. The app integrates perfectly into my "workflow" for reading stuff on the Web. If it's a quick, snappy news article, I'll just read it in my browser. But if it's something long and in-depth, I'll just

click the Instapaper bookmarklet and read it later on my iPhone.

And this operation is even smoother if you use Google Reader as your main interface to the blogs, news sites, and Web sites you like to follow. If a certain article left you with a warm, fuzzy feeling and you want to keep it on your iPhone forever and ever, just choose Instapaper from Google Reader's Send pop-up menu at the bottom of the menu (as shown in Figure 15-6). It uses the account information you provided to Reader in its Settings page to hand the URL off to Instapaper, and from there it pushes onward to its inevitable destination on your iPhone.

r even more to know that her d
and admired.

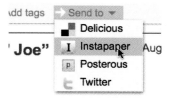

Figure 15-6
Instapaper is even integrated into
Google Reader.

The "free" edition is, well, free. For
a measly stinking five bucks more, you get
a "paid" edition that allows you to organize
your saved Web pages and offers a slightly
more muscular reader. Who cares about
the features? Instapaper is an iPhone "must-
have" and it's just five dollars. Buy it, and
keep Instapaper in business!

THE OTHER CO-BEST ANSWER: STANZA

Go back to Chapter 9, the chapter on
electronic books. Stanza — the finest desktop and iPhone book reader available — has
a nifty little feature: It can convert any Web
page, contained in a single URL, into a fairly

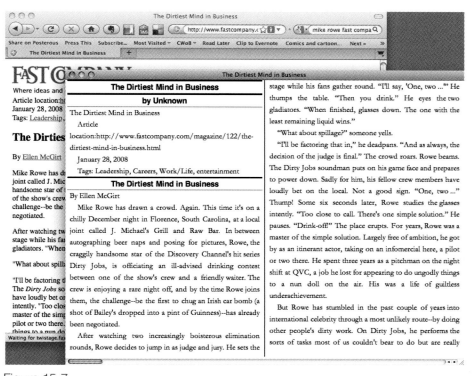

Figure 15-7
Stanza turns Web pages into electronic books.

slick electronic book that can then be read by Stanza's desktop or mobile editions.

It's dead-simple, simpler than what I'd normally use an itemized list for. In Stanza, just choose File ▶ Open Location and paste in the URL of the Web page, and in seconds that page is transmogrified into a very pretty electronic book (see Figure 15-7), ready to be synced to the iPhone edition of Stanza.

It's good to have both Stanza and Instapaper in your toolbelt. Stanza creates a much prettier e-book, and its iPhone reader is far, far better than Instapaper's. But Instapaper is much easier to use. Click a bookmarklet and you've got it. Click a menu in Google Reader, and you've got it.

TWO FREAK SOLUTIONS FOR WIKIPEDIA

Wikipedia is Google. That's to say that it's become part of the culture of modern humanity and it's seized the role of "online reference tool" that there's really no way any other service will ever come along and challenge it. The information you find on Wikipedia can't be taken as gospel (not even the articles about the Gospels) but to quote a line from *The Hitch-Hiker's Guide to the Galaxy*, in the places where it's incorrect, at least it's *authoritatively* incorrect.

So it's good to have a couple of solutions for downloading Wikipedia information to your iPhone where you can be sure it'll always be at hand. If you're curious to find out how to tell a poisonous snake from a non-poisonous snake solely by examining a fresh snake bite, for example, you really don't have time to move to the top of that butte to the north in order to get a better wireless signal. You'll be glad that you

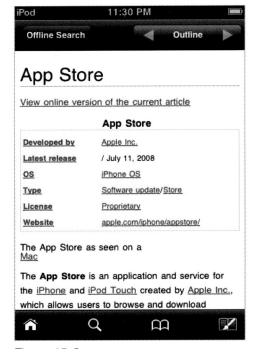

Figure 15-8
Putting all of humanity's unverified knowledge on the iPhone, with TiniWiki

loaded up your iPhone with every piece of data you thought you'd need for your week-long badlands adventure.

Taking the Whole Damned Wikipedia with You

There's an iPhone app named TiniWiki from mContext (www.tiniwiki.com) and it's utterly barking mad.

Maybe I shouldn't judge. What do *you* think? It costs $5.99 and *it downloads the entire Wikipedia into your iPhone* (see Figure 15-8). All 6 million entries. It'll take up nearly 7 gigabytes of storage, but at least if you're ever stuck somewhere without Internet access you'll still be able to get all the salient production details about the *Happy Days* spin-off *Joanie Loves Chachi.*

See? You agree with me: barking mad!

But cool. *Awesome,* even. And it seems just a *tad* more sane when you learn that you have the option of just downloading certain "volumes" of the Wikipedia instead of the whole trough. And for six bucks, it's a hell of a wonderful little novelty app, with the added bonus of maybe providing you with exactly the info you need in an isolated situation.

And it's not insane to want to carry *parts* of the Wikipedia with you. I bring you back to my tales of adventure in Asia. I had an iPhone in my pocket and as such, answers to pressing questions ("If I eat something called a 'Hundred-Day-Old Egg,' will I quite simply die? Or is it just one of those colorful names?") were within reach. For a price. Remember, using the Internet outside of your home country costs beaucoup bucks.

Under those terms, TiniWiki is a neat idea, even if it can eat up fully half of your iPhone's storage. Besides, TiniWiki lets me live that dream I had since the first time I read Douglas Adams's *The Hitch-Hiker's Guide to the Galaxy* as a kid: My iPhone is an electronic device that contains every scrap of knowledge ever compiled.

Mine's even better than the device in the book: It also plays music and video.

Wikipedia Portable Collections

If you want to carry Wikipedia content around with you, you might also try out one of Wikipedia's under-used feature: the abil-

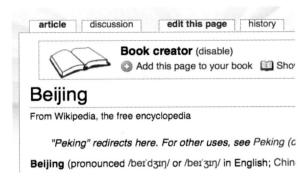

Figure 15-9
Wikipedia.com allows you to make "books" of the articles that interest you.

ity to make "collections" of articles. Look at a small panel of buttons in the left gutter of any ' article, entitled Print/Export, Click the Create a Book link and after a one-click setup, a new toolbar appears atop every Wikipedia article you read (see Figure 15-9).

So if you're preparing for a trip to Beijing, just browse through all the tourism, history, social, and political articles that strike your fancy and click the Add This Page to Your Book button in the toolbar. When you've had your fill, the site can export all of your collected articles into a single, downloadable document:

1. Click the toolbar's Show Book button. Wikipedia will take you to a new page that shows your collection of articles.

2. Drag and drop items in the list of articles to change their order, and give your book a title.

3. From the Download box on the same page, choose a document format from the pop-up menu. PDF should be self-explanatory at this stage. The Open-Document Text option will save it as a nicely formatted (and highly refor-

mattable) word processing document.

4. Click the Download button. Wikipedia will crunch the articles for a minute or two and then furnish you with a link you can click to download your collection.

You can use the PDF file as is with any of the "slap it on your iPhone and read it" solutions I mention in Chapter 20. OpenDocument is a new-ish word processing format favored by Wikipedia because it's an open format owned by no one company. Most modern word processors can import the file. You can export your Wikipedia book into a Microsoft Word-compatible file and then hand it off to Stanza for further e-book transmogrification and final installation onto your iPhone.

MAPS

"Good God, sir!" you exclaim. "I have the Google Maps app! Why the devil would I want to *carry* copies of maps stored on my iPhone!"

Here I cross my arms and patiently wait. You blink once or twice and then feel some small embarrassment.

"You're about to tell me 'What if you're in a foreign country,' right?"

Yes, how perceptive of you. Map data is still data. *Lots* of data. Because don't forget that Google Maps is always downloading map information as you go. Plus, although GPS covers the entire planet, it's a fatal mistake to simply assume that your iPhone will be able to find a cell tower no matter where you walk or drive.

The App Store is now bursting with apps that download entire regional road atlases to your iPhone and offer you turn-by-turn spoken directions from point a to point B.

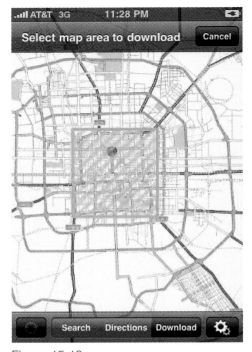

Figure 15-10
OffMaps will download actual, specific map data.

And they get the job done but actually, I'm here to tell you about an extremely little nifty app called OffMaps (`www.offmaps.com`) by Felix Lamouroux. It's just $2.99.

Let's go back to Beijing, since it's done so well for us throughout this chapter. As you prepare for your trip (or via the free Wi-Fi at the Raffles Hotel lobby near Tiananmen Square), type "Beijing" into the app's search box. It'll center its map at the city or address you specified.

Now, you can download any map region you desire. Just tap the Download button and draw a square around the region (see Figure 15-10). OffMaps will download every last scrap of map data and install it on your phone.

Presto. OffMaps acts as a replacement for the Google Maps app (aping its basic "where am I/track my movements" feature), plus it adds a boatload of neat location-specific tweaks as well. What's interesting nearby? OffMaps will pull up relevant Wikipedia articles about your location.

OffMaps works because it doesn't use Google Maps' licensed data at all. Instead, it downloads its maps from OpenStreetMaps. That's

Figure 15-11
iNewsCaster's news harvest

sort of the Wikipedia of mapping data. It's free to everybody, and because the public is encouraged to enhance the data with information about nearby restaurants and services, it tends to have even more information than Google can provide.

MAKING NOISE: INEWSCASTER

But what if you're not in the mood for using your eyeballs today? Meaning: You're acting all petulant because of a perceived slight that your eyes made over the breakfast table. Or maybe it's just that you're driving and you want to listen to blog posts for a half hour instead of reading them and killing many, many people.

Magnetic Time (`www.magnetictime.com`) has a nifty product for both PCs and Macs. iNewsCaster is an RSS reader that works like any other newsreader app ... up

to a point. As for the apps I cover in Chapter 13, you just provide the app with the URLs to the syndication feeds of your favorite blogs and news sites and it automatically downloads and presents all the new, unread articles for your pleasure.

Decidedly *unlike* the others, iNewsCaster actually *reads* the articles into an iPhone-compatible sound file, using a soothingly natural synthetic voice.

It's 30 bucks, but you can download a free trial to see how well the thing works for you.

The Windows Edition

Figure 15-11 shows iNewsCaster's main window. As you can see, the app has been busy, grabbing headlines from a bunch of different sources.

You can add sites to iNewsCaster's watchlist with just a few clicks:

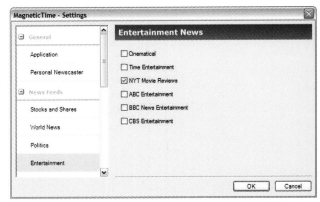
1. Click the Add Feeds button, located in the Common Tasks pane of the main window. iNewsCaster's Settings window opens (shown in Figure 15-12).

2. Scroll the pane on the left until you see the News Feeds section. A number of popular newsfeeds are built right in, organized by category. Just click the checkbox of any feed that you'd like iNewsCaster to keep an eye on.

Figure 15-12
Adding newsfeeds to iNewsCaster via its built-in feed library

3. You can also add the feeds of your favorite sites and blogs manually. To do that, scroll the list down to the very last item and click on Custom Feeds.

4. Click the Add button. A dialog box appears.

5. Paste the URL to your favorite site's newsfeed into the dialog and click OK. (see Figure 15-13). Repeat for each of your custom sites and blogs. Turn once again to Chapters 13 and 14 for tips on how to locate the URL for a site's newsfeed.

iNewsCaster automatically checks each of your subscribed feeds for new content, and downloads any fresh articles it finds.

When you want to convert these articles to spoken audio files:

1. Click the checkboxes of all the articles that seem interesting enough that you'd like to listen to them in the car or during your morning run.

Figure 15-13
Adding a feed of your own

Figure 15-14
iNewsCaster for Macintosh

2. Click the iPod button at the top-right corner of the screen. That's it; iNews-Caster starts grinding down all these articles into spoken text.

The Mac Edition

The Mac version of iNewsCaster operates in nearly the same way as the Windows edition. The layout of the buttons is just a little bit different (see Figure 15-14).

- To add subscriptions, click the Add Feeds button at the bottom of the window. This opens the app's Preferences dialog box, through which you can select feeds that have already been wired into iNewsCaster and add feeds of your own.

- To convert feeds into audio files, select articles of interest from the list and then click the Export button.

iNewsCaster and iTunes

No matter which app you use, the result is the same: a pile of very natural-sounding spoken-text files in iTunes, ready to be synced to your iPhone or iPod Touch.

The files are automatically added to a new playlist in iTunes called iNewsCaster. The app also identifies the tracks' artist as iNewsCaster, so it's easy to build smart

---

TIDBIT

As great as iNewscaster is, you *might* be disappointed with some of its feeds. You're eagerly settling in, expecting to have all of the *New York Times*'s film reviews read to you, but all you hear are brief summaries!

Well, that's not iNewsCaster's fault. Not all feeds contain the entire text of the article. Some sites prefer that you use feedreader software just to see what's new and interesting. If you want to read the article, they want you to visit the actual site, where you might be tempted to read other articles and maybe click on some ads. So their site feeds contain only article summaries.

---

playlists (see Chapter 1) that automatically load just (for example) the most recent 10 converted tracks that have a running time of more than five minutes.

A Free, Point-and-Shoot Solution for Mac Users

If you're using a Mac, there's a simple solution that falls short of iNewsCaster in just one regard (it won't automatically make audiobooks of new Web articles as they're published) but superior in two others (it offers point-and-shoot simplicity and it's free). Just create an Automator workflow that converts the current Safari Web page into an audiobook.

It's much simpler than it sounds.

1. Launch the Automator app and create a new workflow.

Figure 15-15
A magic "make this Web page an audiobook" workflow for Mac users

Figure 15-16
Converting audio to text in Mac OS X 10.6 Snow Leopard using Automator actions

2. Build the workflow you see in Figure 15-15. You create a workflow by dragging actions from the list on the left side of the Automator window into the right side of the window. To locate each of these individual actions in the Actions library, just type their names into the Search box. Automator will locate them for you.

3. Just to keep yourself sane, I've added that final step to the workflow: Instead of slapping these audiobooks into the library where they'll get lost, add the new audio file to a specific playlist. Choose a playlist from the pop-up menu. Maybe you'll want to create a new one just for this content.

4. Try it out. Open up a Web page in Safari — something with just a little text, like the Safari home page — then switch back to Automator and click the Play button. In a few seconds, you should hear a cheerful beep indicat-

ing that everything worked fine. Go to iTunes and play the audiofile ... it'll be named "This podcast was a Web page" or whatever you chose to put into the Text To Audio File action.

5. If it all worked fine, choose File ▶ Save as Plug-in in Automator.

6. Give this workflow a name (such as "Convert this Web page to an audiobook") and choose Script Menu from the Plug In For pop-up menu.

Your automatic workflow will appear in a script menu alongside the Safari menu. Just select the workflow from the pop-up whenever you're looking at a Web page that demands the audiobook treatment.

If you're using Mac OS X 10.6 Snow Leopard, you can go one better: Instead of using a tool for converting Safari text, you can create a service so that any text anywhere in any application can be quickly converted to audio and added to iTunes. Here's how:

1. In Automator, create a new workflow and select the Service template.

2. Build the workflow you see in Figure 15-16.

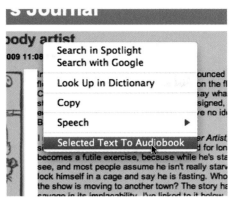

Figure 15-17
The magic of Automator

much as they please, but my heart is forever barred against sympathy.

Because (dangit) I've been stuck in an airport with no bars on my cell phone and nothing to read. *I will not let that happen again.* And so long as I'm diligent about saving or Instapapering anything I read online that's halfway interesting, I'll never go hungry again.

3. Save and name it. How about "Selected text to audiobook"?

From now on, you can convert any text in any window in any Mac app to an audiobook. Just highlight the text and Control+click or right-click to bring up the contextual menu (see Figure 15-17). Choose the Automator workflow, and the magic happens.

One word of warning: It can take a few minutes for Automator to convert a particularly long article to text. Yeah, that's why I had you open the Google home page when testing this out.

ENDING INFO-HUNGER

When I was a wee lad, the people who were running the Internet were fond of screaming "Information wants to be *free!*" in between shoveling double-handfuls of granola and hemp dental floss into their mouths.

Well, I'm of a later generation. I have absolutely no problems incarcerating data and depriving it of its liberty. Its family members may petition the governor as

16

Podcasts

The Skim

Here's a spoiler alert, in case you haven't figured it out yet: The basic purpose of the Internet is to provide hundreds of thousands of jerks, dweeks, geeks, freaks, flakes, egotists, ignoramuses, nutjobs, loners, twits, arrogant pinheads, and delusional Travis Bickle aficionados a way to share their unique articulations of individual insanity with a potential audience of millions of total strangers.

Podcasting was invented when members of the above groups realized that the human population could insulate themselves from these messages by simply sealing themselves inside a metal automobile or any place where Wi-Fi signals can't penetrate or where Internet users can't read text.

Still, as podcasting became part of mainstream communication, the level of content available via podcast was raised. Now, the same shows you tune in to all the time on public radio, local stations, and national TV networks can arrive on your desktop (and thence your iPhone or iPod Touch) at regular intervals at no charge.

I should warn you that the folks who podcast from major networks and the like are (generally speaking) no less stable or egotistical than the Internet freelancers. But at least you know they're probably making a comfortable living. A full belly tends to stifle baser urges to inflict stress and mayhem upon society.

WHAT HAPPENS WITH A PODCAST

Podcasts combine all the best technologies and infrastructures of the Internet in ways that you, the user, can safely ignore:

- Someone in the world sits down behind a microphone and records a show. He or she uploads it to a server somewhere on the Internet.

- The server also contains a little file that keeps track of each episode. It contains a description of the podcast and a synopsis of each individual episode. And, most important for your purposes, a record of what date and time the show was first posted to the server.

- You've told iTunes that you like this show, so iTunes periodically checks this file. It's *called* a "subscription," but not to worry: It's free, free, free. iTunes automatically downloads new episodes as they appear, and adds them to your iTunes library.

- And because you've also told iTunes to automatically copy new podcasts to your iPhone or your iPod Touch, each morning when you snatch the device from its desktop dock and toss it into the front seat of your car, your morning commute is filled with fresh content that (a) appeared from thin air without your having done anything at all, and thrillingly, (b) didn't cost you a penny.

Apart from the "it doesn't cost you a penny" thing, the second-most-thrilling thing about podcasts is that the content is controlled by the same fundamental principle that guides *all* the content that you encounter on the Internet, viz:

"On the Internet, nobody can hear you say, 'But what's the point of this, really?'"

Which means that there's a truly dizzying array of content available. Any jerk with a $10 microphone and a two-bit opinion has access to the exact same means of putting his or her words in your ears as any of the Big Four networks. So during that morning commute, it's entirely possible that you'll be listening to last night's polished, professional, and highly illuminating broadcast edition of *ABC News: Nightline*. Then you move to the next podcast, which is a heavy-metal show by some guy named Jason from Salt Lake City, who's complaining about how he got this *awesome* Motorhead tattoo on his back, but now he feels cheated because he's the only person who never gets to actually *see* it.

When iTunes started supporting podcasts, it totally changed the way I used portable players like the iPhone. And (oh, dear) it completely killed any remaining interest I had in traditional, broadcast radio. I get the best programming from all over the world, and it's available to me any time I want to hear it. As opposed to radio, which limits me to whatever happens to be on whatever station I happen to be able to receive in whatever city I happen to be in.

(Think about your least-favorite national radio personality. I mean, come on: Do you *really* think they'd have a career if listeners had any choice in the matter?)

There's a three-pronged approach to filling your iPhone with podcasts:

1. Locate a podcast that seems at least 38 percent interesting.
2. Tell iTunes to subscribe to that podcast.

ly Zaltzman and John Oliver implore
s week John and Andy celebrate all t

Figure 16-1
Your first step into a larger world

3. Configure your iPhone to automatically load new episodes as they land in
your iTunes library.

THE ITUNES PODCAST DIRECTORY

Apple maintains a huge and fairly ginchy

searchable directory of podcasts, and you
can access it straight from iTunes. But
Apple is highly ecumenical and embraces
podcasts from all sources; it's happy to
subscribe you to a podcast that the iTunes
Podcast Directory has never heard of.

The iTunes Podcast Directory

To visit the iTunes Podcast Directory,
click on Podcasts in the iTunes window's
Sources list and then click the Podcast
Directory button in the lower-right corner
of the window (see Figure 16-1).

Click the Go to Podcast Directory button
to proceed. You're quickly connected to the
entrance to the iTunes Podcast Directory

Figure 16-2
The front doors of the iTunes Podcast Directory

Figure 16-3
iTunes's Top Podcasts: It's all a popularity contest.

Figure 16-4
Podcast categories on the Directory's front page

(see Figure 16-2).

The iTunes Podcast Directory lives on one of Apple's servers on the Internet, not on your own hard drive. So you'll need to have a live connection to the Internet in

TROUBLE

One word of caution: If you're running out of room on your hard drive, subscribe to video podcasts with caution. Each one of these shows can take up five to 10 times as much space per episode as an audio podcast. You'll forget about that until iTunes has been downloading a nightly newscast for three weeks, and suddenly your PC or Mac is throwing up all kinds of "Hard drive space critically low! Everybody panic!" errors.

order to access the thing.

And at this point you should regard yourself as not unlike young Charlie Bucket in *Willy Wonka and the Chocolate Factory* — no, not the Johnny Depp movie, the *good* one, the one that has a scene where the kids get to run through a little park made entirely out of candy and sample to their hearts' delight.

Obviously there's lots of eye candy here at the front door. Individual podcasts get front-row attention, usually because they're new or suddenly hot, but your first clicks should probably go to the Top Podcasts list (see Figure 16-3). It's a ranking based on popularity, which almost always means they're well-produced shows with terrific content, and new episodes come out regularly.

The iTunes Podcast Directory's front door is studded with links to "featured" podcasts. Why *these* podcasts and not others? Because they're all produced with a professional attitude (even if they weren't necessarily produced by professional broadcasters) and are both popular and regularly updated.

But by no means should you conclude

that there are only 100 news podcasts in the directory. To see the entire list, go to iTunes's omnipresent directory menu, click on Podcasts, and select a category (see Figure 16-4).

Click on any one of these category names and you'll be taken to the front page of that particular category, which will have its own Featured Podcasts and Top Podcasts lists.

Incidentally, iTunes's main search feature (that big Search box at the upper-right hand corner of the iTunes window) searches the Podcast Directory as well as the music store. So if you know precisely what you're looking for — and you don't mind sifting through a bunch of music tracks that also match your search query — you'll save a couple of steps.

Again I cite the Fundamental Principle of the Internet: Apple isn't interested in stopping people from making their podcasts widely available, so if the podcaster submits the show's URL to Apple and there are no legal issues involved, Apple adds the podcast with little ado. So you'll find lots and lots and *lots* of noise, with a few gems mixed in.

Thus, the Featured Podcasts lists, and the iTunes Store's Search box are far more useful than scanning through thousands and thousands of individual titles.

Learning More about a Podcast

No matter how you hit upon a podcast

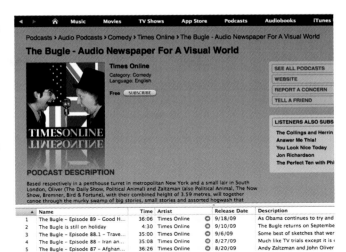

Figure 16-5
Looking at a podcast.

of interest, you can find out more about the show by clicking its little square poster image (if it's a featured podcast) or the circular arrow button next to its title (if it's turned up in a search or some other listing). Either way, iTunes takes you to the podcast's main directory listing (see Figure 16-5).

Here you'll find a description of the podcast, a list of all the shows that are available at the moment, and possibly some user comments. Clicking the Web site link opens up the show's official Web site in your Web browser. Double-click on an individual episode (or its Get Episode button) to download that episode immediately and listen to it in iTunes.

Subscribing to Podcasts through the iTunes Directory

If you've spent some time noodling through the Directory, you've spotted Subscribe buttons here and there (such as the one in Figure 16-6). Yes indeed, this but-

Figure 16-6
The Subscribe button

Figure 16-7
PodcastDirectory.com helps you to find podcasts by a specific location.

ton does precisely what you think it does. Click it, and iTunes subscribes you to that podcast. It starts off by downloading the latest episode and adding it to your personal iTunes library. And from that point onward, iTunes will automatically download new episodes. That's all there is to it.

OTHER PODCAST DIRECTORIES

As neat as the iTunes Podcast Directory is, Apple didn't invent the concept of podcasting and it doesn't own it, either. Nobody does. So there are plenty of podcasts available that don't appear in the iTunes directory.

But honestly, if you eagerly download a show that doesn't appear in the iTunes directory, be prepared to have your heart broken. Getting listed in iTunes is (a) free, (b) a simple, well-documented procedure, and (c) a fairly automatic approval from Apple, unless you're doing something naughty, like explaining how to sneak an old Band-Aid into a bottle of beer and seal it up again to make it look as though it came from the factory that way, so you can maybe scam a free case out of your local liquor store.

I find the biggest advantage of the alternative directories is that they highlight different shows and organize their content a little differently. Which means there's

a good chance that there's a terrific podcast buried deep inside iTunes where I'll never find it, but which I'll trip over on Odeo.com by accident.

Some swell podcast directories:

- **Podcastalley.com.** A strong front page. It's a directory, but it's also backed by lots of info *about* podcasts and podcasters. Another one of those directories that's excellent for discovering a podcast you'd never heard of about a topic you didn't think you'd be interested in, which nonetheless becomes one of your can't-miss shows.

- **PodcastDirectory.com** brings some new twists to the game — among them is its ability to search for podcasts by location of origin. So if you're spending the weekend on Cape Cod and you're specifically looking for local content, Podcast Directory can quickly zone you in (see Figure 16-7).

- **Odeo.com.** It's very iTunes-like in that it's well organized by categories and

Figure 16-8
Apple's own little podcast icon; clicking on this icon on a Web page might subscribe you to a podcast.

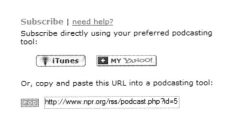

Figure 16-9
Hunting for a podcast's RSS feed

makes it easy to spot the popular and most heavily updated podcasts. I like it for the same reason I use both Google and Yahoo Search when I'm looking for something on the Web: Having two different "periscopes" on a certain target means that you're not just relying on one set of recommendations.

SUBSCRIBING TO A PODCAST

Naturally, subscribing to a podcast you discovered without the help of the iTunes Podcast Directory, or just by browsing around on the Web, isn't a simple as clicking a friendly Subscribe button.

Umm ... unless the podcast has a friendly Subscribe to this Podcast in iTunes button or link. It might incorporate some flavor of the icon in Figure 16-8, which is Apple's own special "this is a link to a podcast" button. It might just explicitly say, "Subscribe with iTunes."

Or something else entirely. The thing is, these people who create Web pages are all mavericks. They're wild stallions, unbroken, untamed; they may bend your precious rules but dammit, they get the job done. Et cetera.

But it isn't terribly complicated. Remember earlier, when I told you that every podcast is represented by a simple file somewhere on the Internet? All you need to do is give iTunes the address of that file.

I apologize in advance for this, but I am forced to introduce a technical three-letter-acronym into the proceedings.

That three-letter acronym is RSS. It's the simple, worldwide standard that powers podcasts (and blogs and all sorts of Internet services). Technically, the address you're hunting for is known as an *RSS feed*. Figure 16-9 shows you the sort of cluster of information you might encounter on a podcast's Web page (in this case, it's from an NPR show).

You see a friendly iTunes button, which takes you directly to a Subscription page in iTunes. Good, we can always use more examples of that, eh?

But if that button weren't there, the colored button that reads RSS 2.0 would command your full and immediate attention. It represents a link to that RSS feed that you want to give to iTunes. It also says "Syndication," which is another tip-off that it's a link to the podcast feed. "Feed," "XML," and "Pod" are other triggers.

To copy the link:

161

Figure 16-10
Manually subscribing to a podcast

1. Right-click (or, on the Mac, Control+click) on the link to open the contextual menu.
2. Choose Copy Link or Copy Link Location (depending on the Web browser you're using) from the contextual menu. Once you've copied the link to the podcast's RSS feed, just hand it off to iTunes.
3. In iTunes, choose Advanced ▶ Subscribe to Podcast.
4. Paste the URL into the text box and click OK (see Figure 16-10).

And from that point onward. iTunes treats the podcast the same as it would if you'd found it in the iTunes directory. It adds the podcast to your list of subscriptions, downloads the most recent episode, and then downloads future shows as they're published.

MANAGING PODCASTS

You can see all of the podcasts you've subscribed to by clicking Podcasts in the Library section of iTunes's main window (see Figure 16-11).

If iTunes knows that there are episodes that it hasn't downloaded — for instance, it's a new subscription, which would mean that iTunes only downloaded the latest show — you can manually download it by clicking the little Get button next to its title.

If there's an exclamation mark (!) to the left of the podcast's title (note *ABC World News* and *Are We Alone?* in Figure 16-11), that means there was a problem when trying to update that item. Either the server where the audio files live isn't available, or the podcast has been discontinued, or perhaps the universe doesn't believe that you're one of those people who deserve to have nice things happen to them.

Updating a Podcast Manually

By default, iTunes automatically looks for new episodes of your podcasts on a regular basis. If you want iTunes to look *right freaking now* — you're about to leave the house for a three-hour drive to your folks' house and you don't want to be 18 minutes in before you realize that you've already heard everything on your iPhone — just click on the Refresh button in the lower-right corner of the iTunes window. Make sure you're looking at your list of podcasts first; if you're looking at your music library, that button will say and do something else entirely.

iTunes will update all your subscriptions immediately, automatically downloading any new shows that you don't already have. If you'd like to update just one show, choose Update Podcast from the podcast's contextual menu (to get that menu, right-click — or, on a Mac, Control+click — the podcast's name). Only that one podcast will be updated.

Sometimes, for reasons known only to iTunes and perhaps Alex Trebek (who has the whole stack of question cards and therefore knows all the answers in advance), iTunes will come to believe that a certain podcast has become inactive. That its authors are no longer creating new

Figure 16-11
A glorious cornucopia of free content

episodes, that you're no longer listening to them, and thus there's no reason to keep checking for new shows.

So if a favorite show seems to have dropped off the face of the earth, it's a good idea to do a manual Update Podcast from the contextual menu. Click on any podcast in the list and then choose Edit ▶ Select All to, er, select all your subscribed programs. iTunes will take nothing for granted and will check *every last one* of those shows for new episodes.

Unsubscribing

If at some point in life you discover that *Shawn and Kyle's Super-Awesome Weekly Movie Podcast* is neither weekly, nor is it consistently about movies, and "barely adequate" is a stretch, let alone super-awe-

some, you can unsubscribe to the podcast by clicking on its title and then clicking the Unsubscribe button in the lower-left corner of the iTunes window.

Changing Podcast Settings

The lower-left corner also sports a Settings button, which is where you tell iTunes how it should manage all of your podcasts as a group (see Figure 16-12).

Here, you can tell iTunes how frequently it ought to update your podcasts, and what it should do with them once you've got 'em. Through the Check for New Episodes pop-up menu, you can tell iTunes to check hourly, daily, weekly, or manually (which means that it's entirely up to you to remember to click iTunes's Update button and check for new episodes).

163

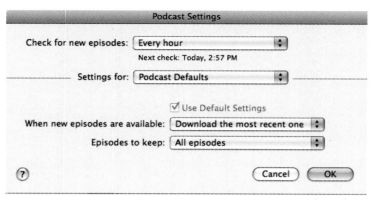

Figure 16-12
Podcast Settings let you tell iTunes how it should update your podcasts.

And what should iTunes do when it finds new content? The When New Episodes Are Available pop-up menu offers three choices:

- **Download All** grabs every episode you don't have. If *The Jeff Boring McDullsworth Show* has 230 half-hour episodes available, then iTunes is downloading all 230.

- **Download the Most Recent One** does what it says. It assumes that you're not, you know, obsessive-compulsive about this sort of thing and you just want whatever's newest. But iTunes kindly grabs all the information about the shows it didn't download, and adds that info to the podcast's program listings so you can peruse them at your leisure.

- **Do Nothing** seems like a waste of a good resource. But at least it's fairly easy to understand. Instead of downloading any new episodes, iTunes simply adds information about those episodes to your subscription listing.

After iTunes updates your podcast sub-scriptions, the new content will be snug and secure in your iTunes library, and any info about shows that it didn't download will appear in the listing.

You also can also tell iTunes how to manage the shows you've downloaded. If you've subscribed to dozens or hundreds of podcasts, you can fill up your hard drive pretty quickly; that's a big worry if you've subscribed to lots of video podcasts. You can tell iTunes to delete every show from your hard drive as soon as you've heard it, or just hang on to the freshest couple of episodes. By default, I like to have iTunes keep every show that gets downloaded because I enjoy listening to my favorites again months later.

SYNCING PODCASTS TO YOUR IPHONE

Normally, you'd use the standard iPhone prefs pane to choose which podcasts get synced to your device. Click on the name of your iPhone or iPod Touch in the Devices list to reveal your sync preferences, and then click the Podcasts tab. You'll see a huge spread of options, shown in Figure 16-13.

By default, iTunes selects Automatically Update all Unplayed Podcasts for you. Every podcast that appears in iTunes is automatically copied into your device, where they appear in its built-in Podcasts list.

Fabulous. This works peachy-keen if you

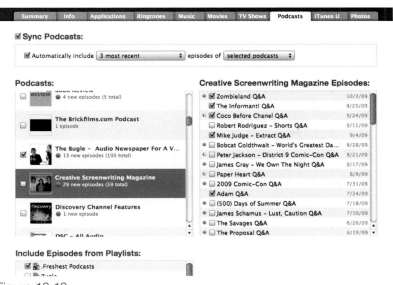

Figure 16-13
Deciding how podcasts wind up on your iPod

iTunes to be a bit more selective about the content it sends to your iPhone. iTunes 9 allows you to specify on a podcast-by-podcast, and even an episode-by-episode, basis which shows get synced to the device. It's espe-

have a modicum of self-control and don't subscribe to more podcasts than your poor little 8- (16-, 32-, …) gigabyte device can handle.

Otherwise, you're quickly going to run out of space on your iPhone or iPod Touch. Picture yourself there in the car, laughing merrily at the acres of bumper-to-bumper traffic. There is a song in your heart because a two-hour delay gives you all the time in the world to listen to a recent podcast you downloaded which features three hours with the creators of *The Matrix*, in which they admit that the first movie was sort of okay but then the final two were just self-indulgent, pretentious nonsense.

And then you discover that none of it got copied to your iPhone because everything you've downloaded over the past week is still choking its capacity.

So clearly, it's a Good Thing to allow

cially handy; sometimes your favorite episodes are months old.

Personally, I manage my playlists via the traditional way … but I also create smart playlists just for my podcasts (see Chapter 1). For one big reason: The iPhone can't "mix" podcasts on its own. It will happily play every episode of *The Bugle* one after the other, but it won't do something as simple as "Please play the newest dozen unlistened podcast episodes, one after the other."

That's a big deal during my hour-long commutes, y'know?

For example, Figure 16-14 shows a smart playlist I set up that always ensures that the newest podcasts land on my iPhone. The first line says, "This playlist should only contain podcasts." The second and third lines omit video podcasts (which are bad, bad things to have playing while you're driving).

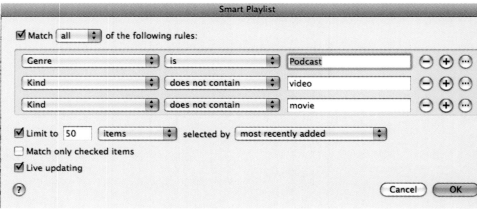

Figure 16-14
Taking greater control over iPod content with smart playlists

The playlist always contains 50 podcasts, and as new podcasts arrive, the old ones are pushed out. So this playlist always contains the freshest content from my podcast subscriptions.

Success! Because my normal mechanism for listening to podcasts is this smart playlist, once I've heard the latest *Martini Shot*, the iPhone starts playing the newest

> ## TIP
>
> Be sure to turn to Chapter 14 for one of my favorite iPhone tricks. Your iPhone can download certain podcast episodes directly from the Internet. But by bookmarking the podcast's RSS feed in Safari, you can have the latest episode streamed through your iPhone or iPod Touch, directly from the server, without wasting time or space.

SMODcast because it's the next item in the playlist. Hours and hours of uninterrupted music and nobody has to die because I was fiddling with the iPhone on my dash instead of looking ahead to check for stalled-out school buses. That sounds like a pretty fair deal to me.

Podcasting is such a wonderful thing that it's utterly *astounding* that you humans haven't discovered a way to wreck it yet. A world full of free, rich content that lands on your iPhone as though delivered by pixies while the shoemaker slept. I've been at this since there were less than 500 podcasts in the world and I'm still amazed by the content.

Hey, here's a tip: Search for "Magnatune" in the iTunes podcast directory. It's a music publisher with a freaky way of doing business: It hosts dozens and dozens of regular podcasts featuring recordings from its library. An hour of Mozart, every week. Or Bach. Or Jazz. Or Xanthanian Typewriter-Swallowing Music. No ads, no cuts, no commercials; it's like a radio station.

The idea is that if you like some of the music in the podcast, maybe you'll visit www.magnatune.com and buy some of it on CD. I should, um, probably do that sometime.

It's also slightly remarkable that Apple is the one maker of portable devices who supports podcasting so aggressively. Just think for a moment: Apple makes jillions of dollars a year by selling people content through the iTunes Store. And yet they use that same entity's massive resources to connect their customers to hundreds of thousands of hours of free content. Go figure.

Well, I'm certain you'll find a way to ruin this entire concept. I had a favorite brand of cookie and I wondered just *how* this perfection of delectability could possibly be ruined. But you people came through for me: The company replaced the high-quality chocolate with stuff that was mostly paraffin, and dumped so many preservatives into the recipe that they never were quite crisp.

And some people have no faith in humanity. Pish-tosh! Put your shoulders into it, Mr. and Mrs. Humanity, and I'm absolutely certain that within one generation, podcasts can be worthless and intractable junk of absolutely no value or interest to anybody.

17

Downloading Music from Places Other than iTunes

The Skim

Downloading Music for Free ♁ Freebies from Commercial Music Sites ♁
Freebies from Music Blogs ♁ Googling for Tunes ♁
Downloading Music for Pay

Apple is famous for end-to-end solutions. And although that
sounds a little bit naughty, it just really means that by creating a world in which you sit down at your Apple computer and
launch an app that Apple created for managing music and connect to
Apple's online music store and syncing the music you bought to your
Apple portable music player ... well, then Apple has a big opportunity
to make sure that nothing goes wrong at any step along the way.

It also has an opportunity to dissuade you from giving any other
computer, software, or music company a shot at your cash.

So, yeah, I guess it really *is* just a little bit naughty.

The iTunes Store is actually quite a marvel. I've always held that
I'd rather live under a dictator who anticipates and satisfies my every
need than live in freedom, if freedom entails that all I have are 10
earthworms for dinner and a further 90 that I'm fattening up for market so that maybe I can come home with four beans to feed the favorite of my nine children.

But Apple's hardly your sole source of online music. There are plenty of ways to get your hands on free music that are in fact perfectly legal. And in recent months, two large online music retailers have discovered a way to sell music to iPhone and iPod users that goes iTunes one better.

DOWNLOADING MUSIC FOR FREE

You're not a cop, are you?

Seriously dude, could you lift up your shirt or something so I can see if you're wearing a wire? Because if y'are, I wanna say that I have no intention of illegally trafficking in pirated music, and if there's any evidence or anything that I did, then it was entrapment and stuff.

No, no, I hope I didn't offend ya or nothin'. But I had to ask. We've been gettin' hassled a lot, y'know. Can't be too careful. Particularly *now*. Because The Man's been coming down hard on downloading unprotected music off the Internet. And I've got this *awesome* plan that lets us all download truckloads of music every day and there ain't a *thing* that the recording industry or the feds can do about it.

The secret — you gotta swear you won't tell nobody else — is simple: *You make sure you don't do anything that's actually illegal.*

Yeah, I know. I was pretty proud of that scheme myself, after I shook the final few bugs out of it. You should have seen the look on the dude from the Recording Industry Association of America's face after he confronted me on my doorstep with network logs proving that I'd downloaded hundreds of megabytes of MP3s, all triumphant-like, and then learned that I'd done so completely legally, with the encouragement and permission of the files' original copyright holders.

Mind you, he still sucker-punched me in a delicate area and then poured the rest of his takeout coffee on me as I writhed in pain on my own porch, before he stormed off to his car and backed over my novelty mailbox. But let's be clear: The moral and legal victory was absolute.

Why Stealing Music Is, You Know … Bad

Lots of people make fun of the recording industry's copyright watchdogs, and for good reason: Their excesses are, well, so *excessive*. I suppose you could praise them for having an unusual dedication and determination to see their tasks through to the end, even when it's been demonstrably proven that the person they're prosecuting into bankruptcy is an octogenarian retiree who doesn't even own a computer. You could also suggest that they're a separate branch of the evolutionary tree and have seven webbed toes on each foot. But that wouldn't change the fact that piracy is wrong. You want this album? It's a commercial product? Then you gotta pay for it. Period.

And if the moral angle doesn't work for you, do keep in mind that at this stage in the game, detecting illegal music downloads is a fairly simple, automated, and successful process. Rest assured that the recording industry's copyright goons became aware of that illegal file-sharing site well before you did. Also be aware that even if you never provided a name and address, your computer left behind a sequence of digits that can rewind the download all the way back to your house, and that the aforementioned goons can exchange these digits for a name and address with one e-mail to your Internet service provider.

So it's wrong and it's dangerous. And most music sucks, anyway. Do you really want to risk a $3,000 fine over a song from a band that, 20 years from now, you're going to swear to your kids that you never ever liked or listened to?

Becoming a Pawn in a Marketing Plan

Yes indeed, it's possible to (1) download music; (2) download copyrighted music, by name-brand artists; (3) not pay a dime for it; and most bizarre of all, (4) play right into the hands of the recording industry.

It's all down to merchandising, promotion, and the desire to Go Viral. Record companies regularly seed the major commercial music stores with tracks that you can download for free. The most reliable ones:

iTunes Music Store

I know that the basic theme of this chapter is downloading music free of the corporate chains of the Apple iTunes golmothra. But I must remind you that a new smattering of free tracks arrives on iTunes every week. And naturally, the iTunes Store is your first and simplest click. The store's front door always contains a few links to free downloads. Usually you'll find these links at the bottom of the page, as in Figure 17-1.

And it's not just music; *everything* free is collected on that page. Music, videos, books, the whole whack. Naturally, you won't exactly be spending hours and hours poring through the cornucopia of free

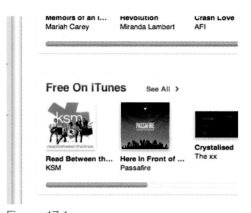

Figure 17-1
Beats for deadbeats: free music from the iTunes Store

selections; usually there are only a handful of freebies available at any given time, and they're only available for a limited time. But iTunes shoppers are such a huge and important part of the music market that music publishers are often willing to give away tracks by chart-topping acts instead of the factory-floor sweepings you'd expect to see.

You do indeed have to look to find these freebies, but if you're not interested in scouring the store yourself, you can just bookmark the Free iTunes Store Downloads blog (www.itsfreedownloads.com). This regularly updated blog maintains a list of not just the free music downloads but also free audiobooks and videos. Best of all, you can subscribe to its RSS feed in your Web browser or newsreader and automatically be notified of new freebies.

Amazon MP3 Store

But if Apple is occasionally willing to let you have a morsel or two of free music, well, Amazon.com is the ice cream truck that got stuck under the low bridge near your house,

MP3 Downloads > Music By Price > Songs > Free

Figure 17-2
Amazon has … um, wow … a *lot* of free music.

whose driver is urging you to help yourself to as much as you can stomach before it all starts to melt.

The top page of Amazon.com's MP3 music store usually stashes information about fresh, popular, and recommended free tracks in the right-hand column. But this link will simply return a list of all of them:

```
http://www.amazon.com/s/
node=334897011&sort=salesrank
```

This URL (entered as a single line) will spit out the delightful results shown in Figure 17-2.

I call your attention to two elements that sort of leap out at you: the preponderance of the word "free!" in the Price column; and the bit at the top reporting that this specialized search for just free music returned 1,256 results.

I should also call your attention to the fact that I've actually *heard* of many of these bands and am happy to add their work to my iTunes library. Don't worry that this isn't the iTunes Store; just click on the Get MP3 link and they'll land in iTunes. I'll explain that in a little more detail later in the chapter.

Helping Preserve Our Cultural Heritage

Or at least that's how you feel when you visit the Internet Archive (`www.archive.org`). It's no mere repository of audio files. As a nonprofit member of the American Library Association, the Internet Archive has taken on a goal of protecting and *preserving* content and making it available to current and future generations.

It's an ambitious agenda. Archive.org shows you Web pages stretching back to the very start of the World Wide Web. Classic books and essays are available as electronic texts. Movies, television shows, old software … and yes, music, all from artists who support Archive.org's cause (see Figure 17-3).

You might think that this audio archive contains, I dunno, public-domain jug-band music transferred off wax Edison cylinders. You would be correct. But it also contains modern tunes by grassroots labels and independent bands, speeches, conferences, and the largest and best-indexed collection of legal concert recordings available anywhere — many from major, currently touring groups.

With tens of thousands of music files available, it's easy to fill an iPhone to the brim from Archive.org alone. And that doesn't even touch on its archives of freely downloadable video and other content.

Finding Free Music

Of course, the sites I've mentioned aren't the only spots where you can find free music; 99 percent of the others fall into a few predictable categories:

- They offer free music, but you can't actually download any of it. It's like a radio station where you can be your

Figure 17-3
Archive.org: free music with a higher calling

own deejay. Which is fine if you're trying to kill some time at work, but not
so good if you want to fill an iPhone.

◻ They offer free music, but chiefly as
a way to sneak spyware, adware, key-
stroke loggers, and other nasty Trojan
horses onto your system. Which is
why you should be careful about Googling for "free music downloads." It's
up there with "free ringtones," "free
wallpaper," and "Do you have the same
credit-card or Social Security number
with a famous celebrity? Take our free
online quiz and find out!" — something of a Red Flag Term for fraud.

◻ These sites offer free, downloadable
music, no fooling, but even the legit

ones offer just a few specific bands
or selected tracks from a band as
a promo. Which is terrific from my
point of view as I've got hundreds of
pages here to fill, but what help would
hundreds of pages of random URLs be
to you, the consumer?

◻ No, instead I must press on and
talk about ways to locate free music
through search engines.

Basic Search

Tech companies have long since given
up on competing with Google and instead
hope to find some sort of niche in which
they can carve out some sort of success.
Google doesn't (at this writing) have a sim-

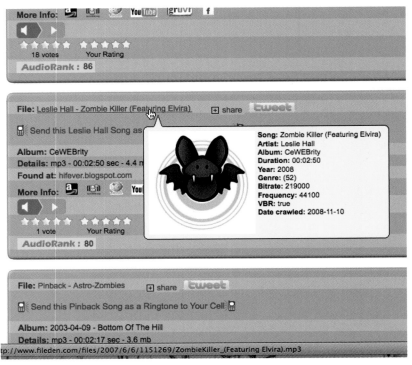

Figure 17-4
Skreemr.com searches for music. But the files it finds may arrive covered in rabies spit.

ple "search for audio files" feature ... okay, cool! Now that I've called this omission to Google's attention, that's the feature it'll add to its search engine.

Until then, this looks like a job for Skreemr.com. Skreemr.com's niche is to be the search engine that searches for audio. So if you just click on Dogpile's Audio tab and type in the name of a genre or a specific band, it brings back the goods (see Figure 17-4).

Beware, though: Some of these tracks might be copyrighted music. Remember, online music pirates are very easy to uncover. It's just not worth the risk.

FREEBIES FROM MUSIC BLOGS

The Web is obviously a powerful tool for a band that wants to promote itself and its music.

And thousands of lower-tier bands offer their MP3s on their personal sites as an enticement to maybe drive 30 miles to a hole-in-the-wall venue just outside of Pittsburgh and pay a $5 cover charge to see 'em play live. But how to *find* these sites?

Welp, you can try a straight-up Google search for the sort of music you like ("Bluegrass MP3 download") and keep clicking until you get lucky. Or, you could subscribe

Figure 17-5
Hype Machine: all the music in the blogosphere, at a glance

TIDBIT

The 3G data speeds and the flexibility of the App Store has added a celestially ginchy new dimension to the iPhone experience: the ability to access streaming music services like Pandora and Last.fm from anywhere in the world and listen to them "live." So when I snark about online music that you can't download, I'm just talking about those teasy sites that only let you hear a fraction of the music that's available, and only under limited conditions. Pandora and Last.fm are important and cool enough that they merit separate coverage in Chapter 18.

music that the parents of today and the kids of tomorrow can't abide.

to any of (let me check), yes, 183,277 music-oriented blogs.

Or, you could visit one blog that keeps tabs on all of the music being linked from all of the *other* music blogs. The Hype Machine (www.hypem.com) is a Web log that follows music blogs. It pops out and links to all of the free new music files that are getting talked about (see Figure 17-5).

The results can be a bit scattershot. Hype Machine gives you the firehose treatment, as opposed to giving you a nice friendly clickable button marked "Music you'd be likely to show half an interest in." But the side benefit is that it doesn't take long before you've bookmarked a bunch of music sites that to your delight, regularly featuring the

TROUBLE

The Web is also obviously a powerful tool for a band that wants to delude itself and its belief in the ability of a Kiss-influenced Christopher Cross tribute band to make it in the industry. All I'm saying is that just because your band's site got more than 210 visitors last month it doesn't mean it's time to tell your boss at the shoe warehouse where he can go stick it.

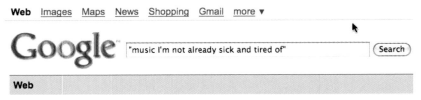

Google "music I'm not already sick and tired of" (Search)

Web

⚠ No results found for **"music I'm not already sick and tired of"**.

Figure 17-6
Searching for music I'm not already sick of via Google's usual interface doesn't work very well.

Googling for Tunes

Eventually, it comes down to this: rummaging through dumpsters and trash cans for scraps of entertainment.

At least that's what it feels like when you start using Google to locate music files. It's a hopelessly random tool for this sort of thing. It works a treat if you click on the search box armed with the name of a fantastic band that you heard playing in Harvard Square on your way to buy comic books, but a search for "music I'm not already sick and tired of" doesn't return the results that it ought to.

And you *know* that the instant I typed that sentence, I had to click over to Google to see what would come up if I actually performed that search. (See Figure 17-6.) Google is the world's authority on search, so I guess this means the problem is with my attitude or something. Duly noted.

Google *could* become a monster tool for finding and downloading free music. But as of this writing, it doesn't appear to be interested in giving us that sort of tool. Google does have a Music Search feature, but all it means is that if you a standard search for "Janis Joplin," it begins its list of search results with a list of albums and music ser-

vices where you can purchase them.

The next best thing is to exploit one of Google's advanced search features. I'll cut to the chase and give you a sample Google search string:

```
awesome bluegrass link:*.mp3
```

"Awesome" and "bluegrass" are straightforward search terms; please find me some bluegrass, and I only want stuff that's awesome.

The meat of the string is at the end: "link" means "return Web pages that link to the following Web address." Any downloadable MP3 file will have a Web address that ends in the .mp3 filename extension. Natcherly, we can't possibly know what that address will be, but Google will interpret the asterisk (*) as a wildcard, meaning "anything."

In total, the search string means "Find Web pages that contain the words 'awesome' and 'bluegrass,' and that contain at least one link to an .mp3 file." Plug this into Google and it's all over but the endless wading through dozens and dozens of pages of results.

Delicious Music

There's a similar trick that uses Delicious. com, the (hypermegasuperawesome)

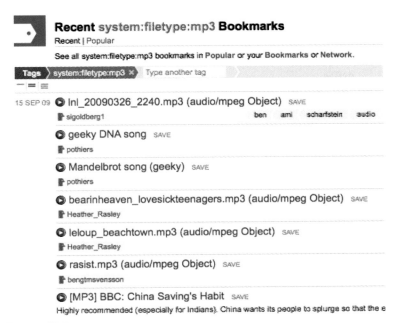

Recent system:filetype:mp3 **Bookmarks**

Recent | Popular

See all system:filetype:mp3 bookmarks in Popular or your Bookmarks or Network.

Tags > system:filetype:mp3 × | Type another tag

15 SEP 09 ● lnl_20090326_2240.mp3 (audio/mpeg Object) SAVE

sigoldberg1   ben   ami   scharfstein   audio

● geeky DNA song SAVE

pothiers

● Mandelbrot song (geeky) SAVE

pothiers

● bearinheaven_lovesickteenagers.mp3 (audio/mpeg Object) SAVE

Heather_Rasley

● leloup_beachtown.mp3 (audio/mpeg Object) SAVE

Heather_Rasley

● rasist.mp3 (audio/mpeg Object) SAVE

bengtmsvensson

● [MP3] BBC: China Saving's Habit SAVE

Highly recommended (especially for Indians). China wants its people to splurge so that the e

Figure 17-7
Delicious MP3 bookmarks: like *American Idol* voting, only not quite so dippy

community-based Web directory. Delicious is a valuable tool for navigating the Web. Its users can "publish" bookmarks to the Delicious.com Web site, and tag their links with keywords that make it simple to find pages that fit certain categories.

Search Google for "poker tips" and Google will return every Web page everywhere that contains those two words. But if you search Delicious, it only returns Web pages that the service's legions of users have personally tagged with those two descriptive words. And (hooray) by definition, the search results are all items that a real human being once considered valuable enough to actually bookmark. So nearly every page it returns is pure Tabasco.

You can indeed search for "free music"

and get lots of productive hits. But Delicious (unlike Google) will search specifically for music files if you know how to ask. Bookmark this URL (as one line):

```
http://delicious.com/tag/
system:filetype:mp3
```

The result is a list of recently bookmarked MP3 files that Delicious's users have located and saved all over the Web (see Figure 17-7).

Do keep in mind that these are unmarshaled, unpoliced bookmarks. So it's possible that you'll find links to illegal downloads. And remember: Downloading music illegally is just plain wrong, and can result in some serious consequences.

RapidLibrary.com

If you're an unsigned band or artist,

177

you're high on ambition but low on funds. Maybe you can't afford to pay for all the bandwidth that even a modestly successful online album eats up.

A centralized file-hosting service called RapidShare has become a popular service for hosting these huge media files; more often than not, when I'm visiting a band's site and it's inviting me to grab a copy of the latest live show, the band's site directs me to a RapidShare link.

It's a great service, but it lacks any kind of a centralized search feature. No wonder: Its purpose is to host individual files, linked from the folks who put the files up there to begin with. But third-party services have popped up to fill the void. The one I use most often is RapidLibrary.com. Type the name of a genre, band name, or the name of a local club that hosts live music, add an "mp3" to the search string, and you'll quickly get a long list of links to Rapid-Share-hosted files.

Two warnings:

First, remember that lots of folks use RapidShare to host illegal files; again I urge you to consider that even if the moral problem doesn't dissuade you from downloading copyrighted music, the legal problem should be a convincer. The RIAA can easily trace a file to an Internet connection and then to a computer.

Second, there seems to be many Rapid-Share "search services" that look ... well, shady. They'll show you a long list of links, but before you can download anything you need to sign up for a special account. And these are the very last places where I'd hand over a credit card number.

I recommend RapidLibrary because I've used it for months and haven't seen any Bad

Things happen as a result. But if sometime after this book is published it asks you for as much as an e-mail address ... forget it.

DOWNLOADING MUSIC FOR PAY

iTunes has indeed become the Google of online music stores. It's impossible for any business to compete with it head-on. The only way you can sell digital music online and really make a go of it is to serve needs that Apple is unwilling or unable to address.

It also helps that Apple is so big and powerful that the record companies are desperate to weaken iTunes somehow, *anyhow.*

Enter Amazon.com and the Amazon MP3 Store (see Figure 17-8). To get this new store off its feet and running (and chasing after iTunes with a two-by-four), the record companies made deals with Amazon.com that allowed the retailer to sell *all* its digital music as unlocked, plain MP3 files with no digital rights management (DRM) of any kind attached, from day one of the store's operation. You buy the track, it arrives as an MP3 file.

Purchasing music is no tougher than purchasing anything else on Amazon. com: Just click a button next to the track or the album. It's charged to the credit card attached to your Amazon.com account and automatically downloaded to your hard drive. If this is the first time you've purchased an Amazon.com MP3, the site also prompts you to install a free "helper" program that automatically adds any downloaded tracks to your iTunes library.

But of course, the MP3 you've bought isn't limited to iTunes or an iPhone.

You can sync it to your iPhone. Your iPod. The e-book reader device that also

Figure 17-8
The Amazon MP3 Store: a worthy competitor to iTunes

plays music. The little $15 music player you bought your 10-year-old. Anything.

Apple ultimately responded to the Amazon MP3 Store by making most of the music on iTunes DRM-free and high-bit rate, just like the Amazon.com offerings. But still, MP3 is *the* universal format. iTunes purchases arrive in your library unlocked, but some devices might not be able to play iTunes's AAC-format music file.

Good heavens. So why *wouldn't* you just switch from the iTunes Store to the Amazon MP3 store and be done with it? Well ...

◻ **The browsing experience stinks.** Why is the iTunes Store so good at separating me from my money? Because it's so easy to just browse. I hear a song in a TV commercial and I just intend to buy that one song. But

there are links to iTunes pages that explains more about the artist. And there's a list of other music that was purchased by the same people who bought this track. And there's a huge list of recommended tracks that are similar in theme or genre. And ... But Amazon.com has merely tweaked the same storefront it uses to sell Danielle Steele novels and lightbulbs. It's easy to get what you came for, but not so easy to buy something that you never new existed, if you follow me.

◻ **No "Complete My Album" or similar features.** And that's one of the great bits of the iTunes Store. You buy one track, and listen to it so frequently that you buy a couple more over the next week. Ultimately you think "Heck with

179

it … I'll take the whole album." But on Amazon.com, you'll have to buy each track separately. There are a bunch of "missing" features like this.

Still that feels like nitpicking. I didn't even mention that tracks and albums are often cheaper from Amazon.com than from Apple. Once again, the record companies want to put as many arrows in Amazon.com's quiver as they can.

But the browsing experience is still a big loser.

Hmm.

Okay. I'm not proud of this, but I'm here to serve you.

I use the iTunes Store to *find* the music I want. And once I've decided that I really do want a copy of the Asylum Street Spankers' "Since I Met You Baby," I tab over to my Web browser and buy it from Amazon.com.

It's cheaper and it's an MP3. My allegiance is to the freedom of DRM-free music and the buying power of that extra dime, not to Apple.

Sorry, Steve. I still love you.

(Just not in That Way.)

18

Audio Streams

The Skim

Eww! Look at the *mess* that you're making!

There you are, blithely listening to audio on your computer. Are you giving any thought to what's happening to all that audio dribbling through the speakers and your headphones? That's right: It's just making a big sticky puddle on the floor.

You should *catch* that stuff. In a bucket, maybe. It's useful stuff — you really shouldn't just let it spill on the floor like that.

Yes, there are utilities that can capture all the sound your computer is generating and send it to an audio file. It's like holding a microphone up to the speaker, only less wire-y.

These apps can also automatically launch specific audio programs and thus act as a sort of "audio VCR," tuning in to your favorite overseas football broadcast via streaming radio, and have it ready for your iPhone by the time you wake up in the morning.

Finally, since we're talking about streaming radio, we might as well talk about two rather super-awesome apps and services for the iPhone and iPod Touch that bring live radio to your device, no matter where you are.

Bad craziness lies ahead.

TIDBIT

As a guy who creates stuff for a living, I ought to acknowledge a question: Is it *right* to "capture" audio to a file? Shouldn't we consider the possibility that the creators of a streaming Internet radio show don't make a podcast (for example) of this show available because they don't *want* people listening on their iPods and iPhones?

I gotta admit that I don't have an aggressive and arrogant answer to that one. It's certainly wrong to use this software to steal a copy of someone else's locked, purchased music, for example, but when the audio is on a DVD that you own? Using an audio-capture utility is almost *righteous*.

Unfortunately, most examples fall in the middle. I suppose it comes down to the advice your parents gave you (if they were good parents, I mean): Would you feel awkward justifying your actions to someone? I continue to record BBC programming because it's free, and the BBC publishes the URLs to its streams openly, and (unlike many radio sites) the BBC doesn't even use Web ads to subsidize the broadcasts.

But your mileage will vary. Please — I say, sincerely — don't be naughty. One day you're going to wonder why nobody creates any *decent* content any more and the answer is because nobody could make any money doing it.

CAPTURING AUDIO TO A FILE

There are utilities for the PC and Mac that can capture your computer's audio to a file.

The function of these utilities is so basic and fundamental that I need to break it out of that preceding paragraph and let it stand all by itself in its glory:

It can capture any audio playing through your PC to a file that you can import into iTunes and put on an iPhone.

Well, that's game, set, and match, isn't it? It's a solution to any and all permutations of the question "How to I get this audio onto my iPhone?" Examples:

- The BBC streams enough incredibly great content that the sheer awesomeness of it all can affect the tides and confuse migrating birds. But there's no "record" button on the Real Audio player that plays the actual content. So once you've heard the BBC Radio Drama version of *Dirk Gently's Holistic Detective Agency*, it's gone for good.

    Solution: Record it while you listen to it.

- You've bought oodles of dollars' worth of music from the iTunes Store or some other commercial music site that locks up your purchased tracks in proprietary digital rights management. You can't take your iTunes Store music and play it on your Zune (pause to spit on the floor) or through a non-Apple home media server. You can't take the tracks you impulsively purchased on Wal-mart's music store and get 'em to work on an iPhone.

    Solution: Play the tracks in iTunes and capture them to plain, unprotected MP3 files in full stereo.

❑ Through the magic of audio chat, you and four or five people are having an online meeting. You'd like to, you know, *record* all this so that when inevitably the whole project fails and takes the whole company down with it, you can have a swift and conclusive rebuttal to the charge that it was *you* who suggested a buddy-cop movie starring the grown-up cute little kid from *The Sixth Sense* and a wise-cracking cartoon motor scooter voiced by Jimmy Fallon.

Solution: Start capturing the output of your chat program to a file, just for safekeeping.

❑ You think that Hunter S. Thompson's stream-of-consciousness rantings in one of the commentary tracks to the *Fear and Loathing in Las Vegas* DVD is *just* the thing to motivate you through your morning run. But you're not terribly interested in ripping the movie with one piece of software and then using a second piece of software to strip the audio portion into a separate file.

❑ You get the idea.

On and on. An audio capture app is the sort of tool where you put it on your hard drive … and then just wait. You can be certain that eventually, it's going to be the solution to *some* sort of problem.

Using these capture utilities is barely more difficult than pushing the Record button on a VCR.

(You kids remember what VCRs were, right?)

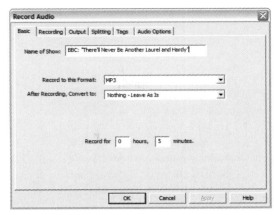

Figure 18-1

Replay A/V at its most basic: preparing to capture audio

Capturing Audio with Windows: Replay A/V

Applian Technologies' Replay A/V, part of Applian's Capture Suite (`www.applian.com`), is an absolute marvel. It's an awesomely sophisticated simple app whose purpose is to take your computer's audio and stick it in amber for all time.

"Snag whatever's coming out the speakers to a file" is barely worth its time. You'll see it stretch its legs later in the chapter. But for now, let's say you've inserted your DVD of *My Dinner with Andre* into the drive or you've pointed your browser at your favorite streaming radio station or … well, you would know better than I what you're going to want to record.

It's a snap:

1. Launch Replay A/V. The main window is shown in Figure 18-2 but for the moment, please choose Record ▶ Record Audio from Speakers. You'll see the simple panel shown in Figure 18-1. The default settings should be

Figure 18-2
Recording a show manually

just fine: MP3, don't have Replay do
anything funny to the file afterwards.

2. Give your recording a name, and then
select a recording time, if you want to
have the recording stop automatically
after a certain decent interval. Press O
when all is as you like it. Replay A/V
will begin capturing audio from your
PC's audio circuitry. The app's main
window will look like Figure 18-2.

3. Start the audio in the app of your
choice. Remember, Replay started
going the moment you clicked OK.

4. When you want to terminate record-

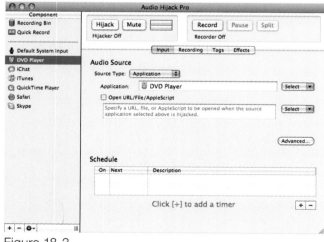

Figure 18-3
Audio Hijack Pro for Macs

ing, click on the program in the Replay
A/V window to reveal its pop-up
menu. Choose Stop Record/Down-
load. This is unnecessary, of course,
if you told the app to just stop automatically after recording for a specific
duration.

5. Go back to the recording's listing and
select View Shows to go to the folder
where the recording was saved. There
it is: a plain MP3 ready to import into
iTunes.

Capturing Audio on a Mac: Audio Hijack Pro

The corresponding Mac app is a lot
prettier than Replay (but don't judge the
Windows app just yet, please). And at the
basic task of "capturing live audio from your
computer," it has a couple of fresh tricks.
Replay A/V just holds a virtual microphone
up to the PC's speaker; *every* bit of audio
gets captured in one stream. Which is why
20 minutes into your capture of a conference call, the sounds of
World War II air combat
fills the audio picture.

Yes, this was the moment
you got bored and started
playing a game while half-
listening to your boss.

Audio Hijack Pro from
(yes, this is indeed the
name of the company)
Rogue Amoeba (www.
rogueamoeba.com; $32)
is more selective. When you
launch the app, it immediately presents a list of every
app it sees which can generate noise (see Figure 18-3).

So you can be very selective in what you mean to capture. Let's convert the audio from my *Raiders of the Lost Ark* DVD to an MP3:

1. Choose DVD Player from the list of apps, and then click the Hijack button. This tells Hijack to capture the audio generated by only this app. If new e-mail arrives while you're recording, the Mail app's "Bling!" won't appear in the movie recording. As with Replay A/V, the default recording settings are perfectly fine. But you can click on the Recording tab of the window to select a file format and choose a duration for the recording. Hijack is now in standby mode.

2. Click the Record button to start the recording.

3. Switch over to DVD Player and start the disc playing.

4. When the movie's over, return to Audio Hijack.

5. Click on the Hijack button again to turn off the recording.

The audio file can be found inside your Music folder, in the Audio Hijack subfolder. As promised, none of the cheerful "new mail!" sounds.

CAPTURING SPECIFIC SHOWS AND STATIONS AUTOMATICALLY

These manually operated apps work great. But there are other features and programs that can record streaming Internet audio in just one or two steps. It's not a case of knowing which, what, where, and when a show airs; just tell the app that you want this show recorded, and the app works out all the details on its own.

TIDBIT

Audio Hijack is a remarkably slick app. I'm just scratching the surface here. You can have it automatically open streaming audio URLs on certain days and times, so that you always catch the news on your local news radio station. You can have it pass control to a script or another app once you're finished, so that whatever you record lands on your Web site without a single extra step. Et cetera, et cetera.

Windows: Back to Replay A/V

Boy, I love this app. Have I told you that I love this app? Well, I do. It sells for $49 but I've recommended other Applian products elsewhere in the book — the company makes a *sweet* app for capturing even tightly-locked-down commercial Internet videos — so I think you ought to spend $99 for the full Replay Capture Suite.

Here's what I mean. The BBC is airing a radio series based on Douglas Adams' *Dirk Gently's Holistic Detective Agency*. I can, um, figure out what time it airs, and what BBC Radio streaming channel it's on and what day and what time. And what time that would be here in Boston. Then stay up and hijack the recording. And remember to do that every time every new episode of the show airs.

But why would I do that? I have Replay A/V!

1. Click the Open Recording Wizard button in the main Replay A/V window. A simplified list of functions

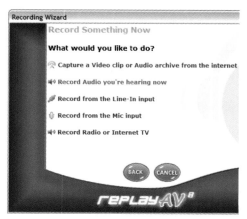

Figure 18-4

The many modes and moods of Replay A/V

appears (see Figure 18-4).

2. Click on Browse the Media Guide. Replay gets in touch with Applian's media servers and opens the home page of their extensive guide to Everything That Happens Via Streaming Audio.

3. Click on the Shows button. A search page opens (see Figure 18-5).

4. Type in details about a show you want to find. In this case, I'm looking for a specific program so I type in the title.

5. Click Find Show. Well, whaddya know … it found it right away (see Figure 18-6).

6. Click the Add button, and Replay A/V does the rest. The app knows what it needs to do and when it needs to do it.

That's it. Replay adds the show and all of its upcoming episodes to its recording schedule. Every time a new episode airs, Replay will record it.

And you can search for all kinds of things. Search for topics, search for locations, search for radio stations. The Replay guide is extremely thorough.

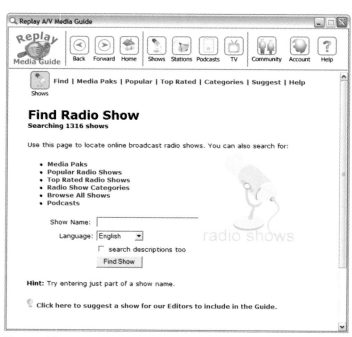

Figure 18-5

Search the world's airwaves in one page.

Macintosh: RadioShift

I wish there were a Mac app that was *quite* as meaty as Replay A/V. RadioShift

Category: Talk - Books
Category: Talk - Comedy

*Dirk Gently has an unshakeable belief in the in
Holistic Detective Agency's only success seer
old ladies. Then Dirk stumbles upon an old fri
into a four-billion year old mystery that must
immediate extinction.*

Dirk Gently's Holistic Detective Agency pl:

 BBC Radio 4

Wednesday
9:30 PM - 10:00 PM Local Time

Figure 18-6
Ask and ye shall receive: the program
page.

— another great app by Rogue Amoeba,
a name that I repeat I am not making up —
isn't as powerful, but it feeds from the same
trough. And it's a lot prettier.

Once again, I want to record a show off
BBC Radio 4. But this time, I'm not thinking
of a specific show. I'm just browsing for content in a specific channel. Figure 18-7 shows
you RadioShift's leadoff search page.

1. Type in a search term. Here I've
   searched for "BBC Radio 4" and the
   app quickly found the station's details.

2. Click on the name of the station.
   A program guide for BBC 4 appears
   (see Figure 18-8).

3. Radio 4 Comedy sounds good. Click
   on the show listing and click the Subscribe button. There's one final little
   detail page but once you click the Save
   button, a new subscription is added
   to the app's to-do list. Every evening
   at 9:00 p.m. Eastern Time, RadioShift
   will tap into the BBC's stream and
   capture the audio to a file, which will
   be stashed inside a RadioShift folder
   inside the Music directory.

It's another "set it and forget it" solu-

TIP

Better to risk stating the obvious than confuse y'all: Replay
A/V can't record any of your
scheduled programs *unless it's
running*. It also can't add new
recordings to iTunes unless
that's running as well. So make sure
that both apps are launched and standing by at all times.

This also means that your *PC* will
have to be up and running at the
appointed hour. Head on over to the
Start menu and choose Start ▶ Control
Panel ▶ Performance and Maintenance
▶ Power Options, and set up Windows
so that the system never hibernates.
You can tell Windows to turn off the
monitor and the hard drive, though.

tion. Recording this material on schedule
becomes the app's problem, not mine. I can
listen to my library of recordings directly
in RadioShift, and send selected episodes
to iTunes so that they can be synced to my
iPhone.

RadioShift is a lovely app. You can search
for specific things, but you can also browse,
browse, browse. By topic, by region, by
category. You can even call up a map of
the world. Cities with streaming radio are
marked with a green dot (see Figure 18-9).
I don't know what they listen to in Reykja-
vik, but I sure intend to find out.

The Mac and PC apps go at the same
problem from slightly different angles, but
the end result is equally terrific: Wonderful programming from all over the world

Figure 18-7
Searching for shows via RadioShift

Figure 18-8
Scanning through the entire program guide for a specific channel

Figure 18-9
Scanning the globe for awesome audio

just magically arrives on your hard drive on a daily basis. And it's all free, free, free.

INTERNET RADIO ON THE IPHONE: HAIL, PANDORA!

One of the iPhone's true transformative software categories is the huge collection of iPhone apps that streams live audio from Internet radio sites. You think it's a neat trick to have 16 gigabytes of music? How about having *millions* of songs? And you never need to sync them up, and you never need to pay for them, either?

I'd wear my poor little fingers to nubs trying to describe all the streaming audio apps. Chiefly, if you have a radio station, a network, or an Internet music service, you're keen to release a free app that lets users access that stream through the iPhone. As yet, there's no one tuner to rule them all.

So instead, I'll champion my two favorite apps.

Pandora

I don't think I could get through my day without Pandora.

Figure 18-10
Building a new Pandora radio station

Pandora represents a powerful new perspective on radio. It's an almost perfect melding of the "I am a deejay" mentality of an iPod/iPhone owner who mixes his own playlist and the "I'm not made of money" sensibility of someone who loves music but who can't pay for hours and hours and hours of tracks at a buck a throw.

So Pandora is a compromise. Give Pandora the name of a band you like. It'll use music from that band as a starting point and draw upon a sophisticated database to choose music that "fits" alongside.

You don't assemble playlists. You create personal "radio stations." You start by installing the free Pandora iPhone app and creating a free user account at www.

191

Figure 18-11
Asylum Street Radio: the cream rises

Figure 18-12
Why, 23 songs in, did the deejay add this song to the mix?

pandora.com.

You can create, manage, and listen to Pandora stations via any Web browser, but let's keep this an iPhone party, eh? Figure 18-10 shows you the first step: tap the New Station button and Pandora asks for a starting point.

Type the name of a band. I'm starting with the Asylum Str ... well, whaddya know: Pandora knows about that band and guesses the name after just a few characters. Click, and it creates the station and starts playing an Asylum Street Spankers tune (see Figure 18-11).

An invisible deejay who knows about every band that ever got a record deal starts playing music. The next song won't be an

Asylum Street Spankers tune; it'll be from a band that it considers to be similar.

Uh-uh ... the next song is from Black Flag. I don't like that song. So I tell the deejay by tapping the thumbs-down button and then tap the Next Track button. By voting thumbs up and thumbs down, the deejay gets a better handle on the sort of mood that comes to mind when I think, "Asylum Street Spankers radio."

Huh? It's playing a Squirrel Nut Zippers song now? It makes sense, but I wonder why?

I needn't live in mystery. I tap and receive an explanation (see Figure 18-12).

And it's a good tune. I want to remember

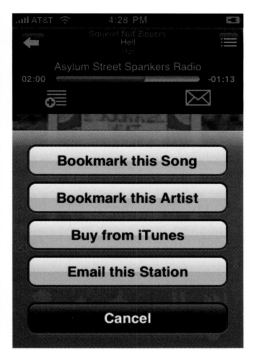

Figure 18-13
When a song is good enough to hold on to

it for later. So I tap the pop-up button (the up arrow) and see a list of options (see Figure 18-13). I can actually buy it immediately via iTunes! Tap, and it's mine.

If I don't have 99 cents to my name, I can just bookmark it so that later on, when I'm at a Web browser logged in to www.pandora.com, I can pull up a list of all the great discoveries.

I'm quite addicted to Pandora. Obviously, the more you use it and the more songs you rate, the better Pandora gets at picking songs you've never heard before but instantly fall in love with. You're like Howard Hughes. You own the radio station and if the deejay wants to keep his job, he'll

focus on making the boss happy. The only real downside is that your deejay doesn't take requests. It only selects songs that fit the theme of the first artist you chose, and will shape future requests on that radio station using your thumbs-up and thumbs-down votes.

Last.fm and AOL Radio are two more great streaming services supported by free iPhone apps. But Pandora is the one I shall forsake all others for.

Rhapsody/Rhapsody to Go

The Rhapsody music service represents not an opponent to the iTunes Store, but an opposite. The iTunes Store model is that of a traditional store. Want to listen to an Elvis Costello album? Fine: Buy it for $9.99.

Rhapsody is "subscription" music. For $15 a month, you're not buying anything. You're merely subscribing to monthly access to a library of millions of tracks. You can search for Costello's *Mighty Like a Rose*; you can *listen* to *Mighty Like a Rose* in its entirety.

In fact, you can do nearly anything with the Rhapsody library that you can do with the iTunes Store library — but if you cancel your subscription, all of "your" tracks and playlists disappear. Again, you don't actually own anything (although Rhapsody makes it easy to purchase tracks as well).

I'm glad that subscription music on the iPhone is no longer an either-or question. I've used subscription music on players like the Zune and enjoyed the experience greatly. The obvious upside is that it makes music exploration far, far more affordable and attractive. You hear a piece of music on TV or at a party and moments later, you're listening to a sampler of that artist's catalog.

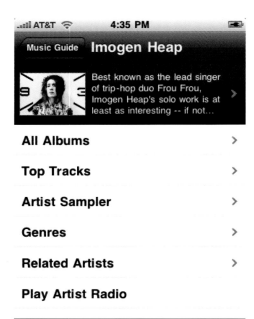

Figure 18-14
Buffet-style music dining via the Rhapsody service

You can manage all your Rhapsody favorites and playlists remotely — build a playlist via the Web browser on your desktop PC, and it becomes available to the iPhone player — but you can also access the entire catalog via the iPhone.

Figure 18-14 shows you the basic Rhapsody experience. Here I've searched for Imogen Heap and am presented with the full buffet: I can play any of her albums or tracks, or just go straight to a sampler of tracks selected from her entire catalog.

The good news — besides the "all you can eat for one low price" aspect — is that all of your Rhapsody music lives on their servers and streams to your iPhone via Wi-Fi or

3G. Which means that you can choose from millions of songs wherever you are in the world, without needing to sync up anything to your phone ... and this library takes up next to no space on your device.

The bad news — besides the "$15 a month and you don't actually own any music" aspect — is that the sound quality suffers a little due to the streaming technology. It's typically like listening to FM radio. Clean and clear, but you can certainly tell the difference between a Rhapsody stream and a music file in your iPhone's music local media library.

I hate to end on a negative note so here's another piece of good news: Rhapsody offers a weeklong free trial. You don't even need to hand over a credit card number. Just download the app from the iTunes Store, create an account on Rhapsody, and start listening to music right then and there.

So do you see what I mean? All those electrons shouldn't just slop out of your desktop speakers and spill onto the carpet. They work their way deep into the pile. Silverfish feed on them. Then they become *super* silverfish who are no longer intimidated by humans.

Keep the insects *down*, my fellow humans. Capture and stream!

Above and beyond protecting our species from insectoid overlords, capturing audio is just too good a bargain to pass up. People wonder how radio can survive in an iPod era. Well, *this* is how radio survives. It delivers the product that radio does best — hours of fresh and often insightful content each and every day — and it delivers it through a medium that lets us enjoy the programming on our own terms.

As for Pandora and Rhapsody ... you'll

get hooked. Just give in and don't fight it. If you're lucky, the money you save by having 90 percent of your music needs sated by unlimited, streaming music will help cover all the tracks you buy from bands you'd never heard of, but instantly fell in love with once these services tossed them in the mix.

Internet Videos

The Skim

Dead Bloody Simple: Vixy.net ⊡
Viva Variety: KeepVid ⊡
Superhuman Video Capture for Windows

Q: What did we ever do before the emergence of YouTube, Hulu, and other Internet video sites?

A: Actual work. We did *actual work*. Lots of it. That's what we did before streaming video.

Honestly. Like you had to even ask! Look at the mighty Boulder Dam, one of the most incredible engineering projects in human history. Beethoven's *Ninth Symphony*, a tune described as "one of the highest achievements of man," a creative work so powerful and inspirational that it served as the hopeful anthem to the closure of an international conflict that claimed tens of millions of lives. Or the Great Pyramid at Giza, whose monumental form and seething mysteries has endured through five millennia.

Ask yourself: "Do you think the people who accomplished these great deeds spent *any* amount of time watching some kid from Encino attempt to play the Super Mario theme using the 12-foot electric arcs thrown off by an enormous Van de Graaff generator?"

Yes, I'm just as depressed about this as you are. But remember: All strength comes from knowledge.

Welp, we're stuck with this sad state of affairs. The *good* news is that the utter collapse of all civilization, though inevitable, won't really start

Figure 19-1

The URL to the YouTube video you're currently watching

becoming a nuisance until our as-yet-unborn grandchildren turn 40. So for now, we can download some of the better videos and enjoy them on our iPhone and iPod Touch.

Ah. But the trouble is that very few of these sites allow you to simply *download* content. Google Video has a straightforward Download for iPod/iPhone button, but it's not available for all videos — and really,

that site isn't the Big Name of video downloads, is it?

I have three favorite ways of transmogrifying online videos from YouTube and other sites. Three? Yes; because sometimes "Simple" and "Successful" aren't the same.

All methods start at the same place: a piece of online video excellence that celebrates the human creative spirit in all its glory. And absolutely *not* just another dopey but adorable video of a puppy trying to work his head free of a cantaloupe rind.

Start off by copying the video's URL from your browser window's address bar (Figure 19-1 shows a YouTube URL), and you're off and running.

DEAD BLOODY SIMPLE: VIXY.NET

Vixy is the sort of Web service that makes you instantly suspicious of the company's motives. It does something awesome and it does it for free, so you're wondering just how the hell Vixy is making any money out of this because it must cost *money* to run a site like this and …

Oh, yes, good point: all the huge ads splashed over the page.

Vixy.net is indeed a free piece of software that runs via a Web site. There's nothing to download and nothing to install. It all happens via your

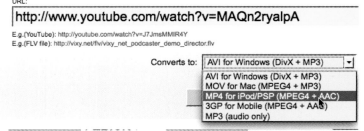

Figure 19-2

Converting videos online, via Vixy

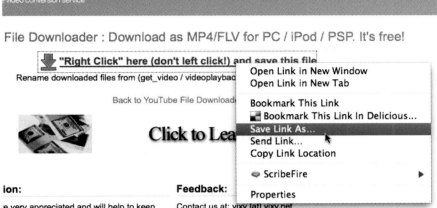

Figure 19-3
Vixy, when your video is ready for downloading

browser. Here you go:

1. Copy the URL of the YouTube video or of a Flash video on the Web that you'd like to download. If your video isn't on YouTube, the URL must be directly to a Flash video file (.flv).

2. Open www.vixy.net in your desktop browser.

3. Paste the video's URL into Vixy's URL box (see Figure 19-2).

4. Choose an iPod/iPhone-friendly file format from the pop-up menu (MP4 or H.264-MP4).

5. Click the Start button. Things will percolate behind the scenes for a moment as the service locates the video file and prepares it for transmogrification. When everything's ready, Vixy moves to the download page you see in Figure 19-3, and the video file should start downloading via your browser automatically. If it doesn't, right-click or Control+click on the Download link

and save the file to your hard drive manually from the contextual menu.

6. Give the video file a name that ends with .mp4 to make sure that iTunes and your computer correctly identifies it as a video file. (Your browser will automatically choose a name identical to the link you've selected; the app's dumb and doesn't know any better.) If you just blithely click OK, there's a good chance that iTunes will refuse to import the file, solely because it's expecting a certain kind of filename. So: Choose wisely.

And that's it. You'll have an MP4 file on your hard drive that you can import straight into iTunes and thence to your iPhone or iPod Touch.

Great! But Vixy has two big drawbacks:

◻ As far as accessing video sites is concerned, it's a YouTube-only solution. And that's definitely the top video site, but it's no help with videos from

199

KEEPVID
download streaming videos

KEEPVID Bookmarklet
1.) Drag this button onto your links toolbar
2.) Click Keep It! when watching a video to download it

RL http://vids.myspace.com/index.cfm?fuseaction=vids.individual&VideoID=40617478   **DOWNLOAD**

sors

AVS Video Converter   FREE Download   FREE **AVS DVD Player**
Recommended Download ★★★★★   ALL Formats Converter   All formats media player

Figure 19-4
KeepVid.com, your universal video grabber

MySpace or the many other places.

❏ It's often unavailable or unusable. Remember, it's a *service,* not a piece of desktop software; you're sharing it with God-knows-how-many other users, all of whom are clamoring for conversions at the same time. In fact, I can sort of expect it not to work during normal human hours. You have a real chance late at night or early in the morning. And let's not forget …

❏ It could disappear at any moment. It's not a piece of software that lives on your PC or Mac, safe and sound. If Vixy keeps losing money or if someone decides to sue, it folds its tents and that's all she wrote.

But it's a great tool. Just don't let it be your *only* tool. Fortunately, there are other implements for your tool belt.

VIVA VARIETY: KEEPVID

Okey-doke: If I want to grab a video from a site that Vixy doesn't support (that is, anything but YouTube), or if it's some unreasonable time of day like 7:20 p.m. and the site is too busy, I simply move on to KeepVid.

Like Vixy, KeepVid is a free service you use via a Web browser. Vixy grabs the video and converts it to an iPhone-friendly format. KeepVid is solely a download tool; you'll need to convert the downloaded file from Adobe Flash format to an MP4 on your PC or Mac. But! KeepVid has the advantage of supporting dozens of different video sites.

Your Vixy skills will translate right over to KeepVid:

1. Copy the URL of the video you want to snag. Again, see Figure 19-1. Just copy it straight from the address bar of its Web page.

2. Go to www.keepvid.com.

3. Paste the URL into KeepVid's URL field and click the Download button (see Figure 19-4). The software on KeepVid's servers will percolate a bit and find your video's actual Flash-formatted file on the video service's server. When it's finished, a Download link appears on the page (see Figure 19-5). If your video is from any service other than YouTube, you'll find a link to a Flash Video file (.flv). That's the standard (but not iPhone-friendly) for-

Figure 19-5
Downloading the Flash video file that KeepVid located for you

mat used by most sites. But! If you *are* snagging something from YouTube, it's likely that you'll see a link to the Flash file *and* a second download link to an .mp4 video file that can be imported directly into iTunes with no conversion necessary! Apple has partnered with YouTube to convert huge chunks of its library to Apple-compatible formats; this is why the iPhone's built-in YouTube player app works so well. Awesome. Obviously, if there's a link to an .mp4 file, that's the one you want. Otherwise, take what you can get.

4. Right-click or Control+click on the Download link and save the file to your hard drive (as with Vixy, look for Save Link As or Download Linked File or some such in the contextual menu that appears). As with Vixy, your browser will choose a filename that makes no sense. Give the file a name that the humans can relate to and make sure it ends with .flv if it's a Flash file, or .mp4 if it's an MP4 file.

Cool. If you were lucky enough to snag an MP4 file, you're done. Go out for waffles. But if it's a Flash file, you'll need to convert it to MP4. Well, slugger, I know that you're feeling kind of blue right now, but

it's about time you realize that life is full of disappointments. It's not our problems that define us, it's how we *overcome* those problems.

Sorry. I have no kids and my innate parenting and nurturing skills sometimes need to find an outlet.

You just need to process those video files with a conversion utility. Though it's a crowded market, there are two great ones for PCs and Macs that are free for the downloading.

Stick around for a bit and I'll tell you about that stuff but let's not move on before talking about a limitation of KeepVid: It, too, can't snag video from every source. Now that more and more networks and studios are "getting it" about digital content delivery, networks are creating whole services for the purpose of giving you free access to that episode of *House* that you missed last night.

But they're still the enemies of the proletariat, in so much that they've set up their servers in such a way that it's almost impossible for a service like KeepVid or any other mortal utility from locating and downloading the video.

Hmm. If only there were a *superhuman* utility that could capture *any* sort of streaming video.

Well, that's for later. For now, let's convert that Flash file to something your iPhone can deal with, shall we?

Windows: Applian's Replay Converter

Google "iPhone flash video converter" and you'll find dozens and *dozens* of apps and Web sites that want to handle the job for you. Nearly all of these are poor-quality rehashes of open-source conversion tools. Some of them are free, but you visit the site and wonder if this tool isn't going to search your hard drive for credit-card numbers and transmit them to a Zybloborgian crime syndicate. Others are commercial apps, but they're woefully overpriced for what they deliver.

Among all that chaff, I can recommending two Windows utilities. The best of the free conversion apps is Videora's iPhone Converter, downloadable from www.videora.com. Flash video goes in, iPhone-compatible video comes out.

But the one I want to show you is from Applian. It's called Replay Converter, and you can download a free demo from www.applian.com. And it's the good kind of demo: It will work forever on YouTube videos. Other formats will be watermarked until you give Applian $30.

Thirty bucks! Wow! But actually, I'm encouraging you to send Applian $99 for the full Replay Capture Suite, which includes all Applian's megasuperhyperawesome utilities for capturing all kinds of media (video *and* audio) to iPhone-studly formats. Stay tuned to the end of this chapter and you'll see why I'm such a big fan of Applian.

Replay Converter is a simple, one-window utility (see Figure 19-6).

1. Click the Add Files button. Select one or more Flash files via Windows' standard file picker.
2. Click Convert to Video File in the bottom tier of radio buttons.
3. Choose iPod Video/High Quality in the Target Format pop-up menu.
4. Click the Go button. And then there's the usual amount of percolation while the app engages in hard-core math. Eventually a set of MP4 files is depos-

Figure 19-6
Converting Flash to something actually useful, with Replay Converter

ited on your hard drive. Unless you specified a new location for the converted files, they'll appear in the same folder as the original Flash files.
5. Drag the little buggers into iTunes and enjoy.

Macintosh: Video Monkey

Hello, hello: This is more like it. Video Monkey (see Figure 19-7) is precisely the sort of app that Windows users are hoping to find. It's a transcoder that's so good, there's really no need to mention any other … and it's free. Go to www.videomonkey.org and download the freebie. It makes the whole process simple and efficient.

1. Add files to Video Monkey's conversion queue. You can either drag the files right into the list or you can bring up the standard Mac file picker by clicking the Add button.
2. Select a size. The Convert To pop-up button lists formats for all Apple devices and a few from the other side of the fence. But All Apple Devices gives you great quality, so just leave the setting where it is.

3. Select the Add to iTunes checkbox to have Video Monkey add the result-ing video files to your iTunes library as soon as they're fin-ished.

4. Click Start to get the ball rolling.

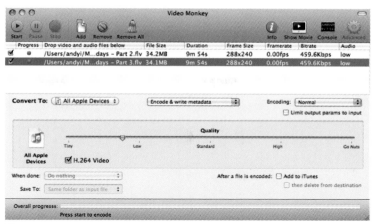

Figure 19-7

Video Monkey: one Mac transcoder to unite them all

And as usual, this is an excellent time to get to know your spouse and chil-dren a little better. Because this conversion is going to take a while and, yes, you'll be *that* bored.

There is indeed the Quality control in Video Monkey, but it's generally not worth messing around with. You're starting off with a video file that was compressed for YouTube so bumping that controller up won't really make the video look any better.

Technically you'll get better video if you click the H.264 Encoding option. But the increase in quality isn't dramatic and the increase in conversion time is devastating.

Check it, and you have enough time to actually take the family out to a session of kite-flying followed by a picnic lunch. Leave it unchecked and you're back at your com-puter before you've finished one game of Sorry all the way through.

Eventually, Video Monkey will complete the conversion and announce that it's done so by saying something clever.

Bravo.

SUPERHUMAN VIDEO CAPTURE FOR WINDOWS

Okay. All of the above methods have lim-its in that they don't work unless the video service has done next to nothing to hide the locations of the video files on their servers. So the *really great* services (like Hulu.com, which hosts network prime-time shows in their entirety a mere 24 hours after they've aired) are out of the running.

And what about live, streaming video? Lots of cool things happen in real time via streaming. Such as your video chats with your friends, Congress debating a grease and petroleum-derived coatings and lubri-cants subsidy surcharge on C-SPAN, that sort of thing.

The most useful type of utility for this problem is one that does a complete end-run around the problem of locating the source of the video. It's streaming into your PC; a super-utility would just tap into that stream and divert the flow into a video file at the same time that your browser is playing it through a window.

Applian makes an *insanely* good Windows-only app called Replay Media Catcher (see Figure 19-8). And it's another $40 but (holy cats) wait until you see how well it works and how easy it is to use. Suffice to say that *this* is why I was recommending that you give Applian $100

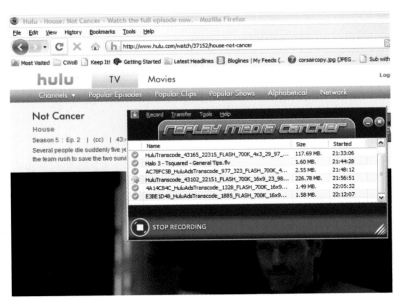

Figure 19-8

Capture any streaming video with Replay Media Catcher, software that merits applause.

for its full suite of capture utilities (which includes Media Catcher) instead of going with a freebie Flash converter. By the time you buy all the Applian products I so earnestly recommend in this book, it'll be a big bargain. And once you see how well these things work, you'll be sold.

So: back to last night's episode of *House*. I *could* buy it from the iTunes store for two or three bucks. Or! I could do this:

1. Launch the Media Catcher app and open Hulu.com in my browser.

2. Click Media Catcher's Start Recording button.

3. Switch over to my browser, navigate to the newest *House*, and start playing it. If I switch back to Media Catcher, I notice something cool: It has *automatically* sensed that a video stream

has opened up. Every time Hulu (or any other app running at the time) starts a stream, Catcher opens a new capture file for it. The truck ad before the episode? Captured. The episode itself? Captured. An interstitial ad for macaroni and cheese? Captured. As the name suggests, Media Capture doesn't download the video directly from Hulu's servers. It acts like a VCR, recording the show in real time as it plays. When the show's over, Media Capture automatically closes the file and takes a very smart guess at the name. This episode of *House* has the show name *and* the episode title.

4. Click the Stop Recording button. The app has already saved the file, but this action prevents it from continuing to

capture and save every stream it sees.

At this point you will be sort of fumbling for more things to do but trust me: That's all there is. I now have a 42-minute Flash video file of the episode. All I need to do is convert it from Flash to MP4. The same utilities I recommended in the last section will work just fine for that.

Incredible. I've been using this utility for a few months now and still I say: incredible. Figure out how much dough you've spent downloading TV shows from iTunes and tell me that Replay Media Capture is overpriced. You can't, can you?

I try to be on guard against major expenses that are secretly just gateways to a series of *additional* major expenses. Like a game console. Or a boat. Children. That sort of thing.

And the iPhone and iPod Touch are no different. It's a swell device in and of itself … but what's the harm in buying this *one* episode of *Saturday Night Live*? Just *one* series pass to *Lost*? Eventually, you have an iPhone chock-full of video entertainment and a house with lots of bare spots on the wall where your great-grandfather's valuable art collection used to hang.

But there's a hell of a lot of great content floating around in video sites. And it's all free. True, Hulu wanted you to buy that episode of *Family Guy* from the iTunes Store instead of capturing it and YouTube wants you to have to keeping coming back to the site and watching commercials instead of simply adding the video to your media library.

Be fair, though. I'm sure that when the semipro skateboarder who *thought* he'd be teaching hundreds of fans how to do a 720 Sherman Helmsley with a Half-Weezie lay-

TIP

Honestly, exactly what goes on over there at Applian? The folks there make capture utilities that are simply supernaturally good. There's absolutely nothing like Media Catcher for the Mac. Nothing. And this utility is one of the reasons why I have a copy of Windows installed on my MacBook. When a utility is good enough to warrant shutting down your system of choice and rebooting into a whole different operating system *just* to do this one thing … well, that's one hell of an app.

It's also a reason for Mac users like me not to act so cocky. An OS is the greatest thing in the world until you find that *one* app for The Other System that your machine can't run.

I'm not used to being on the wrong side of that fence. It's dark and scary.

back, but instead wound up teaching hundreds of thousands of office workers that a steady job with good health insurance is nothing to scoff at, he didn't want the video to be seen by 2,283,911 mocking hipsters (as of 4:24 this afternoon). We can't always get what we want.

Oh, unless you want to see John Lennon's interview on the *Dick Cavett Show* on our iPhones. That's totally doable.

PART V

The Office

20

Putting Terabytes Worth of Files on Your iPhone

The Skim

Why Pushing Files is a Great Idea ◘ Simple but Limited: E-Mail ◘
File Types the iPhone Can Open without Help ◘ Cloud Storage ◘
Hail, Dropbox ◘ Air Sharing: Finally, the Holy Grail ◘
And Then, There Was Pogoplug

write about and review technology for a living. When I refer to "the box of smartphones in my office," I literally mean a box filled with smartphones. When a new phone arrives for review and I can't find space for it in the box, I send some of the older loaners back to their manufacturers.

So when I say that I think the iPhone is the best phone out there, that opinion is backed by a certain amount of experience.

And when I say that there's one feature found on even the cheapest smartphone that I sorely, sometimes *desperately* miss … well, that's kind of a big deal, too.

It's such a bloody simple feature: *a memory card slot.* Or failing that, a simple USB connection that mounts the phone's storage on my desktop like any other USB device.

Those things are an open invitation to put a piece of data on the phone and *use* it. On a Windows Mobile or RIM BlackBerry or

Google Android smartphone, there's *nothing* stopping you from putting a file on the device. Drag a file from your desktop on to the phone's icon on your desktop and presto: a copy of a vital report, or just a movie to watch on your flight to Denver, is on your device.

On the iPhone, iTunes alone has the authority to install a file that can be seen by the whole system. Which is annoying enough even if it's a video or a music file. It's *doubly* annoying when you're prevented from copying a Word file, or a spreadsheet, presentation, a PDF — files that the iPhone can open and read, no problem. But iTunes has never heard of the things, so there's no built-in way to exploit that feature.

So you need to take things into your own hands. Via tricks, Web services, and third-party software, you can work around this problem and make the iPhone into something much, much more than it was. And with some slick hardware in your office, you can add gigabytes or even *terabytes* of storage to your iPhone.

WHY PUSHING FILES IS A GREAT IDEA

In general, these are tricks for installing arbitrary desktop files on your iPhone. In *practice*, this basic technique lets you do all kinds of cool and useful things:

- **Play video or audio files without worrying about iTunes's limitations.** I often leave video files at home because putting them on the iPhone takes a little bit of planning. First I need to import it into the iTunes library, then I need to tell iTunes I'd like it copied to the device, then I need to sync it over. By copying it into the

iPhone's storage directly, I go from a file on my desktop to a file on my iPhone in just one quick step, and it opens and plays with just a single tap. It's a big boon for when I just want to watch last night's *Letterman* show and then delete it forever.

- **Play media files that originate from sources other than your home iTunes library.** You're at a friend's house and she's raving about this terrific podcast she's been listening to for the past month. She offers to give you three hours' worth of MP3 files. And you'd love to listen to them on the 90-minute drive back home, but gee, you didn't happen to bring your iMac with you so you can't download and sync the files in. But! No problem: You can copy the files into a folder on your iPhone directly, and play them with just a tap ... the iPhone's built-in iPod app doesn't know it's there, but the OS doesn't care. It sees an MP3 file, you tap to open it, the OS plays the file. Simple.

- **Carry your Microsoft Office files with you and actually use them.** As a journalist, I can leave the house once I've filed my columns but I'm not *really* free to go until I hear from my editor and I know that everything's A-OK. So before heading out to get a celebratory order of strawberry pancakes, I copy all the week's work into my iPhone. If an editor wants to talk about some changes, I can just tap on the right Word file and the Text file containing all my notes, and we can talk about the manuscript together. When I have a presentation coming up, I'll copy the Keynote or PowerPoint file to my iPhone — this way, I can rehearse my slides on the plane.

◻ **Carry your whole work environment with you on your phone.** Thumb drives are nice, but I often forget to take them with me. I *never* leave the house without my iPhone.

◻ **View images at their *full* resolution.** When you sync images to the iPhone, iTunes scales them down to save space. Well, that's very nice ... but what if the file is a detailed map of the labyrinthine college campus you're going to be visiting? The original image shows you buildings, corridors, names. The scaled-down edition is just a purple MIT smidge. When you copy a JPEG to your iPhone manually, it's pixel-for-pixel perfect.

On and on and on.

But the most significant advantage to copying files to my iPhone is the simple fact that *I know they're on my iPhone.* There are lots of cool services for accessing data via the Web or even over the Internet via a neat iPhone app. I'm even going to recommend some of them here.

The trouble is, even the 3G network doesn't stretch everywhere. It's not reachable on a plane and in many parts of New England. And what if you're deep inside a building?

When I'm at the front desk of my hotel and the clerk claims to have no record of my reservation ... well, my confirmation number is no damned use to me on a server somewhere in Oregon, is it? I need it to be *there on my iPhone.* Should I just *trust* that I'm going to have 3G reception in every place I need it?

Et cetera.

Okay, I sense that you're sold. Let's ease you into this slowly. There are multiple approaches with multiple advantages.

SIMPLE BUT LIMITED: E-MAIL

The easiest solution involves no added software or services. Just e-mail a copy of the file to yourself as a file attachment, and then let the iPhone fetch the message. They land in your inbox as an e-mail (see Figure 20-1) and when you give the attachment a tap, the file opens using the iPhone's built-in media reader.

Pro: Dead-simple. And if you manually

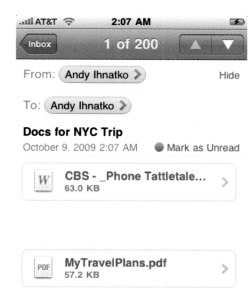

Figure 20-1

E-mail: the simplest way to put files on your iPhone behind iTunes's back

download the file, the docs stay in memory long after you've lost Internet access or put the phone into Airplane mode.

Con: You can't *count* on the data sticking around. As soon as the iPhone needs some more storage space, it'll purge the actual data from memory, forcing you to download it all over again. And remember, your inbox can hold only up to 200 messages at once. If you're thinking about keeping a copy of your campus map, think again; if you have anything akin to a social life, e-mails from friends will wipe it from the rolls in days.

Hmm. Not bad. you should definitely keep that in mind, but you sort of want per-manence, don't you? This sort of slaps at the problem.

FILE TYPES THE IPHONE CAN OPEN WITHOUT HELP

Okay, before I go on: I skimmed over this whole "just give the file a tap and it'll open right up" business. The iPhone has a built-in viewer that supports a long list of file types. All the "tap and it'll open" techniques in this chapter — or elsewhere in the book — will work with any of these kinds of files:

- **Video files** in .mp4, .m4v, and .mov file formats, encoded in either H.264 or MPEG. There are a few more cave-ats (it only supports a certain maxi-mum bit rate, for example) but them's the broad strokes of it.
- **Audio files** in AAC, MP3, AIFF, WAV, and Apple Lossless formats.
- **Image files** in JPEG, TIFF, and GIF formats.
- **Document files** in Microsoft Word, PowerPoint, and Excel formats; Apple Pages, Keynote, and Numbers formats; and PDF files.

Apple keeps expanding this list, so stay tuned to `www.apple.com/iphone/specs.html` for the current roster.

CLOUD STORAGE

Let's go back to the basic function I whined about at the top of this chapter. There's a file on my PC or Mac and I want to use it on my iPhone. I want to just drag it from Point a to Point B. Simple.

Ideally, I'd be copying a file directly from my desktop to the iPhone. Okay, but what if I could copy it to a folder on my desktop, and then Unseen Forces automatically transmitted it to a virtual folder on a server on the Internet? And then my iPhone could access this same virtual folder via Wi-Fi or 3G?

That's good enough, and that's a basic concept known as "cloud storage."

You sign up for an account with a special service that gives you a parcel of storage on one of their servers — typically a flash drive's worth, more or less.

Instead of sticking this "flash drive" in a USB port, you double-click a little desktop app that connects to that server, logs into your account, and then "mounts" that folder on your desktop, where it behaves just like any hard drive. It works like any other folder. Drag files in, edit files inside it, save and open documents inside it from within any app. Plain vanilla, through and through. Neither you nor your computer are particu-larly aware that your files live thousands of miles away.

Cloud storage has two basic advantages. You can connect to this virtual folder from any computer or even any device. If it can connect to the Internet, it can connect to the cloud storage service and access your files. The second advantage is that you don't even necessarily need to formally "mount" your virtual folder at all. You can access all your files via any Web browser.

Cloud storage is practically tailor-made for smartphones. There's even a side benefit: I can't "add" more storage to my iPhone, but accessing a cloud service through my iPhone is like attaching a 1-gigabyte flash drive or even a 100-gigabyte hard drive to my iPhone. It's the perfect storage for "deep archive" files that I'd like to have access to but that aren't so important that it's worth loading directly inside my iPhone's limited storage space.

There are many cloud services and many of them have released apps for the iPhone that connect to the service and let you access your files. Only three are worth serious attention, methinks: Box.net (`http://box.net`) and iDisk, which is offered as part of Apple's MobileMe service package (`www.me.com`).

(And a third, which is so fantastic that you should probably use it instead of the other two. But I'm tipping my hand for the next section, aren't I?)

No, of course they're useful services. They offer distinct little twists that The Third Mysterious Service lacks.

If you're often working on projects with lots of different folks, Box.net is a good answer. Figure 20-2 shows you the basic iPhone interface. It makes it very easy to have a big folder of personal, private storage, and yet "share" individual files and folders with specific people. When you're accessing your storage via Box.net's desktop Web interface, you can even edit any Microsoft Office files you've stored on the service.

Box.net has a number of monthly pricing

plans based on the features and amount of storage you want. They'll give you a 1-gigabyte folder, and all of Box.net's core features for free. For $15 a month, you get 10 gigs and the full buffet of what Box.net can do, including the ability to edit files online.

iDisk (shown in Figure 20-3) is ... well, it's iDisk. Support for iDisk is built into every copy of Mac OS X, and Windows users can access an iDisk with a simple, free download. It's part of the Mac experience. "When you're done with your section of the report, drop it in my iDisk," you say, and if that person is a Mac user, he or she will find that particular function hard-wired right inside the Finder's Go menu. All of Apple's iLife apps use iDisk to share music, photos, and videos. iDisk is just one of the features you get with a $99 annual subscription to Apple's MobileMe service.

That $99 buys you 20 gigs of storage — already much more than the 15 gigs Box. net gives you (for $15 times 12 months, or $180). And if you need more storage, Apple will expand your iDisk for an additional fee.

I like both cloud storage services buuuuut ... no, unless their unique advantages appeal to you, they can't hold a candle to Dropbox.

HAIL, DROPBOX

Okay. So at this point, you know what Dropbox's basic features are. There's a folder on your desktop that behaves like any other folder, only it *isn't* a real folder, it's actually a connection to your cloud storage on a remote server, you can access your files from any Web browser as well, and there's an iPhone app that allows you to access this folder and view the files.

Dropbox (`http://getdropbox.com`)

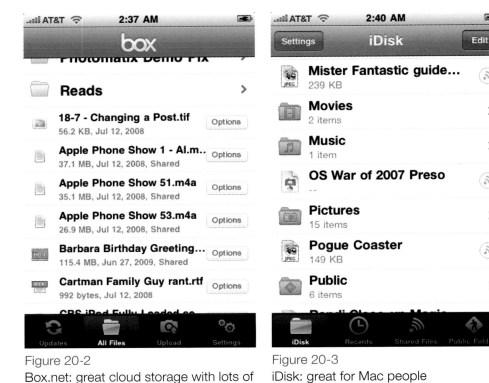

Figure 20-2
Box.net: great cloud storage with lots of sharing features

Figure 20-3
iDisk: great for Mac people

wins the iPhone Cloud Storage Crown thanks to two critical features:

- Your folder is "mirrored" across several of your PCs and Macs. You can install the Dropbox desktop software on every damned one of your Macs and PCs. Each one of these computers will have a for-real, honest-to-god local Dropbox folder on its hard drive (shown in Figure 20-4). If you disconnect from the Internet, it's okay: It's a real, local folder, and it contains real files. Ah! But any file you copy into this local folder will automatically be uploaded to your Dropbox cloud storage *and automatically uploaded into*

every other Dropbox folder on every other machine you own. The preponderance of Mac screen shots in this book has already revealed to you that I use a Mac as my primary machine. Figure 20-4 is a screen shot I saved on my netbook's Dropbox folder. To get it on this Mac, all I needed to do was wait a minute and presto! It magically appeared in my MacBook's Dropbox folder.

- The Dropbox iPhone app can download files directly into your phone's local storage. Figure 20-5 shows you the iPhone app in action. As with the other cloud service apps, I can browse the folders and sub-folders in my

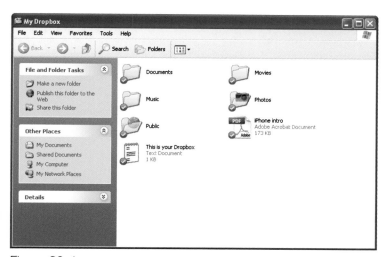

Figure 20-4

Dropbox: one folder synced onto every device you own

the time. When you pick up your iPhone and launch the Dropbox app, the file will be available. And you can keep it permanently.

You can't complain about the pricing, either. You can get 2 gigs of storage for free, and you can get *huge* storage for fairly low money: 50 gigs for $10 a month, or 100 gigs for $20. And there's no size limit on individual files, so you can even use it to access DVD-length video files from your iPhone. Remember, the iPhone has a built-in player for video files that works in both portrait and full screen landscape modes (see Figure 20-6).

Dropbox and tap any file to open and view it. Unlike the Dropbox folders on my PCs and Macs, files don't sync to the iPhone app automatically. (Why not? Because the Dropbox app would need to be running in the background all the time, and Apple doesn't allow third-party apps to do that.) But! If I open a file and tap the Favorite button, the file I'm viewing will be downloaded into the iPhone's local storage and saved in the Dropbox apps' local Favorites folder. I can open and view a Favorite file with the app even with the iPhone in Airplane Mode — no Internet access is necessary.

Dropbox is a clear win for nearly all iPhone users. The desktop apps work automatically and invisibly. You want that file on your iPhone? Just copy it into your desktop's Dropbox folder and it's done. You don't need to tether anything and you don't even need to have access to the iPhone at

Dropbox is the greatest solution for putting your own arbitrary files on your iPhone. Except, of course, for the *other* greatest solution for putting your own arbitrary files on your iPhone.

AIR SHARING: FINALLY, THE HOLY GRAIL

Am I being an unpleasant noodge? I love Dropbox and I use the iPhone app alllll the time. But I still want to be able to simply copy a file from my desktop directly to my iPhone, without having to use the Internet as an intermediary.

Air Sharing Pro from Avatron Software (http://avatron.com) is one of my five

215

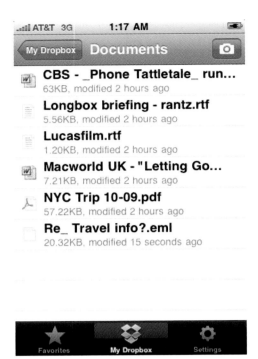

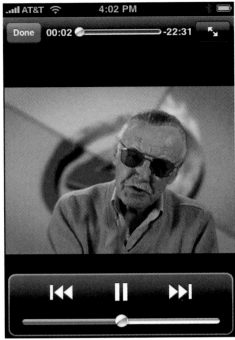

Figure 20-5
Dropbox for iPhone

Figure 20-6
Watching an MP4 video hosted on my
Dropbox

favorite apps for the iPhone. I couldn't get
by without it. Honestly. You need to buy
this app. There's a free edition as well, but
I firmly believe that when an opportunity
to give these people $9.99 presents itself,
everyone should go ahead and do it.

Air Sharing lets you "mount" your iPhone
on your desktop as a real, honest-to-God
network storage device. It does this by
establishing itself on your local Wi-Fi
network as a WebDAV file server. What
is WebDAV? All you need to know is that
Windows, Mac OS, and Linux all support
this standard out of the box. Unlike Dropbox, which requires a free "helper" application, your existing computer can simply
connect to the iPhone and treat it just like

a flash drive, with no extra software needed.

Figure 20-7 shows Air Sharing in action.
In addition to the behind-the-scenes magic,
Air Sharing Pro is one hell of a slick file
manager. It's bloody elegant at organizing
and browsing files, and includes a couple
of very slick little tricks. I can print files to
networked printers, and e-mail files directly
from my Air Sharing storage area.

Bonus: I have full control over security.
I can set it up so that it requires a username
and a password, or leave it completely open.
I can turn off the sharing features entirely,
and just use the app to browse and read the
files I've already copied to my iPhone. Or
I can even just establish a single folder as

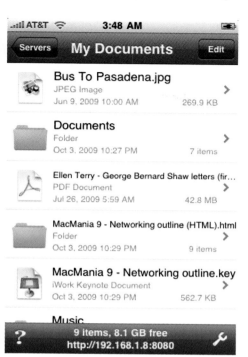

TIP

And just now (doing the last-minute final edits on this whole book), I've received an e-mail from Air Sharing's developers, with a list of new features coming in the next edition: the ability to access any Internet server via FTP, download any Internet file via its URL, and even access your Mac remotely, browse your hard drive via Air Sharing, and download individual files to your iPhone from thousands of miles away.

The developers tell me it ought to be ready for you by the time you read this. Yet *more* reasons for you to earmark $9.99 for Air Sharing Pro.

Figure 20-7
Air Sharing, the perfect solution to putting Any Damned File You Want on your iPhone

a public folder. If I'm physically inside the office, anybody can just throw a file into my iPhone, which I suppose could be the modern digital equivalent of slapping a "Kick Me" sign on my back without my knowing it. But I bet there are legitimate business uses, too.

Activating Air Sharing on Your Local Network

The Air Sharing app is completely inert when it's not running. None of your PCs or Macs will be able to see or access the Air Sharing documents on your iPhone until you launch the app and "mount" the phone on your desktop as a shared folder.

Note the URL at the bottom of Figure 20-7. That's the network address that your computer uses to find your iPhone on the local Wi-Fi network.

Typical of the amount of care and thought that went into Air Sharing is the fact that a set of *detailed* step-by-step directions for mounting the iPhone as a shared folder are hard-wired right in the app. Just tap the question mark (?) at the bottom of the screen and you'll see instructions for Windows (with separate detailed instructions for each edition), Mac, and Linux (see Figure 20-8).

At the end of these two or three steps, a new shared network folder appears on your desktop. It's your iPhone, and there's no difference between this shared folder and any other folder you've ever worked with. Figure 20-9 shows you what my

TIDBIT

When I talk about "copying files to your iPhone" using Dropbox or Air Sharing or any other tool, I don't mean it the way you'd copy files to your PC. Copying a file to your iPhone via Air Sharing makes it available only to Air Sharing. You won't be able to open that text document in the Stanza e-book app, even though the app supports text tiles. Think of this nugget of storage as an isolated flash drive and nothing more.

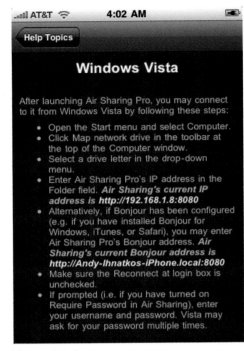

Figure 20-8
No need to check the shipping box for Air Sharing's installation instructions

iPhone looks like to Windows XP; Figure 20-10 is what it looks like to a Mac.

Some random notes on the setup:

- Your iPhone isn't tethered to any one machine. If you're staying with friends, you can mount your iPhone on their PC as easily as you connected it to your home Mac.

- The connection stays active only so long as the app stays active. If you switch to a different app, or if the iPhone goes to sleep, the connection disappears. Something to consider if you plan on copying 1.3-gigabyte movie files to your iPhone.

- Your file storage is a special, separate area from all other parts of your iPhone experience. For instance, you won't be able to use this app to "copy" music to or from your iPhone's music library.

- For a bit of extra security, you can password-protect the Air Sharing directory so that strangers — strangers who have

seen the secret URL on your screen, or are very handy with a network analyzer — can't secretly connect up your iPhone and see your files.

Using the Air Sharing File Browser

Like I said, copying and manipulating files on the iPhone is the boring half of this app's functionality. It's when you're gadding about the metropolis that Air Sharing shines. Just navigate through folders. Want to view a Word document that you copied to your special Hybrid Fish-Ocelot Project folder? Tap on the folder to open it and then tap on the Word document to view it. Want

Figure 20-9
My iPhone, as it appears when I'm using Windows

Figure 20-10
My iPhone, mounted on my Mac desktop

to watch a video? Tap on the video and it starts playing. Ditto for audio files.

And don't just use this app as an alternative media player! It's like a flash drive that you never forget to slip inside your pocket. If you keep critical files on your iPhone via Air Sharing, you'll always have your digital workspace with you as you move from machine to machine and city to city.

It's kind of as if you've created a whole second smartphone within the iPhone. Because none of the other iPhone apps can see or interact with the content you've copied into that folder or its subfolders, Air Sharing is the place you go to play with files and media that you're keeping secret from the rest of the phone. It's such a big part of my iPhone life that it's like a whole separate device that I immerse myself in when I need to manipulate and store files "for keeps."

The only limit to Air Sharing is the limitations of your iPhone's storage. You get the luxury of a direct connection without the

freedom of being able to copy these files to a much, much bigger storage area. If you copy 5 gigs worth of raw video files to your iPhone, you're five gigs closer to a "Some Files Could Not Be Copied" error from iTunes the next time you try to sync a whole month's worth of video podcasts.

But there's a way to add a real, honest-to-Thor terabyte of hard drive storage to your iPhone.

AND THEN, THERE WAS POGOPLUG

Regard, please, the simple box shown in Figure 20-11.

You may call it "Pogoplug." At times I'm inclined to refer to it as "the woman whose hand in marriage I am unworthy to covet."

The Pogoplug has an Ethernet port. You use this network port to connect the Pogoplug to your home broadband modem or network. It has a USB port. You connect this to any USB hard drive. Any drive of any capacity. Terabytes. You can even plug in a hub and connect several drives at once.

After a simple, three-step setup, the hard

219

drives connected to your Pogoplug can be network-attached to any device you own that has access to the Internet. You just install a special free helper app that makes the Pogoplug-attached drives look and behave like anything you have plugged into one of your computer's USB ports.

(You can also access the data on those hard drives via any Web browser. But your eyes are saucer-wide with the potential for transmogrifying your iPhone experience, so I'll skip over that.)

What looks like a simple wall transformer (you can plug it into AC via a long power cord if that's more convenient) actually contains a little computer. One of its tasks is to always tell Pogoplug Central where this little Pogoplug can be found, anywhere in the world.

And it really, *really* works. I traveled from Boston to Beijing and when I connected my MacBook to the hotel Internet two blocks away from Tiananmen Square, the little Pogoplug app automatically contacted www.pogoplug.com, located my Pogoplug in my office half a world away, and my office drive icons appeared on my desktop. Just like that.

There is indeed a Pogoplug app for the iPhone. It does indeed absolutely kick butt. Behold Figure 20-12.

Launching the app connects me to Ryder, a 500-gigabyte USB hard drive in my Boston office.

As with any of these other file tricks you've seen so far, tapping on any viewable file (picture, movie, audio, document) puts it on the screen. And like the Dropbox app, I can tap a Download button to copy the file directly into the Pogoplug app's iPhone storage (see Figure 20-13), where the file

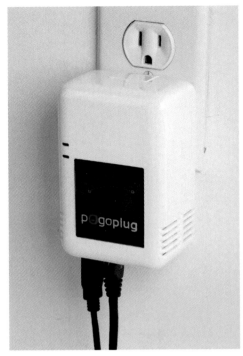

Figure 20-11
Pogoplug: unlimited storage for your iPhone

remains safe and sound whether I have Internet access or not.

The damned thing works. *It works!* I confess that I wasn't completely ready to accept that when I first set up my Pogoplug. But it's absolutely the perfect storage solution. Unlike "cloud" solutions, copying files to my storage takes less than no time. When I wanted to put thousands of songs on that drive, I just unplugged the drive from the Pogoplug and connected it to my desktop for the transfer. When I want to expand my storage capacity, I just swap the drive for a bigger one … or just attach a second drive via a USB hub.

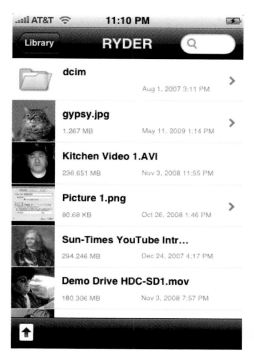

Figure 20-12
My hard drive, mounted on my iPhone
via Pogoplug

Figure 20-13
Viewing and downloading files from
a hard drive, via Pogoplug

And, I repeat, this whole "locate your Pogoplug no matter where it is in the world" absolutely works. I think it's the only such solution that actually functions as advertised. Even in *Beijing* it worked flawlessly.

The Pogoplug is just $99 from www. pogoplug.com. $99! I'm shocked. There are no subscription plans and no monthly fees and no bandwidth restrictions. $99 and you own it. Period.

It's insane. It transforms the iPhone from simply awesome to megahypersuperawesome with bacon bits. This one simple, affordable device obliterates the problem of having to *choose* what media and data you want to put on your iPhone. Make a copy

of your entire iTunes library and copy it to your Pogoplug. Now, every song and video you own is "on your iPhone." If you use your Pogoplug simply as your home network server, you'll never be caught away from your house without an important file. Just pull out your iPhone and *get the file that you were working on this morning.*

I'm babbling now. I should probably move on.

So what's the best solution to the problem of carrying arbitrary files with you? Dropbox, Air Sharing Pro, or Pogoplug?

I like all three. They're three different approaches to the same problem. I use Air Sharing to turn my iPhone into a virtual flash drive. It contains all the files that I *always* want with me.

But it's a minor hassle to mount the Air Share volume on my desktop. So I often use Dropbox for casual "I want to put copy of my travel itinerary and confirmation numbers on my iPhone" sort of things. I just save the file to a local folder and that's all there is to it.

I use the Pogoplug because it's a killer device for anyone who uses computers and travels. The fact that I can access every file I own and every one of *The Bugle*'s 100-plus podcasts without taking up space on my iPhone is a tremendous bonus.

All three are killers. And all three underscore the wisdom of George Carlin's old "A Place for Your Stuff" routine.

He described your house as nothing more than "a place for your stuff." When you go on vacation to Maui for a couple of weeks, you need to pack a *smaller* version of your stuff. Then a friend of yours suggests that you spend the weekend at the beach house of a friend of his, so you fill a knapsack with an *even tinier* version of your stuff ... et cetera.

The key to my happiness and security as a nerd is the ability to keep creating smaller and smaller versions of my digital world.

On my desk in the office, I have the big, quad-core big-screen desktop machine with 2 terabytes of attached storage: My Stuff. My MacBook in the living room is a smaller version of my stuff.

So what happens when I'm headed someplace and I just don't want to bring a computer with me?

Of course, "no computer" is translated in my head as "*some* kind of computer, certainly." The iPhone, equipped with these three apps, allows me to create probably the smallest acceptable version of My Stuff. I have my e-mail, I have the Web ... and I also have a gigabyte or two of files from my desktop to read, amuse, edit, and just surround myself with a slight static-y feeling of security.

Don't ask me why I need to have an eight-year-old manuscript of a novel I stopped thinking about three years ago. There's no sensible answer and the one I make up wouldn't make me look very good. I'm just grateful to have a working solution.

Calendars and Contacts

The Skim

H mm. So I suppose I can't talk you out of this idea. No matter what I say, you're going to use your iPhone or your iPod Touch to store an address book and a personal calendar.

No, I don't approve. I've examined this from all angles and you can't escape the realization that address books and calendars each increase the risk of human social contact. That sort of thing can really cut into the time you have available to translate *The Wizard of Oz* into Klingon.

If you're using Microsoft Outlook or the standard Mac OS X apps (iCal and Address Book) to manage your calendars and contacts on the desktop, you have this bit covered already. iTunes automagically syncs your data to the device. Move on and thanks for reading this intro. Here, take a free tip on how to make ice cubes: If you use hot water, they'll come out looking nice and clear instead of cloudy. Off you go.

But Microsoft Outlook and Apple's iCal and Address Book are the only apps that iTunes supports directly. If you use another app to manage that big wobbly mound of names and phone numbers and agreed-upon dates and times when humans can step right up and break your heart, you'll need to bring in some help.

DEALING WITH NON-STANDARD CALENDAR AND CONTACT APPS

If you use a nicely managed company mail system, the concept of copying your desktop address book and calendar to your iPhone seems like a ridiculous thing to call a "problem." It all simply works because (whether you know it or not) your office uses Microsoft Exchange Server to seamlessly and constantly push and pull all that data between every calendar and address app you use — whether it's on your desktop or your phone.

In truth, this chapter is more for those unfortunates among us, for whom neither the iPhone's built-in sync features nor a system like Exchange are any help whatsoever.

I shall now address this group directly: Hello, unfortunates. Your problem is that you're using some sort of obscure address book or calendar app that isn't hip with the times. In researching this section of the book, I came across at least seven alternatives that are still in *some* sort of common use.

Or, you have all your contacts locked inside the phone you had before you succumbed to the siren call of the iPhone. You never bothered to manage your contacts and calendars with a desktop. Or, the phone came with some crikey underpowered desktop app that doesn't have any useful export tools.

Well, I can't address each of these apps and phones specifically. Instead, I offer you the secret to solving the problem: Google Sync (www.google.com/sync). Google Sync is a set of tools and services that allows most handsets to sync to Google's own calendar and contact services.

It does this by offering you a free Microsoft Exchange-compatible mail account. That's all Google Gmail is, really. So you sign up for Google Sync, sync your FitzMellon 2828 Smartphone to Google ... and then use Google Sync to sync that same pile of data back down to your new iPhone. And support for Google Contacts is built right in to iTunes; just click the Sync Google Contacts button in the Info pane of your iPhone's syncing prefs.

Google Sync works as remarkable glue. As I investigated app after app and phone after phone, even if I couldn't find a direct "sync this phone or app's data with the iPhone" utility I could certainly find one that brought this antediluvian piece of tech into the world of Google Calendar and Contacts. And once the data is on Google, it can sync downward into just about anything.

HOW CALENDAR AND CONTACT DATA GET FORMATTED

Still, there might be a circumstance under which Google Sync isn't a desirable answer. Like, for instance, you don't want all your personal information in the hands of Google, where God knows who can get their hands on it.

(You can trust Google. But you can't necessarily trust that nobody can figure out that you chose "password" as the password to your Google account.)

Instead, to get all that data into your iPhone or iPod Touch you're going to have to use one of iTunes's approved apps as a go-between. That is, instead of iTunes automatically syncing all your data every time you plug your device into your desktop, you first manually export all of your

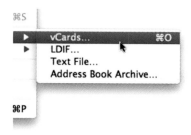

Figure 21-1
The Mac's Address Book app can
import vCard data without any help.

Figure 21-2
SyncWiz: making Microsoft Outlook into
a much better class of idiot

DiscoAppointmentsAndFolks data to Outlook, or iCal and Address book. Once the
"approved" app holds all your data, you plug
in your iPhone and iTunes updates it.

See? iTunes is still working with the
familiar apps it knows and loves.

There are two industry-standard formats for moving contact and calendar data
between apps and platforms:

- **vCard** format is used for address book
  data.
- **iCalendar** format is used for calendar
  data. And just to make sure there's as
  much confusion on the matter as there
  can possibly be, it's sometimes short-
  ened to "iCal." During explanations
  like these, it's inevitably lengthened to
  "iCal, not to be confused with the calendar app that ships on all Macs."

Most modern apps can export their data
in both of these formats.

Importing vCard and iCalendar Data into a Mac

Importing the data into the Mac OS is
alluringly cake-like. Apple's iCal has an
easy-as-pie Import command in its File
menu. Just point it at the exported data and
you're in business. Ditto for the Address

Book. Choose File ▶ Import ▶ vCards and
then navigate to the file that contains all of
your exported contacts (see Figure 21-1).

Importing vCard and iCalendar Data into a Windows PC

On the Windows side, things are just
a *bit* trickier. And here I'm using "a bit
trickier" to act as an efficient substitute for
about two pages of passionate screeding
about why the devil an important, industry-
leading app like Microsoft Outlook doesn't
directly support the most popular contact
data interchange format on the whole
bloody planet.

iCalendar data imports just fine. But
what's up with the vCard support? It can
import vCard data, but (oh, dear God) *only
the first name in the file.* If you have 500
names in there, it'll stop with "AAAAAA
Custom Paint and Body, Inc.," ignoring all
the rest.

So unless you're a way more patient
person than I am, you're going to want to
go to http://sync-wiz.com and buy
SyncWiz, a conversion and synchronization
plug-in utility for Outlook (shown in Figure

Figure 21-3
Importing a vCard manually via Mail

for a living.

Come to think of it, if I worked at UPS I'd probably be on a group dental plan.

Damn. I just brought myself down without even planning it …

THE CHEAP, MANUAL OPTION

All of the above utilities and ideas are based on the idea that you have loads and loads of contacts to move from an old device or app to a new one. But what if you just want to bring a single contact over in a simple, efficient manner?

If you can export the contact into a vCard file, you're in luck: vCards are one of only two kinds of data that your iPhone will simply integrate into its internal libraries without any outside help. Just e-mail the vCard file to yourself and fetch the message on your iPhone.

Tap on the vCard and your iPhone creates a new contact with that information (see Figure 21-3).

Just tell your iPhone whether you'd like all of this info to be added as a new contact or as new info for an existing one. As part of your iPhone's contact database, it'll be synced back to your desktop the next time you dock your iPhone. Or it'll go out immediately if you have push data enabled.

21-2). It also integrates into the app seamlessly, adding *actual* support for vCard, instead of this purely ceremonial feature that Microsoft slapped in there. And it's quite reasonably priced at $25.

It's wonderful that even the simplest, most straightforward, and most reliable feature on this whole phone has at least one or two gotchas, isn't it?

When I call this little parcel of frustration "wonderful," I speak of course from the point of view of somebody who makes his living explaining things to people. Thank God the world of technology is so badly scuffed, dinged, and rusted out in places. If all this stuff worked the way it ought to, I'd probably be loading trucks at the UPS depot

Clippings, Notes, and Lists

The Skim

"I write doo-dads, because it's a doo-dad sort of town." Thus wrote Dorothy Parker ... brilliant columnist, poet, and wit.

I suppose just for the sake of balance and accuracy I should also include an additional Parker quote:

"*BATS!* Giant, hairy bats! Circling my typewriter and pelting me with copper spoons filled with jam! *AIEEEE!!!*"

She was a treasure of American literature but she did drink quite a lot, you know.

Nonetheless, she had a solid point there about doo-dads. If anything, the communal town in which we all live is even doo-daddier than it's been since the days of the Great War. Your life is filled with little bits of information that defies any sort of ready organization or catchall filing system. Still, you need 'em. What's the address of that luncheonette on Lexington Avenue you wanted to visit on your way to the Metropolitan Museum of Art? What are the museum's hours? What bus do you need to take to get from the museum to your friend's place in SoHo afterward?

One afternoon in New York City, three absolutely essential doo-dads. And this was just for a *fun* afternoon. When there's business and meetings and money involved, you can accumulate dozens of these things over the course of a week.

WHY NOT NOTEPAD? HOW ABOUT NOTES?

Now then. If you've spent any amount of time playing with your iPhone, the phrase "creating tons of pieces of seemingly random and unconnected information with barely any sense or order about it" conjures up one thought: "Notepad."

("Also, 'This very book,'" says the editor of my newspaper column, on occasion.)

But there are a few problems with using the iPhone's Notes app for actual notes.

TIDBIT

If you're a Mac user — particularly a longtime Mac user — I can explain what I mean with one word: "Scrapbook." One of the most useful apps ever, for any machine. Cut something from somewhere, paste it into the Scrapbook … bang, it's there. You didn't have to tag it, outline it, save it, or anything. It was just an endless timeline of Things That Were on Your Screen at Some Point That You Didn't Want to Forget About.

If a future update to the iPhone OS included a simple "save what I'm looking at to the Scrapbook" feature, then Nokia and Palm and all the other phone makers could just go into the frozen yogurt business for all I'd care.

Chiefly: The Notes app isn't very flexible. It's really just a more colorful version of what was available on the first Palm Pilot PDA back in the Nineties. Not exactly a feature-horse, is it?

And second, there's the usual hassle of iPhones and iPods: Your sole conduit for putting info on the device is a copy of iTunes on one specific computer. If someone tells you, "Oh, but if you're going to the Metropolitan Museum, don't go into the Egyptian wing on the first Tuesday of the month; that's when the moon god raises all the mummies from the dead and sends them on a rampage in a sickening harvest for human flesh" and you think, "Golly, I should probably have that info handy," you're out of luck if you aren't at the keyboard of your desktop computer at that moment.

Yes, notes are most useful when they become ubiquitous. Which is why I also like to move slightly beyond even iTunes's built-in "Notes sync" feature. It's good stuff. You can do a two-way sync between the notes on your iPhone and the ones you create in Microsoft Outlook or Apple Mail. But you can do a lot better than that.

Fortunately, there are plenty of tools to handle those random bits of trivial data ranging from quick jottings to essential information.

NOTES AND EPHEMERA: EVERNOTE

Ever since I got my first one, my smartphone has been a lint trap for little scraps of info. It's like that pad of paper that I used to keep in my shirt pocket. An address, a phone number, information about a book I wanted to buy or a book I wanted to write

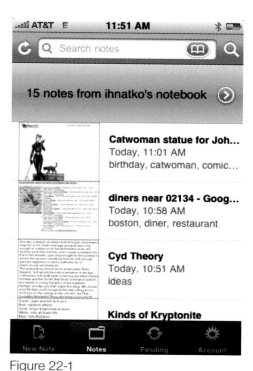

Figure 22-1
Evernote: your big friendly wobbly
mound of information

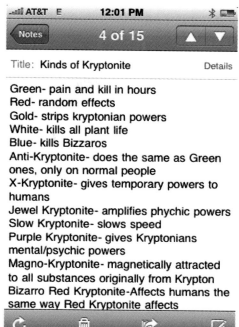

Figure 22-2
Retrieving a note in Evernote

... just a free-floating barge of bagatelles.

Evernote (www.evernote.com) is an
online service and a free iPhone app that
really doesn't care if you want to carefully organize your life and your info or if
you just want to plop it all in one careless
heap. It's all about helping you capture data
wherever you are and getting it back to you
whenever you want it.

For that reason, there's never any need to
keep your PC, Mac, iPhone, and home and
office hardware synchronized with fresh
notes; it's all stored on Evernote's servers.
You can download client apps for every
platform imaginable, or just read and add to
your notes from any machine with a Web

browser. You can e-mail or text info into
your account.

It's this flexibility that makes Evernote
a winner. Keeping your notes on a server
does mean that you can't access them when
you're away from an Internet connection, but
otherwise it's a slick and powerful solution.

Figure 22-1 shows my main Evernote
notebook. I can establish multiple notebooks for different kinds of info, but I prefer
to just have everything together in one
place. Here you can see a gift I'm trying to
find for a pal, a list of diners that I pulled
off Google, an idea I jotted down for a story
about Cyd Charisse, and of course a list of
all the different kinds of kryptonite and the
effect that each kind has on Superman.

233

Figure 22-3
Recording a new voice note

TIP

Evernote has an incredible invisible feature: If you take a photo of something with text in it — a whiteboard, a street sign, a menu, anything — *it'll convert the image text to searchable text.* So if it's the end of the meeting and you're looking at a list of names of the people who've committed to bringing food to the company potluck and arson project, don't bother tapping all that information down. Take a snapshot. When you search for "coleslaw," Evernote will retrieve the photo of the whiteboard.

(See? It's good not to get caught without this sort of info handy.)

And as the Search field implies, I can quickly type in a keyword to bring up any note I want. Otherwise, your notes are presented in the order in which they were last viewed or edited, to keep the freshest stuff at the top.

Tap to read a note (see Figure 22-2). And once a note is open, you can edit it or e-mail it to someone who can get some use out of the thing. Like, Lex Luthor or somebody.

It doesn't matter where I was when I recorded this info. But the Evernote iPhone app offers a full range of note types, which you can create by tapping the New Note button. You get:

- **Text notes**. Just go on ahead and type.
- **Picture notes**. Either select a photo from your iPhone's Picture library, or tap the Snapshot button and take a photo live and in person.
- **Voice notes**. Tap the button and a control panel for a voice recording appears (see Figure 22-3).

Every note you make can be tagged with descriptive keywords to make them easier to find later on. You can even bookmark popular searches like "office project turducken" so that narrowing down 429 notes to just the eight that are related to your ongoing breakroom culinary goal is just a tap or two away.

And if you give Evernote permission, it'll even tag the note with the location you were when the note was created.

As you might expect, Evernote's desktop clients are more muscular than the iPhone

edition. Figure 22-4
shows the Mac edi-
tion. The desktop
version actually
downloads data
from the Evernote
server, for a start.

You can also
grab plug-ins that
make it dead-
simple to send
information from
any Web page into
a new note. Just
drag the clip to
Evernote book-
marklet from the
Evernote.com's
Download page
into the book-

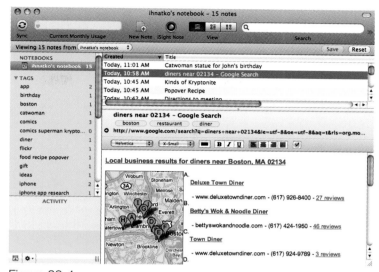

Figure 22-4
Desktop Evernote clients are available for Windows and Mac
(Mac version shown here).

marks bar of your browser (if you're using
Firefox, you can install a plug-in). From
then on, any time you see something online
that's worthy of capture, just highlight it
with your mouse and click the Clip to Evernote bookmark. A little window will pop up
that allows you to tag and otherwise modify
the new note before it's added to your soup
(see Figure 22-5). If you select nothing, the
whole page is noted.

LISTS AND TO-DOS:
ZENBE LISTS

List and task managers are those very, very
"noisy" categories of software in the iPhone
App Store. That is, there are way too many
to choose from, and the one or two best ones
outclass the others by a laughable margin.

Zenbe Lists is one of those head-and-
shoulders-above apps. It's my favorite
because (like Evernote) it's so flexible.

There are some wonderful apps for managing complicated goals and projects, but
only Zenbe is clear and powerful enough
to handle just about anything that can be
expressed as a list.

Shopping list? Sure. To-dos? Yup. Bat-
ting order for the Little League team you're
coaching? Can do. Record of your gas mileage on a tank-by-tank basis? No sweat.

It doesn't have intense management
features that support the "Getting Things
Done" model of whatever. But it lets you
create multiple lists. It lets you attach
notes to each item. It lets you reorder those
list items. It lets you check off items once
they've been completed ... but it doesn't
actually delete the item until you say so; it
just grays it out (see Figure 22-6).

Suffice to say that Zenbe Lists justified at
least $18 of the purchase price of my new
iPhone.

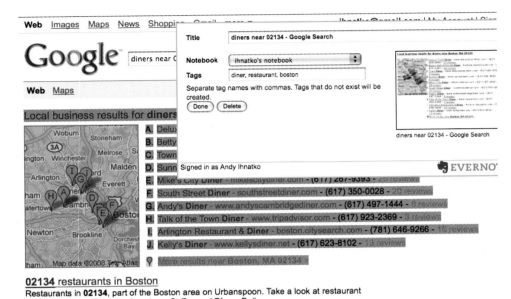

Figure 22-5
Converting info on the Web to a note in your Evernote notebook

Oh, how much is Zenbe Lists? Free. Come on, why would they *charge* for an indispensable piece of professionally designed iPhone software?

(Yes, sarcasm. Well-spotted, sir or madam!)

Unlike Evernote, your lists are stored right on your iPhone; head on through that tunnel without a care in the world, because access to your data doesn't rely on an Internet connection.

But like Evernote, Zenbe for iPhone is merely the mobile projection of the Zenbe Online Empire. Go ahead and use Zenbe list for days, weeks, months, even. If at some point you discover that you run so much of your life through this iPhone app and that you'd like to work with your lists even when you're behind the wheel of such an arcane device as a "desktop computer" — or you'd

simply like to share your list data with your desktop apps — head on over to http://lists.zenbe.com and create a free user account with Zenbe.

And presto! You now can synchronize your iPhone lists with your central account and access your data from any machine with a Web browser (see Figure 22-7).

There's one catch, but it's minor: You need to explicitly tap the Sync button on the iPhone app to synchronize the handheld and the Web editions of your lists. Oh, big deal.

Evernote and Zenbe aren't the only two "collect, organize, and manage random bits of information apps on your iPhone" apps. In fact, if these kinds of apps were sacks of cement, we could convert the Grand Canyon into a useful and far less-dangerous parking lot.

I encourage you to explore the App Store's Productivity category more fully. And let me tell you why: First, it's possible that you'll find a notes app that's more in tune to your personal data collection needs than Zenbe or Evernote. Second, it's actually far more likely that you'll download two or three different examples, look at three or four others, and then simply give up and acknowledge that I've picked the two winners.

Evernote and Zenbe aren't the two apps that do absolutely *everything*. But I'm certain that they're the two apps that offer the greatest flexibility, and offer the best ability to handle whatever need happens to strike you at any given moment.

Figure 22-6
One life, multiple lists, via Zenbe

Figure 22-7
Accessing your lists online via Zenbe's online interface

23

The Office

The Skim

General Approaches ◻ Spreadsheets ◻ Onward to Databases ◻
The Sad State of Writing on the iPhone ◻ Presentations ◻
The Dullest Chapter? Or the Most Exciting?

very year, I start working on a chapter for the new edition of
iPhone Fully Loaded by reading the chapter from the previous
year's edition.

This year, the topic of getting Microsoft Office docs on your iPhone
infused me with enough nostalgia that I wound up tracking the subject through every edition plus *iPod Fully Loaded*, the book series'
predecessor. The first edition relied on lots of clever tricks and generic
text-bashing utilities to brute-force to get data from Word documents,
spreadsheets, and databases into a format that the iPod could handle
in even the most *rudimentary* form. When the iPhone came out, it
could open certain files directly but still required a bit of massage.
And there were a few Web sites that allowed the editing and creation
of content.

Last edition's bagatelle on this subject began with cautious paragraphs. "As I write this," I said, "the App Store has only been open
for a few months and we've *still* yet to see a single decent database or
spreadsheet app." And then there was a note from my editor to please
insert some blank pages right about here. Much like setting out an
empty place setting for Elijah during a Passover seder, I felt that these
blank pages symbolized the awesome Microsoft Office-style apps

that would arrive for the iPhone at some unknown point.

(I couldn't get my publisher to get on board with this idea. It's possible that the staff had a point when it argued, "Don't be an idiot.")

So now it's another year and another edition. And Office apps for the iPhone are still a bit of a mixed bag. Simply *reading* Office files is still a matter handled well by the iPhone's built-in document viewer (see Chapter 20 for instructions on loading any arbitrary file you want on your iPhone, Office document or no).

But editing them is a different story. You gotcher Word, spreadsheet, database, and presentation files. At this writing, the App Store contains individual apps for editing these kinds of files but it's not a diverse selection of awesome solutions. You want "the best," but for the most part you have to settle for "the best you can get right now."

GENERAL APPROACHES

There are still three credible general approaches to using spreadsheets, data-bases, presentations, and documents on an iPhone:

- ▢ **Use the built-in viewer**. Simple. Get the document on the iPhone and open it with a tap. Chapter 20 lists the full range of document types that your iPhone can display without any outside help. For our purposes here: The main file types created by Microsoft Office and Apple's iWork suite are all covered. You won't be able to *edit* any of this data, but it's a perfectly fine answer if you only need this document for reference purposes.

- ▢ **An online Office suite, optimized**

for the iPhone. You punch a URL into Safari and presto: You're looking at a fairly sophisticated set of apps for working with documents and spreadsheets. It's not a "real" app but who cares? You're getting the job done and moreover, getting it done for free. And as you'll see, at least one of these "fake" apps is in many ways the equal of anything you'd buy in the App Store. Bonus: Moving data from your desktop is simple. Just access the site via any browser and upload the file into your Web workspace. It'll be there safe and sound when you visit the Web app via your iPhone at any later date. You can also create new documents and download them to your desktop via that same browser interface. The two best online iPhone suites are Google Documents (http://docu-ments.google.com) and iZoho (www.zoho.com), both shown in Figure 23-1. They share the same modus operandi: Each is one site where you can store and edit your documents, regardless of the machine or device you happen to be using at the moment. If you keep your "world" on www.zoho.com, it doesn't matter if you're at home, at work, or in line at the taxi-dermist's. Access to the site means access to all your documents. iZoho is the better of the two. The apps are far more powerful, and their user-inter-faces are clean and rich. Google Docu-ments features the same Spartan (or shall we say "Soviet"?) design aesthetic as most Google apps, and some of the apps are read-only. I can view a Word file that I've created or uploaded to

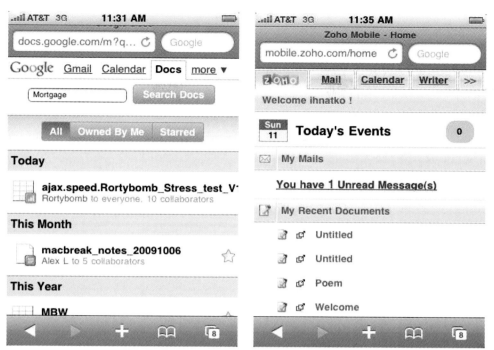

Figure 23-1
Google Documents (left) and iZoho (right): two free online Office suites for iPhone

the service, but I can't edit it. But many people (and even many offices) standardize on Google Documents for workflow and group projects, so it's good to know there's halfway-decent iPhone support.

☐ **An actual iPhone app.** You'd think this would be the ideal. And it is, but anyone who's ever ordered an aqualung by mail-order will tell you that reality rarely lives up to expectations. The App Store has been open for more than a year now. At this writing, the databases are close to what you'd want an iPhone database to be, the spreadsheets are decent but limited, and the word processors are damned-near

useless. Suffice to say that we're still waiting for the developer community to step up to the plate and deliver an Office-style suite or even individual apps that are packed with protein and are generally life-affirming. The best of the lot as this book went to press, Quickoffice's same-named Quickoffice app suite, is just passable.

So this is the State of the Union: Viewing Office docs is covered. Editing Office docs is certainly possible, but there are limits. But truly muscular Office-style apps for the iPhone are still a hit-or-miss proposition, and I'm eager for developers to step up to the plate and deliver the sort of word processor that's so manifestly The Right Choice that it makes all others — existing and future — almost impossible to sell.

The power is there in the iPhone. We just need the software.

SPREADSHEETS

Spreadsheets are a good fit for the iPhone. The built-in viewer can display most Excel spreadsheets with but a single tap (see Figure 23-2).

Online Apps

Google and Zoho's spreadsheet support aren't terribly impressive. You get an intensely plain-vanilla Web version of the spreadsheet that looks about as sophisticated as an assignment from an "Intro to Web Design" class. Figure 23-3 shows the Google Docs' interface. You can browse through the

No Service 🔋	7:23 AM		
◄ Message	**Fuel Economy Data...**		
CLASS	MFR	CAR LINE	DISP
TWO SE	ASTON MARTIN V8	VANTAGE	
TWO SE	ASTON MARTIN V8	VANTAGE	
TWO SE	BMW	Z4 3.0I	
TWO SE	BMW	Z4 3.0I	
TWO SE	BMW	Z4 3.0SI	
TWO SE	BMW	Z4 3.0SI	
TWO SE	BMW	Z4 COUPE	
TWO SE	BMW	Z4 COUPE	
TWO SE	BMW	Z4 M COUPE	
TWO SE	BMW	Z4 M ROADSTER	
TWO SE	CADILLAC	XLR	
TWO SE	CADILLAC	XLR	
TWO SE	CHEVROLET	CORVETTE	
TWO SE	CHEVROLET	CORVETTE	
TWO SE	CHEVROLET	CORVETTE	
TWO SE	CHRYSLER	CROSSFIRE (	

Figure 23-2

The simple way: viewing a spreadsheet with the iPhone's built-in viewer

TIP

One advantage of EditGrid (or Google Docs Spreadsheet) over a "real" app: The site contains mountains of free and intensely-useful spreadsheets that were created and shared by other EditGrid users. So if you're training to run a marathon and you're about to pay $5 for an app that records your training times and advises you of your week-to-week progress as the date looms near ... there's an app for that, but there might also be a free EditGrid spreadsheet. Do a search and if you like what you find, it'll be copied to your Web workspace with just a click.

spreadsheet and make simple cell edits. But it's little more than an viewer by its nature.

No, if you truly want a Safari-based app that can open, read, *and* create — *and even edit!* — spreadsheets on your iPhone, you're gonna want EditGrid. Head to www. editgrid.com from your desktop browser to set up an account and upload a few spreadsheets.

EditGrid has the same basic MO as Google Docs: It's a Web-based app that stores all your data on a remote server, whether you've created it in EditGrid or just uploaded it from your desktop. But the company has thrown all its eggs into the spreadsheet basket. This commitment

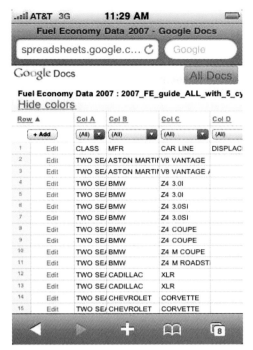

Figure 23-3
Google Docs opens a spreadsheet

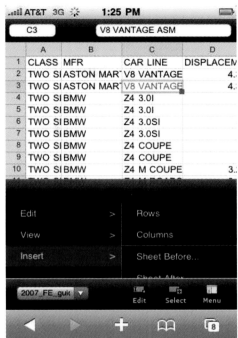

Figure 23-4
EditGrid: *real* spreadsheets on the iPhone

to doing one thing perfectly really shows through when you open one of your Edit-Grid documents on your iPhone, by visiting http://iphone.editgrid.com from your browser.

Figure 23-4 shows off EditGrid's sophisticated Web interface. I've popped up its menus so you can get an idea of how accessible its editing features are, but when all you need to do is view data and perform quick recalculations, the interface hides away completely.

It's ambitious. It's truly an incredible thing of beauty. The fact that it's doing something as sophisticated as running a real spreadsheet through a Web browser ups the awesome into the giga-Elvis spectrum.

You can create new spreadsheet documents. You can edit data, build new formulas, and perform calculations and recalculations. It even charts! Look upon these works, ye unworthies, and despair!

Sorry. What I mean is that it's a swell solution. But it has limitations. You can't expect the 922,028-cell, 21-sheet workbook that maintains and reports on the actuals of your entire division to plug right into an iPhone and work flawlessly, though EditGrid supports workbooks with multiple sheets and a long range of calculations. You do have to think in terms of a "palmtop" edition of your desktop spreadsheets. Do you need the full 21-sheet workbook? Or is

TIP

Some limitations and complaints appear to be common to every spreadsheet app in the App Store. You can expect that any iPhone spreadsheet app you buy won't necessarily work with every workbook you try to import. You can expect that many of Excel's or Numbers' most powerful math and analysis features are missing. And the biggest disappointment: These apps tend to crash a lot. You're force-feeding them huge mounds of data and insisting that they perform a calculation workload that's only slightly lighter than what Spock had to do in order to teach the *Enterprise* how to time-warp.

It's a recipe for disaster, so be forewarned.

there a *subset* of that big monster that still contains all the data and calculations you're actually likely to need when you're away from your computer?

And let's not fault EditGrid for this. I think it's the unavoidable baggage of a small screen and a low-power processor. EditGrid deserves to be considered alongside the best of the "real" iPhone spreadsheet apps. It's not as fast or as powerful (and remember, if you don't have Internet access, you don't have access to your worksheets) but it's useful, easy, and free.

A Real iPhone Spreadsheet App: Spreadsheet

Commercial software has a true Darwinian element, make no mistakes about that. It often takes years for a single app to stand out and overwhelm all other species that were competing for the same resources (that is, consumer bucks).

We're still in an early stage of spreadsheet application development. No one app is making everybody happy, which encourages developers to create more and more apps, which causes confusion in the marketplace, which makes consumers more timid to buy, which means less money to develop new spreadsheet apps and improve the old ones ... it's a bit of a mess.

My favorite spreadsheet app so far is the creatively

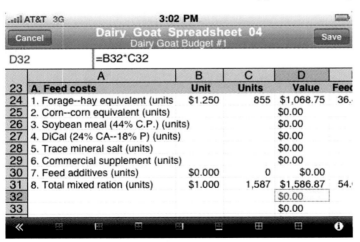

Figure 23-5

Spreadsheet: my fave full-on native iPhone spreadsheet app

named Spreadsheet from Softalk (www.
softalkltd.com), which costs $7.99. No
iPhone app is perfect at this writing, but it
has the best combination of features, from
my point of view:

- ▢ **It's pretty**. And I think that's important. Much of the point of an iPhone
  spreadsheet is to simply carry a "print-
  out" of essential data and enter in new
  information as you acquire it. Softalk's
  uses pretty formatting and simple
  navigation.

- ▢ **It good enough**. Normally, that
  phrase is damning with faint praise.
  But in a mobile spreadsheet app, you're
  not necessarily looking to cram all of
  Excel 2010 into the phone — you just
  want enough of its features to make
  the iPhone a credible alternative to
  dragging a notebook or a netbook
  around wherever you go. Based on my
  day-to-day use, and in conversations
  with people who spend as much time
  working on numbers as I do working with words, I'm convinced that
  Spreadsheet is the most compatible iPhone app as of this writing.

- ▢ **It's good at creating new
  spreadsheets**. Most of the others
  seem to be designed as "players"
  for your existing desktop spreadsheets. Spreadsheet is useful for
  building quick calculations and
  creating data tables on the fly.

- ▢ **It has a workable interface**.
  This is kind of a Holy Grail for
  spreadsheets. Even a *brilliant*
  multitouch interface is a clumsy
  answer at best. A spreadsheet,
  with its beehive-like grid of cells
  and thousands of niddly little

bits of data to be targeted, updated,
and recalced, is *truly* a keyboard-and-
mouse driven beast.

Spreadsheet offers no breakthroughs. The
interface is a bit cramped and it's a bit kludgy
in places. But it's the most iPhone-like and
least-clumsy spreadsheet app … and honestly, after your first couple of hours with
it, its tools for editing formulas and sheets
starts to feel natural (see Figure 23-5).

Turn on its file-sharing feature and then
enter the URL printed on the screen into any
desktop Web browser to access Spreadsheet's
file importer. You can then import and
export Excel's .xls files between the iPhone
app and your desktop. There's also an e-mail
feature … any spreadsheet can be e-mailed as
an attachment right from your phone.

ONWARD TO DATABASES

Why am I talking databases after spreadsheets and before word processing? Because
it's a gentle, cool, leafy oasis. Here we have
two perfectly swell solutions for putting
desktop databases on an iPhone *and* actu-

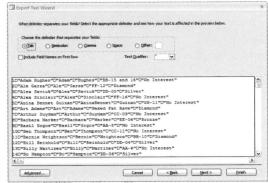

Figure 23-6
Turning database info into table data, which
can then become a spreadsheet

ally using and editing them. No tricks, no warnings ... just good software.

Free and Easy Read-Only Databases

If all you actually need to do is *view* your data, you don't even need to bother with an iPhone database app. Spreadsheets and databases have always been close cousins, to the extreme that many folks use tables of spreadsheet data *instead* of a database.

I've already established that the iPhone's built-in spreadsheet viewer is perfectly fine, as are the reader features of Google Docs, iZoho, and EditGrid. All you need to do is export your database into a CSV file.

"Comma-separated values" is the Esperanto of data. Any spreadsheet app can import a CSV table without any difficulty, regardless of its size.

Some desktop database apps can actually export data directly into an Excel spreadsheet. Six of one, half a dozen of the other. But the Excel solution will probably give you more control over

how the table is formatted and presented.

The export method varies from database app to database app. Figure 23-6 shows how Microsoft Access exports databases. Select the fields you'd like the exported file to contain and the app spits out a text file.

The basic format of a CSV file is a text file in which every line represents a new database record, and the individual fields within the file are separated by tabs. As you can see in Figure 23-6, I've set up Access to spit out the data properly.

A "Real" Database App: HanDBase

At $9.99, HanDBase (www.

Figure 23-7

HanDBase: a no-compromise, "real" database app

ddhsoftware.com) is in the "slightly pricey" range of App Store downloads. But be honest: You would have wasted the money on celebrity magazines and gum anyway.

And HanDBase is a full-featured database app. Its only serious limitation is that it's a "flat file" database: You can't have a record that includes links to other databases, but beyond that, it covers all of the core features of a desktop app (see Figure 23-7).

In many ways, HanDBase is the most valuable $9.99 you can spend in the App Store. After all, so many of the dinky little $0.99 or $2.99 apps in the store are little more than databases. The shopping list app: just a database of shopping items. Exercise tracker: database of workout information. Bowling league manager: a database of bowlers.

These are easy things to build in HanD-Base, either on a desktop or without even leaving the iPhone. It's that second aspect that makes the app so valuable. It's one thing to think ahead and realize that you're going to need a certain database or a certain tool next week. You head for the App Store and buy what you need. But HanD-Base allows me to design an app and a database on a moment's notice, right during the situation when I need to start collecting and organizing information.

Assuming that someone else hasn't already built a HanDBase database to handle that exact same need. DDH Software has a long legacy of building HanD-Base apps for mobile devices. There are hundreds of useful, pre-built databases available for free downloading from www. ddhsoftware.com.

Whether you're acquiring databases from

> **TIDBIT**
>
> Let's not leave this section on databases before I sneak in a mention of Apple's own database app. Bento is technically published by FileMaker. But Apple holds the pink slip on that company and as a result, the company makes a line of Mac and PC database apps that share the basic design and aesthetics of any of Apple's iLife or iWork products.
>
> Bento is a desktop database for the Mac. FileMaker has also released an iPhone edition that can sync data between a desktop and iPhone database with great agility. It's a nice app — but even if you're a Mac user, HanD-Base is your first choice. It's far more powerful and has a much more vibrant user community. Bento is a better choice if you already manage your professional or personal life with the desktop edition and you just want a simple, slick way to bring that data with you when you're away from the keyboard.

your desktop or downloading them from elsewhere, you can move them onto your iPhone easily. HanDBase has a Web-based interface for importing and exporting that's damn slick (see Figure 23-8).

THE SAD STATE OF WRITING ON THE IPHONE

You were expecting a self-deprecating joke about the quality of this book, weren't you?

Your bitterness is woefully misapplied.

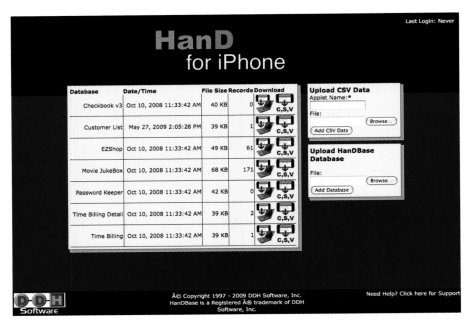

Figure 23-8
Moving databases into and out of your iPhone with HanDBase's Web-based tool

Please, allow me to deflect your hatred toward the developer community instead. There aren't any decent word processors for the iPhone at this writing.

And keep in mind that I'm writing this roughly 18 months after developers acquired the ability to design and publish iPhone software. Dear God.

I admit I'm being a bit of a grump about this. But I *am* a writer, which means that my life is one of solitary desperation even on a *good* day. It also means that I want to have a good word processor on every device I own. Something that moves beyond simple text editing and can at least offer basic formatting and style options.

I don't necessarily insist that an iPhone word processor should let me write a 20,000-word novella, but I think a 1,000-word newspaper column should be well within its abilities. Right?

And so I say: There are no word processors for the iPhone. There are apps in the App Store that *call* themselves word processors, but each one falls short in one way or the other. Either it has a decent editor but there's no way to move documents in and out of the phone easily, or it's barely powerful enough to edit an e-mail, or it was designed by someone who, as a kid, once came home from school earlier than expected and walked in on his Mom having sex with a newspaper columnist and has been bearing a grudge ever since.

There are plenty of Notes-style apps that are geared toward writing hundreds of separate notes of a paragraph or two each. But no word processors.

What I'm hoping for is a decent word processor. I tried 'em all, and each and every one disappointed me.

Notebooks, by Alfons Schmid

Then I looked for a *great* notes app and I found more or less what I was looking for: Notebooks by Alfons Schmid (www. alfonsschmid. com). For $5.99 you get an app that's surprisingly good for

The App Gap * Google Docs • EditGrid • Bending databases to your will

Every year, I start work on a chapter from the new edition of "Fully Loaded" by reading the chapter from

Figure 23-9
Notebooks: less than a word processor but far more than a notepad

viewing Word docs, and fairly great at editing text and HTML docs imported from your desktop. It's not as good as editing Word docs directly, but either format can be used as the "common ground" between Word and your iPhone.

I think Figure 23-9 tells the whole tale.

Yup, it's the Microsoft Word manuscript for this very chapter, complete with formatting and style changes intact, imported just seconds ago. What you see in Figure 23-9 is exactly what I'm seeing in this Word window (only smaller). That's sort of like running a sub-four-minute mile: It marks the app as a true elite and a professional app.

Here's what I mean. I often file an article or a column and then take off for the afternoon. But I usually bring along a netbook so that if my editor e-mails me in the afternoon and asks for some changes, I can rewrite a paragraph or two and get it back in his or her hands. If I sync the file to Notebooks before I leave the house, though,

I can easily handle that sort of challenge without carrying any excess baggage.

Notebooks shows its limits when you try to use it to write things from scratch. Don't forget that it's "an incredibly feature-rich notepad" rather than "a competent word processor." Typing page after page with the onscreen keyboard is a major drag, but that's par for the course with any iPhone app. But I do wish that the app offered some basic formatting options, such as boldface and italics, or font changes. If I could define styles, I'd be over the moon.

But I'm excited about Notebooks, and I recommend it highly to anybody who likes, or needs, iPhone word processing. It's certainly an effective tool for when The Muse seizes you by the hand and pulls you into the hedges for a bit of a kiss-and-cuddle.

Notebooks scores high for its import and export features. For once, I have an app that *does not* swap docs with a desktop via an onboard Web server. Pity. Instead, you need

249

to download a free sync app for your desktop and it doesn't always work properly (as of this writing, anyway).

It offers some damned nice network sync alternatives, however. It can connect to any WebDAV-based machine or service, which includes any PC or Mac, and most online storage services. I can just give it the details of my MobileMe account and presto: I can download any compatible file in that remote folder, and push my Notebooks documents back up. If an editor wants to send me an edited chapter for my approval and comments, he or she can upload it into my WebDAV folder's Public directory. Then I can grab it, make the changes, and e-mail it back from Notebooks.

I'm still holding out for what might be termed a "real" writing tool for the iPhone. But Notebooks will tide me over very nicely

until that arrives. And if Schmid were to add just a few features to Notebooks, I'd happily give him another $9.99 for the upgraded edition and designate it as The Only iPhone Word Processor That Ever Needs to Exist.

Quickword: a Late Addition

It just goes to prove that the iPhone App Store is a constantly moving target. A new update to Quickoffice's $9.99 Quickword app (www.quickoffice.com/quickword_iphone) has just hit the App Store as I write this. It isn't *better* than Notebooks, overall, but it's strong in places where the other app is weak, so I consider Quickword and Notebooks to be equally good choices.

Where is Quickword strong? In its support for true, native Microsoft Word document creation and editing. Whereas Notebooks only edits text and HTML files (at this writing), Quickword is a true Microsoft Word beast. It supports styled and formatted text and easily satisfies my "make a few quick edits" requirement. There are enough horses under the hood that I could credibly write a whole column with Quickword, too.

Where is it weak? Chiefly in the editing environment. In Notebooks, landscape and portrait modes are more or less an equal writing experience. In Quickword, I often found myself needing to twist the iPhone around because I needed to access a certain feature that was present in one version of the app's UI but not the other. I also wish it had greater organizational features. You can sort through documents by folder, and that should be handy enough for most people. Notebooks makes it simple to create "work areas" of related documents and information.

But Quickword is just as strong as Notebooks when it comes to moving data in and out. It's a similar feature set: You can move documents in and out of the app's workspace via a Wi-Fi data transfer or via your iDisk. You can also e-mail your docs as file attachments.

It's too bad that Quickword only supports the iDisk for remote transfers. The handiest feature of Notebooks is its support for WebDAV. If you have a subscription to any cloud storage service that supports this popular standard, then anybody can give you a document for editing. Because Quickword only supports the iDisk, if you want this slick "my boss sent me this document and now I need to mark it up and return it to her" feature, you'll need a $99 annual subscription to Apple's MobileMe.

If this little section demonstrates anything, it's that the App Store is a moving target. When I wrote this chapter a few weeks ago, Quickword was a nice effort but it was a little lean on practical features. What a difference an update makes. By the time you read this, Quickoffice might have made key improvements. And maybe so will Notebooks. They're both at the top of the heap.

Zoho Writer

If you don't have a regular need for an iPhone word processor (and/or $5.99 and $9.99 seem like a hell of a lot of money for

Notebooks or Quickword), the next best solution isn't an iPhone app at all. Yes, all told, the Zoho Writer app in the online Office suite iZoho Office is superior to all current iPhone word processing apps, save for Notebooks.

Check out Figure 23-10. Not an ungodly-impressive app, I realize. But it covers the basics: You can move a desktop Word doc into the word processor (by sending it into your Zoho workspace), edit it on your iPhone (if you have a connection to the Internet), and move it back to your desktop (back to the Zoho Web site). You can create documents and though the editing features are spare, it's perfectly adequate for either editing an existing doc or dumping a few paragraphs of story ideas out of your head while you're away from a computer.

PRESENTATIONS

Huh?

Oh, right. Presentations. Yeah. Well, the

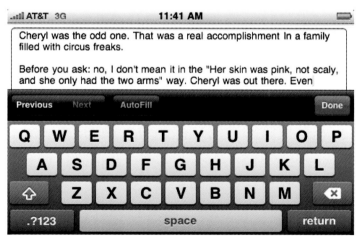

Figure 23-10

Zoho Writer is a distant third, but it's still a decent iPhone word processor.

Figure 23-11
Yes, I'm leaning on a priceless movie prop. Artoo is a support droid, after all.

iPhone's built-in reader can view Microsoft PowerPoint and Apple Keynote preso files without any conversion of any kind.

There you go.

I know you understand what I'm talking about. You learned all about this in Chapter 20, plus once again at the top of this chapter. But I feel as though a section is incomplete without an illustration. So here's a photo of me and R2-D2, taken when I had an appointment at the Lucasfilm campus.

No need to make it any more complicated than that. If you're constantly flying hither and yon delivering presentations, you *could* be tempted to buy a video-compatible iPhone dock, such as Apple's Universal Dock. Then, you could drive all of your presentations from the iPhone. But the output resolu-

tion isn't even low-resolution HD, and I don't think you'd be happy with the results.

Oh! Wait, here's an actual legitimate use of a graphic for this section. If you paw through the App Store, you'll find a small collection of apps that turn your iPhone into a presentation remote for a PowerPoint or Keynote.

Figure 23-12 shows you Apple's own Keynote Remote app, which is typical of the breed. It gives you the expected collection of controls for navigating through your slides, plus information about upcoming slides and your presentation notes.

But I'm not going to delete the image of me and Artoo. I like this photo. My friends and family have been given careful instructions: If I'm ever killed in a crash of some kind, *this* is the photo they're supposed to hand out to the local media for use in the nightly newscast.

THE DULLEST CHAPTER? OR THE MOST EXCITING?

In one sense, this is the dullest chapter of the book. It's hard to get excited about opening spreadsheets and Word documents and the like, isn't it? When was the last time Apple ran an iPod commercial in which energetic young people in colorful clothes danced around a white stage with iPhones in hand, balancing their checkbooks?

But the concept of Microsoft Office-type docs on your iPhone is exciting in two different ways. The iPhone is a freedom enzyme. The power of its data, its apps, and its communications features is often the justification for spending the afternoon somewhere you'd much rather be than your office. Namely ... *anywhere* other than your office. Carrying your work world on

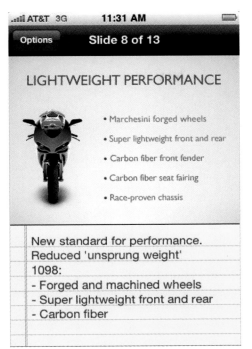

LIGHTWEIGHT PERFORMANCE

- Marchesini forged wheels
- Super lightweight front and rear
- Carbon fiber front fender
- Carbon fiber seat fairing
- Race-proven chassis

New standard for performance.
Reduced 'unsprung weight'
1098:
- Forged and machined wheels
- Super lightweight front and rear
- Carbon fiber

Figure 23-12
Turning your iPhone into a presentation
remote with Keynote Remote.

rental a business expense as well?

I leave this as an exercise for the reader.
And possibly the criminal justice system.

your iPhone lets you do the bare minimum
of productive work necessary to keep the
checks flowing in and retain the power to
take that three-hour lunch.

Better: The fact that you're definitely
using the iPhone as a *business* device to
hold your *business* documents and let you
do *business* stuff makes the iPhone into
a totally legitimate tax deduction. I stand by
that statement.

Those of you who don't fear prison might
want to take this a step further: If you're on
a black-sand beach in Maui and you spend
20 minutes editing a report on your iPhone
... doesn't that technically make the airfare
from Duluth and the two weeks' condo

Index